T H E
UNDERSTORY

M. E. SCHUMAN

THE
UNDERSTORY

*A Female
Environmentalist
in the Land of the
Midnight Sun*

For information about this title or to order other books and/or electronic media, contact the publisher:

Be Free Be Wild Press
meschumancom.wordpress.com
befreebewildpress@gmail.com

ISBNs:
978-1-7379206-0-1 (softcover)
978-1-7379206-1-8 (eBook)

Printed in the United States of America

Cover and Interior design: 1106 Design

I dedicate this book to those who tirelessly
and thanklessly give their lives to protect those
without a voice—and to the creatures that live in the
understory, sustaining an environment for all life.

The Understory: Plants in the understory comprise an assortment of seedlings and saplings of canopy trees; shrubs, grasses, and vines; herbs and moss. Young canopy trees often persist in the understory for decades as suppressed juveniles, hidden in the shadows. Although only a fraction of sunlight gets through the dense forest canopy, the understory has a diversity of plants. The infinitesimal amount of sunlight encourages plants in the understory to adopt a smarter way of living, with less sunlight. As older trees in the canopy die or lose their leaves, the understory plants burst with energy and blossom before the canopy trees block the sunlight once again.

Table of Contents

Prologue

Gazing intently at the bright red coils, knees hugged in tight against my chest, I feel the heat on my skin as I fantasize sitting in front of a fire, deep in the woods. The only sounds I hear are the distant howls of wolves. Eventually, my fingers tire from plugging my ears, and the angry shouting between my parents invades my meditation.

"Damn it, Susie, you are going to set this house on fire sitting that close to the heater," my dad yells.

That was, unfortunately, a common scenario in our tiny, three-bedroom house.

I reflect on those nights as a child so long ago as I watch the red embers burning hot in my wood stove on another cold winter night in Alaska. I have attempted to put my life into words, but there is always something more important to do: the half-acre of garden to weed, water to haul, wood to split and stack, the deck to stain, or snow to shovel—which, I admit, keeps me physically strong. Ah, the endless tasks that need to be done. There was always an excuse.

I think it might be human nature, the need to tell our story.

Whether at a party with people of many diverse backgrounds or an intimate group of few, either in Alaska or in some remote corner of the globe, it was rare not to be around inquisitive people and the sharing of others' life stories. In fact, it has always been exhilarating for me to find out where people are from, how they arrived, and what they do.

And during these incredible exchanges, someone would often pose it to me: "You tell the most mind-blowing stories! Have you ever considered writing a book?"

Until recently, I did not understand how starved I was for these warm and friendly mutual conversations. For months, I had been looking for a home, for a community, and I assumed Washington would be it—the familiar, near family and childhood friends.

But I was wrong. Instead, I found a deep void brought on by the absence of inquisitiveness. I felt a gut feeling as I asked myself: Do others tolerate me out of pity rather than an eager desire to exchange caring words? They appear to have no interest in anything I have to say, or what I have done, or where I have been the last 30-odd years. No, I am merely a tolerated invader of their secure bubble. I see it on their faces.

If there was a family illness, wedding, high school reunion, or funeral, I universally dropped what I was doing and made the trip to Washington. It was rare that a family member or friend would travel to spend time with me in Alaska. Consequentially, I filled this gap with my Alaska friends and "family."

A recent event, my niece's wedding, helped deliver that message like an arrow straight into my heart. The piercing truth came when I learned I hadn't made the A-list for the number of people who could attend the wedding under Covid restrictions of 30 guests.

My cousin was pissed—not that she, too, was not invited, but pissed that I wasn't. She felt so sorry for me. I pretended it didn't hurt, but it did.

This contrast became clear soon after my arrival from Alaska to my long-familiar stomping grounds in central Washington. I was walking with a girlfriend along a forested trail of asphalt, when we came upon a sign warning people to be aware of *a moose*. I was immediately excited and pushed ahead. My girlfriend stopped and said to me, "Moose are dangerous. You need to be very careful around moose. You don't know what to do around them!" I was stunned; speechless. In this undemanding, simple life, I quickly realized I did not fit in. It is one thing to be alone in the wilderness, another to be alone in an urban setting.

Since then, in contemplating my existence among eight billion other human beings, I considered maybe it would be fun to write about my life. I found the whole idea of leaving a legacy appealing but also somewhat daunting.

I had an inauspicious beginning. I was small, premature. And I wanted out. My mother said it was my nature. She said I never wanted to sit still. To hold back. To be quiet. I was like a bull in a china store, she would say. Invincible. When my brother, one year older than me, could start school, I cried desperately to go. He also was the reason why I never knew my real name was Michelle.

I have traveled all over the world, exploring the mysteries of life under the sea from Yap to Honduras. I have walked on endless, unspoiled ground of nature's creation, from seas to mountain spires. I have rafted endangered rivers, such as the Bio Bio in Chile and the Zambezi, in Central Africa. I have been touched by a Mountain Gorilla, and watched the tears fall from the eyes of a baby elephant as it mourned its mother, a bloody emptiness where her trunk and face were missing because of ignorance and self-indulgence.

I have observed a grizzly sow playing with her three cubs on sun-drenched slopes on the western edge of the North American continent. I have borne witness to the sobering spectacle of hundreds of female seals dragging their blackened, distended bellies through the oozing black death spread by human greed, simply to give birth. The amazing journey of life: pain, love, sadness, cruelty, joy.

My neighbor stopped as he was leaving my house. "Michelle, you need to tell your story, to help other women. Women like you."

A story to help *other . . . women . . . like . . . Me?* Wow. That stopped me in my tracks. I am independent. I had a career. I am a survivor. And yet, there I was, after all my sacrifices, all my accomplishments, being called to join my sisters in that circle of women I tried so hard *not* to be part of.

I can think of a thousand reasons not to write. For the first time, I can think of one reason why I should. Because I can. And so, this is my story. I will call it a thinly fictionalized memoir of my life.

Some of my characters' names are fiction, mostly to protect the guilty; but my story, desires, adventures, dreams, and despair are all true.

CHAPTER I

Grit

I *got his text as my dear friend, Coug,* dropped me off at the Anchorage International Airport. I showed her my iPhone, shaking my head.

"Don't you dare do it," she said. "He always gets what he wants from you." She hugged me as tears flowed from our eyes. "Promise me? Promise now?" she demanded. I nodded my head. "I love you, Michelle," she said. I waved as my friend of twenty years hesitantly drove away, leaving me on the sidewalk. I took a deep breath, lifted one bag with each hand, stared at the terminal doors, and walked through.

The sound of water dripping on bamboo alerted me to a text. And then another. The ring of friends as the word spread. *How well they know me.* It took every ounce of willpower not to give into his demands.

My hands quivering, I deleted his text.

1

After the ghostly empty TSA check-in, I wandered to the one and only pub open and ordered a beer. I took a sip of the amber liquid. The faint smell of hops stimulated my taste buds as the foam clung to my lips. For a brief period, the chatter of conversation and clinking dishes coming from fellow travelers at the sparse tables in the airport bar slowly diminished as I closed my eyes. It was so vivid.

I saw the younger version of me, with brown, chestnut-streaked hair as it hung straight, nearly to my waist, as I boarded a plane, departing the Spokane airport. I was wearing faded denim jeans, flared over the tops of my dirty white tennis shoes, gripping the tennis racquet against my chest.

The year was 1978, and I landed six times in the Lone Star state. It was my first time on a plane. It was exhilarating.

A petite, elderly lady sitting in the seat next to me grabbed my arm and said, "Sweetie, don't look out the window." But I did. I loved it. Open, rolling grasslands of the Texas prairie.

I arrived in Port Aransas to meet my fiancé, Rick, a PhD candidate in the Texas A&M marine aquaculture program, for the summer term. As I walked down the steps of the plane, I glanced up. He was standing in the terminal's shadow, his sandy, shoulder-length hair messy and blowing in the breeze. I caught my breath as my heart beat so hard I thought I was having a heart attack. And then I ran. His hug was suffocating, and I didn't care. It was late August, in a state I had never been in before, with the man I loved.

My summer job as a Range Conservationist with the United States Forest Service (USFS) in the eastern Cascades had finished. We had a few weeks before fall semester started at Washington State University (WSU—pronounced *WAZZU* by the locals). Rick decided he did not want to pursue a PhD in aquaculture and instead was pursuing a PhD opportunity in mechanical engineering at WSU, allowing him a shortcut without going through the Master's program.

However, he needed a break from school, so he planned to work before going to graduate school the following summer. I had a couple of weeks, so we planned a road trip together from the Texas Gulf in his 1965 Chevy van back to Washington. This was to be my first big road adventure, as I had never really traveled outside of Washington before that, except to work in Oregon.

Rick and I had met in the Blue Mountains of Oregon, working for the USFS during the summer of 1976. I was a recreation tech and Rick, a smokejumper. We were both planning on attending WSU that fall. I was 18, a wildlife biologist and pre-vet major. Rick was 23, zoology and pre-med. Rather than go to college after high school with a full academic scholarship, he felt it was his patriotic duty and enlisted in the Army, bound for Vietnam. He became a paratrooper and served more than two years.

I would remind him throughout our brief marriage, "If I knew you then, you would not have gone." He would reply, "If I had known you then, no way would I have enlisted." Then he would add, with that half-cocked smile, showing his dimples, "If I had, it would have been safer to stay in 'Nam." I would smile at him. "You got that right."

My new co-worker and roommate for that summer of 1976, Jan, was from a small town near Spokane, Washington. She was also 18 and a work-study employee from WSU with a major in engineering. We had never met before that enlightening summer, but we became the best of friends. She would eventually be the maid of honor at my wedding.

He was doing calisthenics with his smokejumping crew. A dozen shirtless men, sweat glistening on their tanned bodies in our front yard at the Tollgate Ranger Station. I only noticed one guy. He was lean, muscled, sandy-brown hair, and fit. He looked at me and smiled. That was it. I was hooked. Done for.

We had just arrived at the station after a long day cleaning the scattered campgrounds. Jan was sitting in the passenger seat of our two-ton USFS green truck, the back end filled with garbage. We got out and stared.

Jan saw this play out and said, "What about your rule?"

"What rule?"

We both grinned. She, too, had her eye on a jumper.

My rule was not to get serious. Summer was for fun, but when school started, it was all work.

Although Jan and I were only recreational techs, cleaning outhouses and hauling garbage, we soon learned that was not the only crap we had to deal with. If I had only known then that this harmless, inconsequential summer job was but a preview into a culture that would haunt me throughout my career in the sciences, my life choices might have been different.

For five days, "Frenchy," a gruff, gray-bearded French Canadian, was our nemesis. He showed up at the station one day and said, "*We* need to lay a new pipeline to one of the recreational facilities."

While he sat on the tailgate of the faded-green USFS truck, smoking a smelly, brown cigarette, he lectured us as to the problems of hiring girls in the federal government.

Muttering in English with a French accent, "Women belong at home having babies, not taking jobs away from men." We were a "captive" audience as *we*—Jan and I, not Frenchy—dug a trench 18 inches wide, 30 feet long and 20 inches deep. It took us five full days, not because Jan and I did not know how to use a shovel or were weak or lazy. It took us five full days because, every morning, we dug a new trench.

Each morning after we arrived at our trench, we would continue our "dig." Frenchy would light his cigarette, look at the "ditch" and mutter in French, *"Il est faux"* (it is wrong). *"Fille stupide"* (stupid girl), he would say while pointing to an untouched area of ground a few inches from our current trench. Rather than get mad, Jan would look at me, smudges of dirt on her porcelain face, her big blue eyes sparkling with mischief, shrug her shoulders, and mouth, *"bâtard fou"* (crazy bastard). I would giggle and then mouth back, *"bâtard paresseux"* (lazy bastard).

What Frenchy didn't know was that both Jan and I had studied two years of high school French. My French teacher had only three students in my second year. He'd been stationed in France during WWII and was tickled when he could teach us French slang. He, too, had a captive audience, as the three of us girls sat in awe of our wonderfully warm, smiling, theatrical French teacher.

Anyway, this went on for an entire week. Jan and I would arrive, pick up our shovels, fill in the current trench, stab the dulled shovel blade into the raw dirt, and begin anew. Our hands caked with grime and calluses, Jan and I would smile as we walked into our tiny, pea-green colored kitchen. There on the kitchen wall was our newly hung sign, with the bright red words from Aesop's Fable:

> *"Some men are of more consequence in their own eyes than in the eyes of others."*

"Ma'am, are you finished? Ma'am? Can you hear me?"
In a daze, I looked up at a very frustrated server.

"I am sorry. Hard to hear with the masks on," I apologized, embarrassed.

At least my mask and glasses hid the tears falling from my eyes, bringing me back to the reality of my current situation.

I gulped the remaining tepid beer and stood up from the table.

How cruel and beautiful memories can be. These thoughts took root in my mind as I boarded my plane leaving Anchorage, Alaska, on May 6, 2020.

It's like walking outside on a crisp fall day, watching the golden leaves waving in the branches of the aspen and birch. The air filled with that bitter aroma of high-bush cranberry and a hint of dried grass. And with the flash of morning light, the trees are bare. Tangled branches naked. The ground covered with mustard-colored leaves, blackened with a scent of mold lingering in the chilled air.

If I had known that the intersection of my life with Rick's would change the direction of my future—and his—in such a horrible way, would I have changed it? Would I have chosen a different path?

CHAPTER 2

Transition Bound

U nder the cloak of candlelight, the smell of basil and pepperoni overwhelming the tiny bedroom, Rick knelt on a bended knee and asked me to marry him. I was graduating from WSU at the end of the winter semester of 1979. He had driven from Richland, where he was working at the Hanford Nuclear Plant, on his break from school, surprising me not only with his visit but with a proposal.

Our plan was to marry May 26, 1979. When we told my parents, they were thrilled. And then they made me a proposition. My mom needed back surgery. She told my dad she slipped and fell on the ice. The truth? She fell roller skating. For my dad, that would be irresponsible, and very likely cause a knockdown drunken fight between them. The surgery, curiously, was timed with my graduation after fall semester.

Hesitantly, I said, "Yes." It was not at all what I had planned, but my father explained he could not take time off his job at

Grand Coulee Dam, a good three-hour commute away. He pleaded with me.

My brother, who lived a block away, was busy with work.

Of course, I said, "Yes." I found a job with the local Fish and Game as a biologist conducting non-game surveys, with flexible hours, which allowed me to take care of my mom and work.

One of my biggest issues with being home was the cigarette smoke. The toxins cause my lungs to close, although my mother said all of that was in my head.

After my arrival, I cleaned and scrubbed the tiny house. At first, I thought I would need to paint, but after washing off years of the yellowed slime of nicotine, the walls and cupboards sparkled. My father, always a farmer at heart, had a beautiful garden, and his dahlias were stunning. I scattered seed of white shasta daisies to give a look of wildness, as I worked in the yard, where we would have the reception.

And then, one morning as I got on my bike to ride the three miles to work, I got a call that set the tone for the rest of my life. The USFS offered me a wildlife-biologist position in Bozeman, Montana. Elated! MSU had a wonderful graduate program in engineering. When I got to the office, I called Rick immediately.

Rick, however, was not so receptive. He grew quiet in response to my excitement. Federal positions such as this were rare, I explained.

"That's a great opportunity. I am sorry you have to turn it down."

"Why would I turn it down?"

He wanted the security of professors he knew, and as rare as the federal biology job was, a doctorate offer was even rarer. WSU was a place he was familiar with, and he had already enrolled for the summer session. And what about the wedding? His tone was dusted with anger.

My parents made it clear there were limited funds for our wedding, which required Rick and me to make do on a limited budget. I designed our invitations, and we limited the guest list to forty. *Hmm*, I thought, *they had not yet been mailed.*

We could elope? Or go to the justice of the peace?

I explained all this to him until he reminded me of my godparents, Uncle Joe and Aunt Rose. They were coming from Wisconsin.

"And what about your dad? He wants us married in the Catholic church."

It was bad enough I had to miss my graduation ceremony. It appalled my mom that I would have to pay to graduate. I could not pay for a wedding and pay for my graduation. And now I had to make a choice between my career and my wedding. I wanted to get married to Rick and for him to be my husband. But...what about what *I* wanted?

Dammit. I broke my rule. I fell in love. *I will make this work. For Rick and for us.*

"You'll see. It'll be fine. I promise," he told me.

The small wedding was wonderful. The weather was sunny and clear, as friends and family helped Rick and me celebrate our day. Close friends decorated our Chevy van with beer cans streaming from the bumper, toilet paper strung with flowers, inside the cab, and then we were off on our honeymoon to Hawaii.

We had a blissful honeymoon and then went directly to Pullman, where Rick got his Master's in mechanical engineering in two years. He bailed out of the PhD program after the first semester, afraid he could not keep up a 4.0 GPA. I worked full-time in grants and research while my range and wildlife professors bugged me to get my Master's. Instead, I picked up more pre-vet and soil-science classes and left research to work in the plant-pathology lab, while beefing up my application for vet school.

In 1981, Chevron offered Rick an engineering position in Concord, California, the last place I thought we would live. Is there any rangeland in East Bay? Where would I work?

As a concession, Chevron promised me a position in the environmental group if Rick accepted the position. I compromised, and we went to California.

After months of discussions and pleadings, there still was no movement on my position with Chevron. Rick said to be patient. They wanted to make sure he was happy with his position. I was going insane with the traffic, the people, and no job. I felt like a homemaker in suburban hell.

Finally, I accepted a temporary job with the Bureau of Land Management (BLM), in Carson City, Nevada, working with wild horses. Another rare opportunity for federal employment. I worked four ten-hour days, allowing me to visit Rick on the weekends.

Two months later, I got an offer to work as a range conservationist in Anchorage, Alaska, with the United States Department of Agriculture (USDA). This time, Rick could not say "No."

On July 2, 1982, I was on a midnight flight to the largest city in the state known as the *Greatland*. Alone. I knew not one person in Alaska. Everything I had was in a backpack on the plane or in an apartment in Walnut Creek, California. And I was excited. For the first time in our marriage, Rick and I could work and live, not only in the same state, but in the same city.

Chevron had an office in Anchorage, and it was part of the oil consortium on the North Slope. He planned to transfer there after I arrived and got settled. It meant temporarily being apart, but that was of small consequence in the big picture. We phoned my parents to fill them in on our plans. As always, there were endless questions from my family when I disclosed our new adventure on the phone as they struggled to piece together the details.

And my dad. Oh, my God—my dad.

I can still hear my dad's words and the image of him whenever he would get upset with me. He would rub his bald head, get red in the face, and say, "Goddamit, Suzie! For Chrissakes."

"Suzie" was my nickname. It was the only name I knew when I was little. My brother could not say "Michelle" and instead started calling me "Suzie." No one knows why, but it stuck. Still, there were many occasions when my dad seemed to forget any of my many so-called names, like when he was talking to his brother, my godfather, Uncle Joe, in Wisconsin.

After we told him we were engaged, I overheard him say on the telephone, ". . . and whatchamacallit is getting married." My mom just grinned and shook her head. That was my dad. You would think he had half a dozen kids instead of just the three of us.

He was always thin and wiry, a gentle man. Until those Irish Catholic genes mixed with alcohol. Then it was a stormy, and sometimes violent, episode. As the middle, sensitive kid, I took it upon myself to do whatever I could to prevent those.

He spent ten hours a day kneeling on cold, wet cement working as a mason on Grand Coulee Dam, the brainchild of President Roosevelt's public works projects in the Pacific Northwest. I believe my dad left his legacy, along with his blood, sweat, and tears, in every layer of cement that spans the mighty Columbia River.

These enormous concrete structures—and my dad's role in creating them—always impressed relatives. Frequently, us kids got to tag along on these family tours. He was showing us a structure along the side of one dam. It was like a massive set of stairs for a giant.

"What are those?" I asked my dad.

"Fish ladders," he said. "They help the fish get upstream."

I contemplated. "But dad," I asked, "Fish can't get up those— can they? Won't they die?" I asked.

"That dam puts food on the table and clothes on your back," my mom snapped at me. I felt bad, but I believe my dad knew the fate of those fish as well.

Before the war, my dad, a talented baseball player in high school, had the potential to play ball in college. But his aspirations were to be a veterinarian.

I had hoped to make him proud someday, as I had dreamed of being a big-game veterinarian since the age of four. I loved animals. My grandfather, my mom's dad, whom I never knew, was known as "the cat whisperer." He trained cats, according to my mom. I found that somewhat ironic since my mom, raised in a rough neighborhood in Denver, associated cats with rats, and, therefore, cats were never to be part of our animal menagerie.

That changed one Easter morning when I brought home a gray-and-white tabby kitten, the first of many. How could she say "No" to me as I hugged the kitten, my big brown eyes pleading, dressed in my yellow Easter dress? I am convinced my animal fascination and love for all living creatures is in my DNA. I reminded my parents several times of that fact. I hoped that, one day, they would take my career choice seriously.

I began taking care of the neighborhood pets by the age of six or seven. Unfortunately for my mother, this included taking care of any animal, domestic or otherwise, and bringing the creature to our tiny home. Shortly after complaints of missing pets started circulating in the neighborhood, my mother made a deal with our neighbors.

The neighbors officially hired me to take care of their pets as needed. This kept the pets out of harm's way and made me proud I could help them. I got paid to take care of animals and get work experience. This position taught me responsibility and alleviated mom's embarrassing task of explaining to the neighbors what had happened to their disappearing pets. The money from pet sitting went into a papier mâché piggy bank I'd made in second grade. On its side, I scribbled with pink sparkle letters, *"college."*

At age 13, I asked my parents if I could spend a summer on the dairy farm in Wisconsin. I expressed the need for farm-animal experience. They said, "Of course!" I remember packing a small suitcase weeks before my bus ride to Wisconsin. As the day came closer, my mom became very nervous. I should have realized that something was amiss with my mom's behavior, because it was very much the same way she acted when my dog, Jingles, supposedly died.

My parents assumed once summer started, my interest in the farm trip would dissipate and be replaced with hanging out with my friends and swimming at the pool. It was quite an unpleasant scene when my parents told me that my aunt and uncle could not have me for the summer. It did not deter me from my goal; I am also very stubborn.

Throughout school, I aced every science course offered and worked for the local vet, starting at age 15, despite my earlier escapades. Although, in my mind, my earlier intentions were totally justifiable.

I should explain a very important but traumatic period in my childhood. I came home from school one afternoon, and Jingles, my beagle, was not in the backyard waiting for me. My mom called me into the house and, with tears in her eyes, informed me that Jingles had died.

Too upset to go to school the next day, I stayed home to care for my distraught cat while mourning the loss of Jingles. Tiger, the cat, was so listless I insisted my mom take us to the vet. While in the reception area, I heard a howl and a deep, loud baying. And then another. I knew that howl and ran from the reception area to the outdoor kennel, and there was my beloved Jingles. A miracle!

But no, our reunion was not to be. The vet and my mom attempted to explain the truth to me. By that point, I was a very hysterical young girl. Jingles had bitten a neighbor lady, they explained, and they had no choice—Jingles was going to be put down. We drove home in silence as I cuddled my cat, my tears soaking her gray fur. Along the way, I devised a plan.

That night, I snuck out of the house and took my parents' brown Chevy station wagon. With the car in neutral, even someone of my small stature could push it down the street making no noise.

Unfortunately for me and my dog, it was a botched theft. A friend, sympathetic to my cause, was an accomplice in the rescue. We decided it would be safer if she stayed home while I drove to the clinic. Once I rescued my dog, I would meet her in the alley behind her house, where I would leave Jingles with her. I would return the station wagon and run back to her house. It was a plan devised by a kid determined to have her dog back.

While my girlfriend nervously paced in her backyard, her mom woke up and noticed a figure with a flashlight walking back and forth. She recognized the figure, ran out, and asked her young daughter what the hell she was doing. My girlfriend, so scared that I would get caught—*and* her, as an accomplice—spilled the beans right there on the spot.

Our moms, with my friend in the back seat, rushed to the clinic and saw me in the car headlights, as I climbed the fence. Jingles bayed into the night air.

My mom, quick as lightning, yanked me down by the legs, threw me into the Chevy station wagon, allowing me no time to escape. A police car with siren and lights on sped past us. I did not talk to my mom or my friend for weeks. The matter, according to our mothers, was settled. Although, deep down, I know that, if my mom had seen the look on my face, she would have climbed the fence herself to rescue my dog.

However, three years later, notwithstanding the scene at the clinic, Cy, the vet, whether out of guilt, kindness, or sympathy, gave me a job. My daily tasks included cleaning kennels and bathing the animals. On rare occasions, I attended surgeries.

Once, I assisted with the most fascinating surgery: a re-section of the intestine on a Black Angus steer. Yes! A steer! The surgery was the most amazing thing I had ever witnessed! I dearly wanted to stay with the steer during recovery, but I had a regional tennis match that afternoon that I nearly missed.

My tennis coach arranged for the school bus to pick me up at the clinic on the way out of town. I was the strongest female tennis player on the team, playing both first singles and on the first mixed-doubles team. I still had spattered blood on my shoes when I boarded the bus as I whispered "Thanks" to the tennis coach. He smiled and nodded his head, as he knew I worked two jobs, and was happy to oblige. He also knew that my family did not support the idea of me playing tennis.

I came from a track family. My brother was state high-jump and pole-vault champion. My younger sister excelled in sprints.

I, too, was good in track until I had a ski accident, fracturing my right ankle. Thinking I could never excel, I started exploring tennis in my sophomore year. I would go to tennis tryouts in the morning and track after school until the track coach saw me with the tennis coach. Busted. I made my choice and joined the tennis team, and as a result, became the black sheep of the family again.

In defense of my parents' adamant aversion to tennis, I can only say that first, they did not understand the game; second, they thought it was for the rich; and third, although they had said nothing, maybe they had hoped I could get a track scholarship. Athletic scholarships for women were rare and, at the time, restricted to track.

Cy, knowing my checkered history and career choice to become a big-game vet, also gave me the arduous task of euthanizing unwanted or dying four-legged creatures.

Unfortunately, there was never a shortage of animals to be euthanized, or what I then called "murdered." Besides our paid clients, our clinic also worked for the animal "pound," as we called the shelters. Back then, there was no such thing as a no-kill shelter.

One day, when Cy returned from rounds, he found a very alive, happy shepherd-cross mutt sitting on the couch. The dog, one of many on death row at the pound, had run out of time. Cy yelled my name. I came into the reception area to find him standing with his vet bag clenched tightly in his hand, his cowboy hat shielding his expression, clearly facing off with the mutt. He did not blink an eye while I defended my reason for a stay of execution for the pound dog.

He shook his head and muttered to me, "The mutt is now your responsibility," and, with a slight grin on his tanned face, he walked down the corridor to his office. The dog became the clinic guard dog, and, much later, Cy rewarded me with a glowing recommendation for vet school.

Regardless of my determination to go to vet school, my parents assumed no obligation to their oldest daughter after high school. From as early as I can remember, they reminded me to work hard and save my money if I wanted to go to college. Once I graduated high school, they held to that conviction. In celebration of my high school graduation, my mom bought new living-room furniture. Not much changed when I graduated from college. She bought me a stuffed dog when I took her to the pharmacy to get medication after her back surgery.

And now, the black sheep of the family, the oldest daughter, was flying to Alaska by herself, leaving her husband in California. It was incomprehensible, what I was doing; they never understood.

Rick loved his job designing oil platforms in California. But the promise he and Chevron had made to me faded in importance. At first, he was angry at me, but Rick's mom, Flo, had an honest discussion with her son. He was so like his father, she told me. His entire focus was on his job. He sometimes worked seven days a week while I took care of our life in California.

I unfolded a small piece of paper, unlined, with bold black words, signed by Rick and me. I gave it to him. It was our pact:

Michelle will delay her career, decline the Wildlife Biologist position in Bozeman, and work at WSU. She will put Rick through graduate school. Upon graduation, we will pursue a location where we both can work in our respective fields.

"Mishie, I am so sorry," he cried as he held me.

"Alaska, here we come?" I giggled, "Promise?"

"Alaska, here we come. I promise you," he said.

CHAPTER 3

Council Field Camp

The puffy white clouds and angled, sharp-edged, snow-capped mountain peaks mesmerized me as they spiraled toward a blue-violet sky. The plane shook as we flew over the long, winding inlet cutting through the Chugach Mountains far below, on time for our 1:00 a.m. approach into Anchorage International Airport. It was July 1982.

It seemed to be an endless flight from San Francisco to Anchorage. And it seemed it was to be an eternal day. Once we landed, I followed the weary travelers to baggage claim, where someone from the office would meet me. I passed an enclosed display of a Kodiak brown bear and stopped. I stood next to the massive animal and looked up, craning my neck backward. It stood on its two hind legs, front paws reaching upward and out, showing the long, straight claws. The massive jaw was open, exposing the enormous canines. It must have stood 20 feet tall.

"Wow. Only in Alaska. How cool would that be to see in the wild?" I remembered saying to myself as I wandered off in disbelief.

Grabbing my backpack, I noticed a pudgy, middle-aged man, face framed with black glasses, beaming at me with a dimple-to-dimple grin. He was heading directly toward me. "You must be Michelle. I am Calvin Miller." He grabbed my pack, nearly out of breath. "But you can call me 'Cal.'"

"I am so glad to meet you," I replied. He had a Midwest accent with a German twang, and he reminded me of Gentle Ben from the 1960s TV show. Bears seemed to be in my sleep-deprived brain at that moment.

I followed him to a big white truck, where a petite woman with a bouffant of red hair was smoking a cigarette at the end of one of those long cigarette holders and appeared to be standing guard. She greeted me with a big hug.

In a Texan drawl, she said, "Let's get you home, sugar. My name is Pat."

They lived in a split-level home in Eagle River, a small town nestled in the Chugach Mountains about ten miles from Anchorage. By now, it was well past 2 a.m., and I was delirious with lack of sleep as Cal rambled on, explaining that I needed to get packed.

Packed? I didn't know what he was talking about. I *was* packed. Maybe he meant *unpacked*. He must have noticed my confusion, as he explained.

"Skippy wants you going to the bush tomorrow." He laughed, "Well, today, I guess. That's the problem in the summer; you never know what time it is." He chuckled again.

"What bush?" I asked. Again, delirious.

"Oh, yes—forgot. You are what we call a 'cheechako.' You leave for field camp. 'The bush' is what we call the boondocks."

19

He then listed items I would need for field camp. Unbeknownst to me, Calvin had never been to field camp, and therefore, really did not know what one would need.

For someone who had never been in an airplane until I was 21, I was already forgetting what it was like to drive a car. In less than 24 hours I had traveled more than 3,000 miles by air. Here I was, again airborne and on my way to some remote location in the bush.

The flight from Anchorage to Kotzebue was 700 miles. And then another 200 miles to Nome. The 737 banked over the Bering Sea and then descended into the tiny village of Nome.

As I arrived at the Nome Airport terminal, one large room, I grabbed my backpack and walked outside. A few hundred feet away, I spotted the hangar with the name Bering Air painted on the outside.

Dressed in my stiff, brown Carhartt pants and my shiny, extra-tough boots rolled down to mid-shin, I relayed the instructions. "Hi, my name is Michelle, and I work for the USDA. I am expected on a flight with Bering Air with a drop-off at the Council field camp?"

I trusted they knew what I was referring to. At that moment, a young, tall man with dark-brown hair and a welcoming smile walked through a door behind the counter.

"I heard they were expecting a new person," he said. "I'm owner and pilot of Bering Air. We are waiting on two guys who are being dropped off at mining camp. Welcome to Nome."

"At least someone knows where I'm going! I certainly do not," I grinned, as he led me to a small plane.

"Have you ever been in one of these?"

I shook my head "No."

"Cessna 206. A solid little plane."

Two husky, heavily bearded miners appeared, and our friendly pilot loaded us up. I sat in the very back, in the tail seat. I found out later that the smallest person always had to go into the back of the plane, with some exceptions. A story for another time.

By the time we dropped off the miners, the weather had changed. The temperature dropped to 34 degrees. I had left Carson City, Nevada, a few days earlier, with a temperature of near 93 degrees. Cool for Nevada on the first of July.

It was July 3 as we flew through a high, gray ceiling of clouds and blowing snow. We landed on a two-track muddied road with a frosting of white. I could barely see out the window of the co-pilot seat, so I wiped the condensation with my sleeve. The dark silhouette of what appeared to be a giant, with black hair appeared, about twenty feet from the right wing of the plane. Standing next to him was a short man, about half the height of the giant. They came up to the plane after we stopped, as the pilot signaled the "Okay" sign for them to approach.

I opened the door and jumped out into the cold mud to meet an outstretched arm belonging to the very tall, nice-looking guy with a silly grin, who greeted me, saying, "I'm Kenny. This is Kusko." He pointed to the smiling, indigenous man of an age I could not discern.

Kusko nodded his head and, ever so shyly, whispered, "Hi."

With his arms stretched out over his head, Kenny said, "Welcome to Council."

Council, known as Kaułiq or Akauchak in Inupiaq, is the nearest site to Nome that has trees, and some Nome residents come to cut spruce trees at Council for Christmas trees.

Even emptied of its passengers, it took the three of us to help push the plane on the wet, muddy, snow-coated airstrip (road). We waved goodbye, as the engines groaned in the increasing wind; the plane circled overhead and then buzzed us before heading back to Nome.

We got into the old Forest Service truck and headed to field camp, my new home for eight weeks. As we approached, I could see a large white canvas tent with a cross frame of poles at either end. As we got closer, I saw about eight smaller, two-person tents of multiple colors that formed a half circle around the larger tent. Kenny said the outhouse was that way, as he pointed in a direction away from camp. You could see a tall structure made of heavy plastic and four driftwood poles. A caribou skull, with bleached antlers awkwardly perched atop a pole, marked the spot.

He led me to a blue-and-white wall tent with a door flapping from the steady wind.

"This is yours."

It was obvious the Velcro on the flapping door was so shredded, especially in this wind, the door no longer worked. I put my pack in a clearing on the floor next to a cot covered with an olive-green mummy bag. Puffs of down were showing through worn seams.

I looked at him, waiting for him to laugh and tell me it was a joke. He did not. He was dead serious.

"Well, thank God it's cold and blowing. Mosquitoes won't be a problem." I was sleeping in a gear tent with no mosquito netting. And no functional door.

I followed Kenny to the white mess tent. Inside it was toasty warm, with a group sitting around an old fuel-oil stove in camp chairs. He introduced me to the crew: Dutchman, the reddish-blond, middle-aged, stocky guy with a reddish mustache and bushy eyebrows, and Scorup, a balding botanist from the University of Fairbanks Experiment Station in Palmer, Alaska.

"And these guys, we keep happy." He pointed at a tall, lean gray-haired man, the helicopter pilot, and a slightly younger man with a stocky build, the helicopter mechanic.

At that moment, a short, plump woman with long, dark hair with gray streaks walked in from an adjoining tent. "And this is Ruth, our cook from Pilgrim Hot Springs."

After a bite to eat, Dutchman walked me to my tent and noticed the flapping door.

"At least a wandering bear can step right in. It would be a shame to ruin such a perfectly good tent with claws," I said.

"Yep," he chuckled. He had a contagious laugh. "We'll talk tomorrow."

I wandered off to check out the outhouse with a 360-degree view. There was no door, so it was an unobstructed view of the honey bucket and a typical toilet seat on top of the plastic, 5-gallon bucket. A set of antlers held a roll of toilet paper. On the walk back to my tent, I stopped. I turned a full circle and took a breath of the cool, clean, glorious air as I saw nothing but miles and miles of tundra. It was heaven.

Until I unsnapped the musty-smelling sleeping bag and noticed a mosaic of circular, white patterns, from an unknown, but highly suspicious, source on the inside. "Sleeping in my clothes is a far better alternative, especially if the tent blows down," I mumbled. Unable to sleep due to the relentless shaking of the tent, I glanced at the flap of the door. It was swirling in and out with the wind. And then I noticed something was attached to the bottom of the flap, slamming against my cot. I scrambled out of the bag and grabbed my coat, which was, originally, on top of the sleeping bag. When the door flap blew in, the Velcro on the cuffs of my coat had stuck to the Velcro on the flap of the door. That was it. I put my coat on, grabbed the white-stained bag and the cot, and headed to the mess tent.

I awoke to the smell of coffee. I surprised Ruth as she brought the coffee thermos into the eating and working portion of the tent. I explained to her my lodging situation. Her bright, dark eyes and her cheerful smile turned into shock and then into what I assumed was her pissed-off look. She looked at my sleeping bag, said something in Yupik, and went back to her kitchen. I later asked Kusko, who was Yupik, if he could translate what she said. He just giggled while his face turned from brown to reddish brown.

By the time the crew staggered in, I'd put my cot in the corner and stowed my gear on top. Ruth rang the kitchen bell; literally—she had a bell and rang it. With her hands on her wide hips, she glared at Kenny and Dutchman. Then she went back into the cook tent.

Dutchman had a very confused look on his face. He had this crooked smile, half grin, half chuckle, with a look of surprise permanently stamped on his face. His bushy red eyebrows raised upward.

"What did I do?" Then he mumbled something about poison in his food. My breakfast was incredible. No one had noticed my cot, much less Billy White stains, the name of my sleeping bag. Later, I find another tent to call home—with a perfectly good door.

The Seward Peninsula spans 18 million acres on the western coast of Alaska. It is a remnant of the Bering land bridge, a strip of land connecting Siberia with mainland Alaska that formed during the Pleistocene Ice Age. This land bridge aided in the migration of humans, and plant and animal species, from Asia to North America.

Across the tundra were scattered remnants of the gold rush; rusty 55-gallon barrels and dilapidated dredges in dried-up creeks. Broken rail tracks extending into nothingness, once clattering with mine carts or trams full of ore, now ghostly quiet.

And to answer that infamous question that makes most of us Alaskans cringe, "Can you really see Russia . . . ?" The answer is "Yes," if you're standing on Little Diomede Island.

The island, at the narrowest part of the Bering Strait, which is about 51 miles long, is all that separates Cape Dezhnev on the Chukotka Peninsula, Russia, and Cape Prince of Wales on mainland Alaska. But Russia's Big Diomede Island is even closer to mainland Alaska, about 25 miles away, making it the closest non-border-sharing country to the continental U.S.

A few weeks after arriving at Council, we were flying in the helicopter and found ourselves in a quickly changing weather situation. We had hoped to get to Wales, Alaska, to collect vegetation and soil samples, but first we had to get through the York Mountains. We had terrible weather, with strong, howling winds, and we were low on fuel—a very dangerous combination. No matter how much you plan for weather, you also plan for the unknown.

Survival is fragile in those conditions, and weather is very much the unknown when working in the field in Alaska.

Our pilot landed on a level piece of ground on a mountain ridge, wind whipping so hard I could not open my door. He had to yell into the mic. Only Kenny had a headset on; Dutchman and I had earplugs. It was obvious what our situation was. The visibility was getting marginal. If we continued course, it was going to get worse. We agreed we would fly over the sea rather than go through the barely visible mountains. The con to this plan? We would fly close to Russian airspace, but our chances of getting shot down were far less than the possibility of flying into a mountain. We played the odds, and that time, we won. We flew over the Bering Sea and made it into Teller with less than a gallon of fuel—counting the fumes. Wales would have to wait.

These pilots were the best in the world, but they paid the price. Demons haunted these courageous men.

We had a pilot who was on loan for a few weeks while they called our pilot away for another project. The substitute pilot always wore a black helmet with a black visor. Yep, he looked like Darth Vader.

Dutchman and I were walking down a long, gentle slope toward the helicopter. You could see for miles. Our packs were heavy with soil samples and plants to identify. As we got closer, we saw our pilot looking directly at us, pointing his sawed-off shotgun in our direction.

We hit the ground. Our radio crackling, we could hear the word "bear." When the grizzly stood up on its hind legs, sniffing at the air, the pilot fired. Not at us, and not at the bear that had been following us. He shot in the air. The blast from the shot sent the bear scrambling back up the slope away from us.

Dutchman and I sat up. We were sure our pilot had finally gone 'Nam on us. This was a term that we used in "sensitive situations" with many of our pilots. This pilot would fly low and fast, weaving back and forth across any river we might have been flying over. He would never fly straight. He had also informed us about his gun that he kept below his seat. I learned over the years that it was rare for a pilot to fly straight, and the reason for that: survival.

He had been watching the bear following us. She had kept her distance, so she was never really a threat. She was a young bear and more curious about these strange creatures walking on her turf. We did not have the nerve to tell him it was him that scared the shit out of us, not the bear.

Every morning in camp that first season, we went through the same routine. I would try to decline a large, high-caloric breakfast like pancakes, eggs, and bacon, and Ruth would look at me, hands on her wide, stout hips, and say, "You may not be home tonight. You must eat a big breakfast." Then she would add, "If you don't eat, I will worry. You need fuel. You are too skinny."

Guilt. She would guilt me to eat. But she was right. I never knew if I would make it back to camp. So, I ate. There were several times over the years that a crew would spend the night in the field. Often, the reason was minor, such as poor weather or a mechanical issue with the helicopter. In the early days, we relied on handheld radios and a repeater, and poor radio reception was not infrequent. But turning a radio off? That would have been grounds for suspension.

I remember the mental anguish vividly if a crew got left in the field. It was an unspoken silence, if a crew was left overnight; survival became the first order of business. The unknown can weigh heavily on one's psyche.

There are not too many places to find shelter on the open tundra. If we were in tussocks, we could squeeze around a tussock, hunker down, and try to keep warm and dry as much as possible, and hope that we woke to the slapping of the helicopter blades in the morning.

Tussock tundra is unique, as grasses such as cotton grass or hair grass grow in stout, round clumps. As fresh shoots form, litter

27

and dead leaves help protect the tender shoots. When the debris builds over time, they form the tussocks. The permafrost below provides a microclimate of moisture and cool temperatures. Over time, with the organic accumulation of grass litter, the tussocks look like large mushrooms on steroids, dotting the landscape.

The cold temperatures, with the insulating, thick, organic mat of tussock vegetation, maintain permafrost soils, which are estimated to contain more than 50% of stored carbon. That is a tremendous amount of carbon. The earth's atmosphere contains about 850 gigatons of carbon. That means there are about 1,400 gigatons of carbon frozen in permafrost. Frozen, but not for long, as climate change is melting permafrost rapidly, resulting in a massive increase in the release of greenhouse gas into the atmosphere.

Flying in helicopters can be extremely dangerous. Helicopter and fixed-wing accidents and crashes are rare, but they happen. It is a common mantra that the more you fly, the higher the percentage you will experience an accident. Back in the day, low bids for government work were a standard operating procedure. That first summer, I found out helicopter contracts fell under this low-bid contracting.

In our Agency, the administrative staff decided who won a contract, based on allocations of money, not value or quality—it was a black-and-white formula.

This process concerned me after that first summer. Where does the safety of a crew fit into low-bid contracts for items such as helicopters? I was curious, so I asked our contract administrator about this. He replied matter-of-factly, "That is the way it is."

I asked, "When was the last time you were in the field?"

His response: "Never."

It was during this discussion that I found out that *none* of the administrative staff had ever been in a remote field camp. I asked the contracting officer if he had ever flown in a helicopter. He quickly responded, "No. I don't like to fly."

Another critical element when working in the field is food. That first summer in 1982 gave me a glimpse into what is important in managing a crew, in a remote field camp in the bush of Alaska. Morale can unite or separate a crew. And the key to keeping a crew happy is wonderful food. And the best way to have wonderful food is to have a good-natured cook.

Ruth was our moral compass! We kept her happy most of the time, and she would keep the camp happy, something the administrative bean counters could not comprehend.

One day, as a surprise, Dutchman and I schemed to give Ruth a morning off from cooking breakfast. As we snuck around the kitchen, as quietly as we could since Ruth's tent was right next door, Dutchman informed me he was going to make eggs-in-a-basket.

He found the eggs and then looked up at me. I had not moved.

My first mistake. I asked, "What in the hell are 'eggs-in-a-basket'?"

With a shocked look on his very serious face—well, as serious as someone with bushy, red eyebrows and a shit-eating grin permanently stamped on his face at 5:30 in the morning can look—he replied, "You cut these holes out of bread and cook the eggs in the hole . . ."

At that point, I cracked up laughing, covering my mouth as tight as I could with my hands, I squeaked, "Why?"

Dutchman was gently breaking an egg into each hole of the bread slices in the skillet. However, because he was giggling, his aim was a little off.

When Ruth stomped into her kitchen with a baseball bat, thinking a porcupine or some other four-legged brave soul had invaded her dominion, we had eggs and shells everywhere, with the smell of burnt toast permeating the air.

We stood there like two kids caught stealing cookies from the cookie jar. Dutchman was holding an egg in one hand and a spatula with egg dripping onto the floor in the other. I was wearing a piece of bread on each wrist, like bracelets, the reason for the last round of hysterics.

"Good morning, Ruth," Dutchman said. "We are cooking breakfast for you." Tears rolled from his eyes onto his very red face.

Ruth was looking at her kitchen. The baseball bat hung at her side.

She said, "What are those?" as she pointed at squashed pieces of bread on her floor.

I blurted, "They are from the holes. We're making eggs-in-a-basket. His idea," I added.

I looked at Dutchman, and that was it. We became hysterical.

Then Scorup and Kenny walked in. They saw Ruth with a bat, and me and Dutchman standing in a mess of yellow goop and white blobs, laughing uncontrollably. And they walked right back out.

We were on kitchen-cleanup duty for a week. She banned us from ever entering her kitchen again without her permission.

Fall was upon us by mid-August. There was a crispness to the mornings as the daylight shortened, and snow dusted the mountain peaks. Hundreds of caribou dotted the plains, migrating north. Golden balls of fur stood out against the bright red clumps of dwarf shrubs of alpine bearberry, feeding on the last few berries.

Bears were easily spotted fishing for whitefish, grayling, and sheefish in the streams.

Evergreen dwarf shrub species such as Arctic heather and black crowberry, only a few inches tall, drooped, with their red and black fruit hanging from their tiny, stout branches. The few remaining leaves of the knee-high deciduous Labrador tea, Arctic willow, and blueberry were dull yellow.

The tundra was alive with grizzly, moose, wolf, caribou, and scattered muskox. The skies were dotted with migrating geese, swans, and cranes. All life was demanding, preparing for the long, harsh winter ahead.

Finally, it was our last night together in Nome. There was one hotel room left, so Dutchman and I shared a tiny, musty-smelling room with two twin beds. The aroma of cigarette smoke was nauseating. I already missed my well-ventilated tent at the field camp.

As we enjoyed our night in the town, Dutchman looked at me, brought up his cold beer, and said, "You won the bet."

"Let me guess—you assumed I got the job to fill an EEO slot, right?"

"Well, in our defense, you were from California."

"Kenny was from California. Was there a bet to see if he would make it?" No response.

"Order me another beer while I use . . . the powder room. Oh, and next year, I design the outhouse."

The fact was I had more field expertise in range science and wildlife-habitat analysis before I graduated from WSU than my male comrades. Why? I took the low-paying work-study jobs, living in remote mountain cabins for USDA or WSU during the summer. At WSU, I always had to manually register each semester, which required an interview with a counselor, to ensure I could work 20 hours a week and manage 18 to 20 hours of science courses, all requiring labs and field trips.

In the Cascade Mountains of Washington and Oregon, I was responsible for collecting thousands of acres of vegetation and soils data for calculating critical habitat components for managing elk and cattle. This type of research required the identification of a few hundred grass, shrubs, herbs, and forest species; the ability to determine land sustainability for elk and domestic animal species; and demanded wilderness survival skills, including the ability to navigate.

By the time I graduated from WSU, I had managed large-game habitat-analysis projects and supervised crews, including a few doctorate candidates, mapping vegetation and soils using aerial imagery, while trekking hundreds of miles in remote wilderness with a backpack and a compass.

In Alaska, rather than map *thousands* of acres of vegetation and soils using satellite high-altitude color infrared imagery (CIR), I mapped *millions* of acres. This job required skills to identify hundreds of plant species, including lichens and mosses to determine the land capability and sustainability for caribou, reindeer, moose, and muskox.

But because I was a female, the bets were always against my success. And for the rest of my career, proving my worthiness never went away.

CHAPTER 4

The Dance Between Darkness and Light

It was a struggle to live in Anchorage after field camp. Public transportation was not reliable; Anchorage was very expensive; and as daylight was disappearing rapidly, winter would soon arrive. It was September.

I jumped at the sound of a phone ringing and constantly forgot to flush a toilet. One very dark and freezing morning, I was walking to work at 6:30 a.m. There was a light dusting of snow, but the sky was clear with stars. I normally had to walk looking down because the plows usually buried the sidewalks in a mound of snow, which also meant I had to walk in the busy street of Lake Otis.

I caught a streak of color overhead, so I stopped to look up. The dark sky was dancing with ribbons of greens, yellows, and reds. I had never seen the Aurora Borealis before. I have no idea how long I watched, but my legs were frozen from not moving, so I ran. Otherwise, I am sure I would have been late to work.

The office was still quiet when I fixed coffee and settled into my cubicle. The amount of paperwork was overwhelming: travel vouchers, time sheets, requests for help. And that was just the busy work! I had eight weeks of field gear to take care of, a hundred vegetation data sheets, splattered with red blobs of smashed mosquito bodies, to analyze and calculate plant productivity, moss species to identify, and a file case of 9x9-inch, high-altitude satellite CIR to interpret and map—more than a million acres of plant communities.

The imagery of deep-red shades blended into hues of pinks appear as abstract art to the layman, but to me? The colors represent diverse plant communities of dense shrubs to lichens.

And by utilizing a stereoscope and stereo pair imagery, which allow me to see three dimensional, I can differentiate between tall shrubs and low shrubs. The crease between my brows, from squinting into a stereoscope, reminds me of the millions of acres I have mapped since the age of twenty.

And I loved it! Rick was right—I needed a break from school. Vet school could wait.

And there I was, sitting in my office—OK, in a cubicle, barely wide enough for a desk to fit, looking at a door. I was finally working in big-game management, in Alaska, no less! And I married the love of my life.

And soon, Rick would get his transfer to the Chevron office in Anchorage. After four years of marriage, living in different states, Anchorage, Alaska, would be our home.

My dad always told me, "Work hard, and it will pay off." For the first time in my life, I let my guard down and believed him.

I called Rick almost every night when I got home. Chessy, my new kitten, would greet me at the door. It was comforting to pick her up, stroke her head, and listen to her soft purr. A neighbor and his very pregnant wife were moving to a new apartment that did not allow cats. While we were talking in the hallway, the young gray tabby ran from their apartment into mine. And like that, she adopted me.

After a long day and a good workout, I was ready to curl into bed with a book. I had just turned the light out when I heard a noise coming from the living room. Then Chessy came running in, jumped on me, hissed, and ran back out. She was meowing and hissing at the curtain of the sliding glass door out to the balcony. The door rattled. I grabbed the only thing I could find—the light on the end table—and then I screamed something and called 911.

The police found footprints in the snow below my balcony. No one was in the apartment below me. And, not surprising at all, they found footprints on my balcony.

"How the hell could that happen?" Rick screamed on the phone when I told him.

There was snow piled up and frozen solid, making the distance between the top of the snow to the balcony about six feet. The police officers theorized someone might have had a bit too much to drink, got locked out of their apartment, and climbed to the wrong balcony. As the police said, it was a Friday night, and the Pines were a happening place.

"Or," I offered, "someone tried to break into my apartment."

The police suggested I change my route when walking home and left.

There is a well-known axiom in Alaska, referring to the male community:

"Where the odds are good, but the goods are odd."

After the incident on my apartment balcony, I told the guys at the gym I wanted to protect myself. Laddy, a retired SEAL, put me on his "get strong" program!

There was talk among the guys at work about the disappearance of several young women, but in a disrespectful and dismissive tone, branding them as runaways and prostitutes.

Later that year, on October 27, 1983, police arrested Robert Christian Hansen, also known as "Butcher Baker," who confessed to killing at least 17 young women, mostly prostitutes.

His killing spree had lasted at least 12 years. During that time, he portrayed himself as a family man, his wife a member of the religious community, and he a prominent member of the business community. Instead of people admitting that he was a dangerous sociopath, even after one of his victims survived, they insisted he was a good and moral man. Hansen was charged with assault, kidnapping, weapons offenses, theft, and insurance fraud. The jury sentenced him to 461 years plus life in prison, without the possibility of parole.

But it wasn't all darkness.

Hallelujah! Rick arrived before the Christmas holidays. We had delayed shipping my car until the Agency committed to a permanent, full-time position. Since arriving in Alaska, I had learned enough in my short time there to stand up for what I needed.

Unexpectedly, my mom told me that she was sending my dad, brother, and sister to Anchorage to spend Christmas with us. I had made it clear to my mom that Rick and I needed to spend Christmas together—just the two of us. My family never had plans to visit. Why now? I asked. She claimed ignorance about that discussion, suggesting it would be nice since she was working over the holidays as a dispatcher at the police station.

Oh, boy, I thought, *not sure this is a good idea, since December is the darkest and coldest time to be in Alaska.*

That was not our plan. It was my mom's. My Christmas present, I suspected. She bought the airline tickets, but apparently, she thought there was room in my tiny one-bedroom apartment for five people.

"It's OK. And we both know it is not your fault," Rick smiled, kissing my forehead. "It will be fine."

We made it work. My sister, Tish, all 5'8" of her, slept on the couch. The only hotel with a room—at a cost suitable to our budget—for my dad and my brother was on Third Avenue downtown. It was hilarious to hear my brother's and dad's stories of what they saw. I had given them both strict instructions to be careful. My dad could be a pushover, but my brother? At 6'4", he could hold his own. Even during the holidays, the tenderloin area of Anchorage was very active.

My brother was having a hard time with the short daylight. We drove to the small town of Girdwood to do some alpine skiing at the Alyeska Resort. The drive to Alyeska, about 30 miles south along the Seward Highway along Turnagain Arm, is the most beautiful in the state. Alas, it was as black as a moonless night, so there was no view to witness. There was a glimpse of light from the late-morning dawn, and, from the chairlift, my brother and sister got a glimpse of a gray sheet of shimmering ice of the Cook Inlet, locked between the Chugach Mountains.

The runs are steep and challenging at Alyeska, but Girdwood is at sea level, and the base elevation is only 250 feet above sea level. The top run is 2,750 feet elevation with a vertical drop of 2,500 feet. Alyeska receives a lot of snow at the top, but as you ski down to the lower trails, they are icy.

Turnagain Arm is within the transition from a white spruce forest to a Sitka spruce-hemlock forest, a dryer south-central region to a wetter coastal ecosystem. Eventually, Alyeska put in some north-face runs at the top, which provided good-quality snow. In the past 12 years, I have been to Alyeska twice in the winter and found it raining both times. Because of climate change, they need a machine to make snow to keep the resort running during the winter.

At least on the drive back to Anchorage, the enveloping darkness got interrupted while we made a stop at the Bird House Bar.

"Oh, my god—you've got to be kidding me," my brother burst out with a laugh as we walked up to the old cabin, half of it disappearing into the ground. "A goddamn fire trap."

And then he looked up. "What the hell is that?"

A dim light eerily shone on what appeared to be a long, blue neck sticking out of the side of the cabin. The bird looked like a cross between a turkey and an ostrich. He smirked, looking up at the bird, shaking his head; then he opened the rickety, slanted door.

He ducked his head and followed us into a place that time had surely forgotten.

Where else could you find a unique experience but at the Bird House? Not in Skinny Dick's Halfway-Inn Saloon near Fairbanks; the Salty Dog on the spit in Homer; the Red Dog Saloon in Juneau; or even at the Red Onion Saloon in Skagway. And that is my sole opinion, from my respective experience.

As you walk through that old, slanted door, you became part of the legend, and the secrets you witness stay secrets. And that was the fascination and magnetism of the Bird House.

My dad felt at home there, and, judging by his antics, he enjoyed himself tremendously. My sister laughed with the bartender and whatever he was whispering in her ear. And my stoic brother, always serious, and completely out of his hometown element, was in deep conversation with his barstool mate, laughing. As I looked at my wonderful husband, he winked and smiled, comfortable, with a mug in his hand, cornered by two lovely women.

The Bird House was constructed around 1903 by an unknown prospector during the gold rush. It had changed hands a few times over the last three decades. Rather than relay the history in my words, I bequeath this history lesson to the reader to explore. And who knows? Maybe the mystery of the Bird House will be unearthed.

I visited the Bird House at least half a dozen times over the years, and I will say this: The Bird House was more than just a bar to get a drink. It was noisy and loud, friendly and crazy. People were at ease. The eye candy, on the walls and the ceiling, could keep you busy all night. My dad purchased some of that eye candy for my mom. He also left his calling card on the door. My brother walked in with a bit of an attitude, but when he left, he came out laughing.

You never knew what to expect when you walked through that disappearing door into the Bird House. Every visit was different. It was like a force coming from the walls, from the ceiling, from the floor, an energy thumbprint left from every living being that had walked through that door. The dynamic was different every time I visited.

The next morning, my dad and brother declared they were going to buy a Christmas tree, although I had no decorations to put on it.

"Maybe we should get a few new ones," Rick said, with a twinkle in his eye.

My brother carried what looked like a big bush up the stairs into the tiny apartment, leaving a trail of green needles.

"Are you sure you want to move up here? You know how much this . . . tree was?" he asked, pointing at the big green bush.

"Seventy-five bucks! People use duct tape to keep their bumpers on their cars. The guy asked us if we needed some duct tape for the tree. I asked him, 'Why? Is it going to fall apart?' For 75 dollars, it better not."

I explained that the tree had traveled further than Santa did with his reindeer, over land and sea, and in the dry winter climate of Alaska, the needles would be on the floor in a few days.

Tish, who was reading on the couch, responded sarcastically without ever looking up from her magazine, "A real Charlie Brown's Christmas tree."

"Yeah, but Charlie Brown didn't have one of these to hang!" Rick grinned as he threw something to Mike.

Mike held the object up by the checkered red-and-green bow and saw the brown nuggets that formed the wreath. "You got to be shitting me!" he said with a shrug, his mouth open. "And how much did this cost?"

"Fifteen buckaroos. Or, more like moose-a-doos," he added as he handed Mike a drink. "Where else can you buy laminated moose shit, formed in a wreath, and topped with a cute little red-and-green bow!"

Tish looked up from her reading. "You got a plastic bag?" she asked me. I pointed to a drawer.

She grabbed a bag, put her boots and coat on, and left. She came back about 15 minutes later, face pink from the cold, and held up a bag of frozen brown nuggets. She put them in the freezer and laughed.

"I am going into the ornament business," she said, lying back on the couch. That was my sis, always the schemer.

We all endured and enjoyed our family gathering. And I am sure my dad, brother, and sister enjoyed their Christmas visit, despite the dark days, and left with plenty of stories to tell.

I don't remember where I heard the phrase, but I thought of it as I waved goodbye to my family when they boarded their plane back to Washington. It went something like:

> "The dance between darkness and light will always remain—the stars and the moon will always need the darkness to be seen, and the darkness will just not be worth having without the moon and the stars."

I suppose I can say the same about the Aurora. If it wasn't for the darkness, how would we ever see those brilliant greens, purples, reds, and yellows dancing among the heavens?

Rick and I had some time to teach ourselvess cross-country skiing. We went to the local Gary King Store and bought ourselves a package deal. We fell a lot, laughed a lot, and experienced the intricacies of avoiding moose—with long, narrow skis hooked to your feet and only poles for protection.

Moose are gigantic animals. They are the largest of the ungulates in the deer family. The Alaska-Yukon species is the largest, with the males weighing as much as 1,600 pounds and the females about 800 pounds. They can stand six feet and taller, depending on the size of their rack, or antlers, which only the males have. Cows can have one to three calves, and twins are common. Like most mothers, cows are fierce protectors of their young. Their long, powerful legs get them through deep snow, but they can be four deadly weapons. If agitated, those legs can strike with such a force they can kill instantly. They look gentle, with that elongated snout, long-lashed eyes, and their slow, graceful saunter.

The eyes of a moose do not brighten in a headlight, as does their much smaller cousin, the deer. The driver does not see them until it is too late. You can imagine what a moose can do to a smaller, compact vehicle.

It was a wonderful New Year's celebration, and Rick and I had some alone time before he, too, had to fly back to California. The fireworks were brilliant against the snow and the crystal-clear night. We huddled under a wool blanket, clasping hot toddies in our gloved hands, and planned for the next chapter of our life together, as the fireworks exploded into the winter night.

To keep the loneliness from creeping in, I kept busy. I signed up for an anthropology course on Alaskan Natives and Culture, at the Anchorage Community College, which eventually became University of Alaska (UAA), convenient for my apartment and work. The added incentive was the free use of the athletic facilities, which included racquetball and a swimming pool. I was an avid racquetball player, even though it did not help my tennis game at all. I signed up for a course, hoping to find people to play ball with.

I finally received my permanent status and GS-9, although still two grades lower than my male counterparts, or about $20,000 a year difference.

Generally, in the federal government, the pay scale an employee qualifies for is called the general schedule or GS. The GS grade levels specify a fixed compensation range for a particular position, in particular geographic localities, within the federal government.

Experience, education, or a combination of the two, generally, determine if a person qualifies for a position and GS. There are 10 steps or pay increases within each grade. It takes 18 years to advance to the step 10 of a grade. There are always exceptions, as I experienced throughout my federal career.

Although I graduated with a bachelor of science degree with a double major in wildlife biology and range science, and a minor in soil science, with two years of summer federal employment as a Range Technician, the Range Conservationist position I was offered was a temporary GS-7, step 1.

This new position was a permanent GS-9 and had been held by Kenny for two years. I was replacing him because, after two years, he was being promoted to a GS-11 in a different position. His wife was pregnant, and he had a family to support. He needed to be home more.

In the early 1980s, it was a typical hiring practice for USDA to hire biologists as term employees or temporary. Term or temporary employees do not receive the same benefits as a permanent employee.

My car finally arrived in May by barge. To celebrate, I took my cat Chessy on a road trip to Portage Glacier. The snow was melting, and I expected the highway would be clear of snow and ice. I checked the tide tables, and a bore tide was scheduled.

The bore tide is a blast of seawater that returns to a shallow and narrowing inlet from a broad bay. In the Turnagain Arm, a bore tide occurs during the full or new moon, when the tidal difference between a low tide and high tide exceeds 27 feet. Although bore tides, or waves, occur all over the world, only a few are large enough to make a name for themselves. The most famous bore tide in Alaska is the one that happens in the Turnagain Arm.

And like everything else in Alaska, it is huge, one of the biggest in the world. The bore tide can get as tall as 10 feet, flowing at a speed of 10 to 15 miles per hour.

Prior to my arrival, the methodology and management of the vegetation survey for the Seward Peninsula largely ignored the scientific method, to say the least. The purpose of this 18-million-acre survey was to provide vegetation data for the management of reindeer. Only indigenous people, normally a subsistence culture, can own reindeer. I walked into a shitshow of a mess. Not only was the mapping not accurate, but the field forms and data-collection methods were not consistent. I called the only person I knew who would give me an answer to my questions, Kenny. He was honest and unapologetic. And it explained why there was such a turnover of people in my current position.

The supervisor hierarchy for me was my boss, the State Range Conservationist, who was supervised by the State Conservationist, the top position at the state level. It was not about ensuring that we followed the high standards of scientific data and method. It was the opposite. What was important was the effort of spending millions and millions of federal tax dollars for an Alaskan program, and making sure the important people got the credit. And in this case, the people who really needed help were not the important people. The goal was not to get results; the goal was how much money was spent and for whom.

Déjà vu. How could I forget that working for the government was not about doing a good job? It was all about not rocking the boat of the supervisory hierarchy. I understood the issues, which is why I certainly did not agree that the two goals were mutually exclusive. I was more determined than ever to ensure that I did my job to the best of my abilities, both scientifically and ethically. Looking back, I realize how naïve I was.

It was the middle of May, and I was anxiously waiting for Rick at the Anchorage International Airport. Snow had melted, and the asphalt ponds were gone. The brown landscape transformed quickly to shades of green. Birch and aspen trees armed with green dots along their branches were patiently waiting to burst into leaves. The glossy leaves of willows extending to the sun's rays provided the much-needed energy for moose, especially the cows, with their large, distended bellies slick from morning dew. The sky swirled with flocks of waterfowl, their honking announcing spring.

A new day, a new season, and new challenges were to follow, but now, my husband was by my side.

CHAPTER 5

Home & Heart

R ick, *dressed in jeans and hiking boots,* could not believe the transformation from winter to spring. "This is incredible!" he exclaimed, as we walked, holding hands, to baggage claim.

Chevron had not yet received his final paperwork for relocating to the Anchorage office, so we were lucky to move into the Chevron corporate apartment. The location was perfect, as it was midway between my office and his. The two-bedroom apartment gave Chessy more room to explore. She quickly got settled into her new surroundings and enjoyed the extra attention from Rick again.

Although we were both busy, we fell back into our natural routine. Every day we talked about those menial details of how our day was at work, and at night we would cuddle. When we disagreed, we would discuss openly, respectfully, and honestly. Well, most of the time, but we had our moments. It was us. Rick always knew me. He knew when he needed to let me vent; he didn't fix me. Or correct me. Or judge me. He just let me be me.

When Rick returned from Vietnam, he'd bought a 12-speed bike and rode from Wenatchee, Washington, to Long Island, New York. In high school, he excelled in wrestling, although he looked like a runner. He was exceptionally bright and had an academic scholarship to WSU.

Later, he told me his bike trip across the United States was a release and therapy. While he was on leave in the States, his platoon had been attacked. He said he should have been there. I always wondered if there was more than just the survivor's guilt that he held so deep inside.

Rick would sometimes have this distant, faraway stare, his expression one of sadness and pain, his eyes veiled with fear. There was a car accident one night on the freeway while we were driving home in Concord. He acted spontaneously, without thought, as he jumped out of our vehicle, putting himself at risk. I saw the same look on our 'Nam helicopter pilots, when there was a potentially dangerous situation. They reacted the same way as my husband.

To relieve the stress of work, we would take short weekend trips near Anchorage. One weekend, we drove south to the Kenai Peninsula. With new fishing poles and hip waders, we tried our luck fishing for red salmon in the Russian River. We camped, fished, and hiked. The scenery was dramatic, the river a turquoise blue. We saw moose and glimpsed the golden brown of a young grizzly walking along the river bank.

Fishing on the Kenai Peninsula is both a blessing and a sin. Thousands of people flock to the famous Russian River, a popular tributary that drains into the Kenai River. The river flows 12 miles from Upper Russian Lake, through Lower Russian

Lake, and empties into the upper Kenai River. With its clear water, the Russian River supports sockeye (red), Coho (silver), and pink salmon.

Another frequent visitor, besides humans, spotted along the Kenai is the Kenai brown bear. These brown bears are a unique and isolated population of fewer than 600 animals and are vulnerable to rapid decline and extinction. In 2013, the Alaska Board of Game proposed to reduce or eliminate the bears by allowing an unsustainable number of bears killed through sport hunts and by baiting. The courts ruled in December 2020 that the Fish and Wildlife Service (FWS) had the authority to regulate wildlife-hunting practices, even if in conflict with state regulations.

The Trump administration defied the authority that the FWS can manage wildlife sustainably on wildlife refuges. All predator species are at risk to baiting, trapping, and killing on refuges. I suspect this will be overturned, but this attitude is frightening.

We spent our fourth wedding anniversary camping at Denali National Park. There was still snow in areas, but the days were warm. And the spectacular Mount Denali was out in all her glory. Or is it Mount McKinley? One thing that never changes in Alaska is controversy, even in the name of the most famous mountain in North America. It took 100 years of debate, but on the eve of the National Park Service's (NPS) 100th anniversary in 2015, under the Obama administration, the name of the highest peak in North America changed from Mount McKinley to Denali.

On our last night, as we cuddled in front of the fire, we roasted marshmallows for s'mores, drank champagne, and toasted our anniversary, watching the peak of Denali twirling between hues of purple to pink, as clouds shielded her snow-topped peak from our view. For us, the mountain would always be Denali, the Great Mountain.

A co-worker of Rick's from the Concord Office, temporarily assigned to Anchorage, became our new roommate. Marc was fun to have around, and Chessy found a new human to tease. It was good for Rick to have a familiar face and friend, especially for windsurfing.

Rick bought a used windsurfer in Anchorage, which was as popular in Alaska as it was in the Bay Area. And to his astonishment, there were endless lakes to challenge all levels, from the beginner to the expert. On the weekends, we would drive from Anchorage to Big Lake, a community in the Matanuska Susitna Borough, north of Wasilla. It is a major attraction for fishing, boating, and other water-related activities.

For us, it was a perfect spot to windsurf, with wind and an enormous expanse of protected water. I was immediately hooked, although Rick had to swim out to get me one time when I could not get the board upright. We were laughing so hard at my ordeal, I forgot how cold I had become. To give me some credit, the boom for the sail was wood, and the board was huge. It was sturdy when upright, but extremely heavy when trying to get the oversized sail out of the water.

Rick joined a local softball team, so I spent many nights watching softball games. Softball and baseball are big in Alaska. Sometimes his team would play at 2 a.m. At least the fields were just a short walk or bike ride from our apartment.

By the end of June, I was completing everything for the upcoming field season. I found myself extremely agitated and anxious. I remember telling Rick several times that, if something happened to me, he should sue the government. Although I was kidding, he knew I was not sleeping and on edge. He finally asked me what was going on.

I explained to him about low-bid contracts, regardless of the quality or expertise of the vendor. That is fine for a copy machine, but for helicopter and gas contracts? I was also arguing with administration and my supervisor about safety gear.

I did find a perfect place for field camp. Moses Point was constructed in 1943 as an auxiliary landing strip for the Air Force, located two nautical miles west of Nome. It provided a servicing airfield for lend-lease aircraft being flown to Siberia by Soviet Red Air Force pilots.

Although Rick missed his project designing an oil platform off the coast of California, he was enjoying the challenges Alaska Chevron provided him. One day he came home after a day of flying to a site off the Kenai Peninsula coast with a co-worker in a small plane, so excited to be back up in the air. He told me all about his pilot and the project they assigned him.

I hoped that flying would not reawaken the demons from Vietnam but, instead, create angelic dreams of Alaska's natural beauty. My husband was thrilled and excited with the opportunities Alaska offered us. At night, however, when we talked, I struggled to hide my feelings of dread. It was a time of high anxiety for me. For some reason, I was more sensitized to risk than I had ever been before. I could not explain it away.

We stayed up late to watch the July 4th fireworks, my first in Alaska, as I was in the bush the first year in Alaska. Although we were losing daylight, after the longest day of the year, summer solstice, the locals start the countdown for winter to arrive. Even in the dusk at midnight, the fireworks are more for tradition than the show itself.

The day finally came for me to leave for field camp. Rick took me to the airport; as he hugged me, he whispered in my ear that everything would be fine. Then he said, "I want you to ask for at least a week off halfway through. They cannot force you to work eight straight weeks out there. If they don't, I will show up with a team of lawyers!" he insisted, halfheartedly. "You do not have to prove anything to them. Or anyone."

"OK. I will see you in a few weeks, then . . . I love you . . . and," I said, seeing the tears forming in his blue-gray eyes. He gave me a kiss, hugged me, and whispered, "And yes, I will take care of Chessy."

"And she you."

CHAPTER 6

Moses on the Sea

The flight to Kotzebue and then on to Nome settled my nerves. As we were waiting to get our bags, Skippy announced he had things to do in Nome. Dutchman and I looked at each other and shook our heads. I told him that the DC-6 was leaving in one hour. He muttered something, and off he went. A man in his own world.

Scorup came up and chuckled. "All things normal. He never helps."

Dutchman looked at me and shrugged. "Trust me. Probably easier this way."

I looked at Kusko and said, "Good thing you didn't get dragged along. I would have probably caused a scene."

The Cooperative Extension agent was waiting for us with our truck. Dutchman winked at me. I grinned back. Whatever Skippy was planning, he would be without a vehicle. We loaded our stuff and headed to Bering Air, where the DC-6 was waiting, along with our helicopter crew, the pilot, and a helicopter mechanic. It took several trips to get our gear from the slaughter facility, what we called our "storage shed," not far from the airport.

"Your boss has 10 minutes, and then we are lifting off."

I shook my head, swearing, and then I told Dutchman and Kusko, "Go," as I pointed to the plane.

I watched as they boarded, and the pilot smiled, gave a thumbs-up, and started the engines. Scorup and I walked over to the Bell 206 chopper, shrugged our shoulders, and strapped in. Our pilot already had the coordinates for Moses Point.

The Bering Sea was sparkling as we approached Norton Bay. We flew past the village of Elim on the northwest shore of Norton Bay, 96 miles east of Nome and 5 miles southwest of the Moses Point landing strip. Elim was formerly named Nuviakchak, in the Malemiut dialect of the Inupiat Eskimo.

The Native culture was well-adapted to the environment. Each tribe possessed a defined subsistence-harvest territory. In 1911, this area became a federal reindeer reserve, and, in 1914, Reverend L.E. Ost founded a Covenant mission and school called the Elim Mission Roadhouse.

The village was incorporated in 1970. In 1971, when the Alaska Native Claims Settlement Act (ANCSA) passed, Elim decided not to take part and instead opted for title to the 298,000 acres of land in the former reserve. The federally recognized tribe in the community, the Native Village of Elim, is an Inupiat Eskimo village with a fishing and subsistence lifestyle, using their fish camp at the headwaters of the Kwiniuk River, at Moses Point.

As we approached the landing strip, we scouted areas for locating the repeater, which was necessary for our one-way radio telecommunication. The golden sand beach looked heavenly and the water inviting, with one small exception: the latitude of 64 degrees N, longitude 162 degrees W made for a chilly swim. By comparison, the latitude of Honolulu is 21 degrees N and 157 degrees W.

There were also a couple of old buildings that we had hoped to use as a makeshift kitchen, dining, and work area. As Dutchman and I stepped into the principal building, our expectations diminished.

"Oh, my god," I gasped. "Please, tell me that is not. . . ."

Dutchman cut in, "I think it is."

"It" covered the room with dark-brown, dried splatters on the ceiling, on the walls, and on the bare wooden floors. Leftover remains of firecrackers and the smell of sulfur still permeated the air.

"At least it's dry! We could scrape it off?" Dutchman asked in a forlorn voice, his eyebrows raised. And then Scorup walked in, and that was all it took. The hysterics began.

"So, your idea of this summer's shitter?" Scorup bellowed.

By the time Ruth arrived on a scheduled charter at Moses Point the next afternoon, we had everything cleaned and set up. We were so relieved to be kicked out of the kitchen and welcomed a hot meal for dinner.

Dutchman could not hold it in any longer as he told Ruth why her kitchen smelled of bleach. Although we were making a joke out of it, we saw that look in Ruth's eyes. She was going to have a discussion with the village elders in Elim.

We got into the routine of field work. The tundra was dotted with our blue-and-yellow tents and the spectacular, blue-tarp outhouse with a rainbow of pink, yellow, and orange engineering flagging waving in the breeze. I had cut out half-moons in the upper quarter of the tarp, and Rick and I had used a heavy-duty glue and duct tape to secure mosquito netting over the moon cutouts, enclosing the top of the outhouse. Heavy-gauge wire was then used to form a peak.

For when it rained, Rick had designed a rain fly, secured with parachute cord. The goal was to allow air and light to circulate but also minimize bug invasion. Inside, there was a custom padded toilet seat, a welcome treat on a cold summer morning. Always, the engineer, my husband.

A week later, a fixed-wing landed on the strip just as we were eating dinner. It was Skippy. He had chartered a flight with Bering Air. He walked in, grinning, and, with nervous energy, asked us what we had been doing.

We all stared at him. Then, as if we had choreographed our response, we answered, "Us?" in unison.

"Oh, gee, I don't know, doing some fishing, getting some field work done," Dutchman said in a sarcastic tone, stressing loudly on the words "field work." "How about you? What have you been doing?" Dutchman demanded.

A few days later, a doctorate student from the University of Anchorage-Fairbanks (UAF) spent two days working with us on a mapping-verification process. It eventually turned out to be part of his research for his doctorate. He was also a pilot. I had flown with him in his plane from the Merrill Field Airport in Anchorage, one of the busiest small-plane airports in the world, to Palmer, where we were meeting with Scorup at the UAF Experiment Station. And wow, was that an eye-opening experience! Not only do you have to be careful of the military airspace on approach to the airport, but you also must be aware of the hundreds of aircraft around you.

After breakfast, I told Dutchman to have a fantastic day before grabbing my field gear and heading off to the plane that had landed on the strip.

"I am sure you will, too, when I am off for the next two weeks," Dutchman smirked.

While Scorup and I were working with my map unit verification, Dutchman was working with Skippy and Kusko for the next two days.

The verification of mapping units requires good visibility and calm weather. Any turbulence can be quite disrupting, if not nauseating, when looking back and forth—from out a window and back to a map-unit delineation on the CIR imagery. We had to verify that the vegetation on the ground matched the plant-community type for the map unit I delineated and interpreted on the imagery. I had mylar overlays on each of the 9 x 9 imagery photos, which allowed notations to be made, but not directly on the image itself.

It was on the second day that we ran into problems. We were flying north of the Bendeleben Mountains on a west-to-east transect. We had barely noticed the dark clouds cloaking the Bendelebens when the gust of wind hit the plane.

Our graduate student was no longer looking at aerial imagery but assisting the pilot. Then those words came over our headphones, "Hold on—it's going to get rough."

And it did. The storm hit fast and strong. Scorup and I were sitting in the seats behind our pilots. We stashed our imagery, tightened our seat belts, and looked at each other. I saw the concern in his eyes. And I know he saw mine. He had flown above the Seward Peninsula enough to realize that this was a nasty one.

At that moment, as our plane bounced up and down and sideways, I said to myself, *This is why. This was why I have felt that pit in my stomach for the last month.*

Although we could not see the broad basin, we knew Death Valley was below us—or wanted it to be. I knew Scorup was going through the same gyrations in his head. The Bendelebens should be southwest of us, and the Darby Mountains should be southeast of us.

Weather changes quickly on the Seward Peninsula, so we were thankful we were flying with Bering Air. We knew our pilot was instrument-rated for these conditions, which could determine our survival.

Flying in white-out conditions creates vertigo; you soon lose the capacity to know if you are upside down or right side up. This brought down the plane John Kennedy, Jr. was piloting from New York to Martha's Vineyard in 1999. It takes years of expertise to trust the instruments, which is why we were happy our pilot was instrument-rated.

I looked at Scorup, "Great. Death Valley."

He smiled. Grabbed my hand.

"We'll be OK. Could be worse; we could be with Dutchman."

Our co-pilot was straining out the window to see. If I hadn't been so scared, I think I could have been airsick! The course that we flew was along the Tubutulik River, which cut through Death Valley. This course would avoid the mountains to the west, follow down the river valley, and out over the Bering Sea and Norton Sound. A much safer route than flying into the mountains.

I don't think any of us said a word as we bounced among the black clouds, rain pounding against the windows and the plane's thin metal fuselage. And then we started dropping through the clouds, skimming above whitecaps of the Bering Sea. Although we were still in a precariously compromising situation, as our plane was not on floats, there was a moment of relief to see outside, even if it was water. Scorup and I never asked about fuel.

And finally, we landed on the strip at Moses Point. Scorup made a crack about needing to go to the outhouse. And then he saw his tent rolling by.

"Maybe dome tents aren't the best design in open tundra by the ocean," I squeaked.

That night, Scorup and I played poker and drank Bailey's and cocoa in Dutchman's tent.

"This isn't fair. I should go back with you guys tomorrow," I moaned. "When you guys get back, I am taking off for a week and going home. If I don't, Rick will cause holy hell."

The next morning, the weather had gotten no worse, but it was no better, either. I informed Skippy that I had too much data analysis to do. I asked the pilot to ensure the safety of my crew, which was Kusko. He got the message loud and clear. The dread I had been feeling was resurfacing.

I grabbed something to eat and went back upstairs to work. Later, I heard Ruth talking with someone outside, who did not sound like our helicopter mechanic. Then she yelled at me to come down. There was an older, indigenous man standing with Ruth. The mechanic was frantically hooking up the battery to the radio telephone.

"What's wrong?" I asked, seeing worry on Ruth's face. "The helicopter?"

The man spoke quietly, in thick Yupik dialect.

"We got a message for you. I rode from Elim on a three-wheeler." He looked at Ruth and then at the floor. Every Sunday, we recharged the battery system for the one-way radio. It had been down all day."

"There is an emergency, Michelle," Ruth quietly said, "from Anchorage."

My head was spinning. First, I thought it was my cat, Chessy. Then I thought it was Rick. A joke or something. I waited patiently by the radio, until the mechanic stepped away. There was chatter, and then I heard my name. And then my heart stopped. Ruth stood behind me. She gasped, putting her hand on her mouth. I clicked the radio button to talk.

"This is Michelle Schuman. I have an emergency message." I clicked. Quiet. Then static. Then a voice. It was my brother. He said Rick and Marc had been in a car accident.

Rick had died.

I don't recall everything he said. My world went dark. My hands shook. Then there was another voice as the mechanic took the microphone from my clenched hand. He clicked the button. "She's here."

The voice told me Rick had been in a car accident. He said he had tried everything to save him, but he had lost too much blood. He was terribly sorry for my loss. I asked about our friend, Marc, also from Chevron. The voice told me he died during surgery.

I remember walking away. The mechanic still had the microphone in his hand. The next thing I knew, I was standing outside. Ruth brought me a jacket. I scared her. She said later that I kept repeating, "I need to go home. I need to see Rick."

Later, I found out that our normally quiet mechanic demanded the Agency send a plane immediately. They refused because we had a helicopter. Ruth told me that our gentle helicopter mechanic, frustrated with whomever was on the end of the line from the state office, screamed into the microphone that he had been trying to reach the knucklehead jackass supervisor currently with the helicopter for more than an hour.

The radio-phone transmitter is a lifeline for field camps and remote villages in Alaska. When there is an emergency, all chatter defers to the emergency. The conversations are not private, but everyone is respectful. In my case, not only did Bering Air take charge when the Agency did not, but villagers I never met came to my rescue.

I was in a fog. Was I still on the plane? Maybe we crashed? The voice on the phone told me Rick had died at 4:37. But my watch said 2:37. How could that be? It was a joke. It had to be a joke. I was numb.

I sat as Ruth made some tea. She told me Bering Air was diverting a scheduled flight from one village to pick us up. Then we heard the rotor of a helicopter, and our mechanic ran out to the strip. I got up and watched when I heard yelling. There was an argument between the pilot and Skippy.

The pilot barged into the door and hugged me. "Goddamn radio was off. He had the fucking radio *off*. Get your stuff. I will fuel up, and we are off to Anchorage."

Skippy came in, telling the pilot that he had no authority to fly the helicopter to Anchorage. And then he moved on Skippy so fast I don't think any of us comprehended what was happening.

After a struggle, our mechanic got the pilot to let Skippy go. I know I said something to Skippy, but I don't remember what it was. Once our pilot calmed down, I told our red-faced, pissed-off pilot that Bering Air was diverting a scheduled plane to pick me up. It should be here shortly.

Later, when I thanked Bering Air, they apologized to me. They had hoped to get me directly to Anchorage, but the weather was dangerous. I will never forget that look I saw in my helicopter pilot. He was someone else. It was that 'Nam look. And I firmly believe Skippy had finally pushed a pilot to that edge. And we all knew it, especially our mechanic.

Ruth and I boarded the plane. The Cooperative Extension agent picked us up and took us to his home. I had missed the last plane to Anchorage. He gave me his phone to use and told me to call home, the Chevron apartment. I think it was the only number I remembered.

A man answered. I recognized the voice. My brain was in overload with so many emotions: happiness, relief, insanity, and anger. This was a horrible joke!

"Marc? What the hell?" I vaguely remember asking him to put my husband on the phone.

I heard sobbing in the background, and then Marc was talking to someone.

"Michelle. Rick died," he whispered, his voice cracking.

I can close my eyes right now and vividly remember where I was, what I felt, what I said, after I heard those words in Marc's voice.

"No. He isn't dead. Because then you should be dead. And you are not." I screamed. "I was told you died during surgery. This is not real. None of this is real. It's a joke."

Ruth grabbed me as I fell to the floor in hysterics. I don't remember what happened next. I had a feeling that someone had slipped me a mickey. I woke up early the next morning, on the couch, still in the same clothes. And very disoriented. I did not have the energy to take a shower.

I could still see Scorup's face. On the plane. It showed fear, his eyes wide; he was holding my hand. We must have crashed in Death Valley.

It was me who'd died. Not Rick. That is why my watch said 2:37. It was the only conclusion that made sense. Everything else was not real. It was illusion. Unfortunately, this type of thinking would haunt me again, much later.

I boarded the plane to Anchorage. I saw people I knew. The president of the Reindeer Herders Association hugged me. He had tears in his eyes, and he told me how sorry he was.

Someone helped me to my seat. I looked out the window at the clouds as they swallowed the wing. They again cloaked me in white, flying through the heavens. I am not religious, but I believe in powers outside of our physical being. I was calm as I thought of my husband—with that wide grin, mustache trying to hide his dimples.

Walking felt sluggish, like I was wearing ankle weights, as I struggled down the stairs from the plane's door to the tarmac. I don't remember feeling anything. And then I saw three familiar faces waiting in the reception area and froze. With red eyes, my dad stared at me with alarm. I was dressed in green-and-red-stained Carhartt's, rubber boots caked with mud, and what was a blue parka, now smudged brown, with unkempt, long brown hair, tied back in a ponytail.

God, when did I last wash it? I thought. *Two weeks ago?*

There was Flo, her face streaked with tears. And then I saw Marc. He was standing next to Flo. His arm was in a cast and a sling across his body. His face looked as though he had been in a bar fight.

Tears flowed from my eyes. My chaotic brain suddenly sent deep, piercing spasms of agony directly into the pit of my gut. I

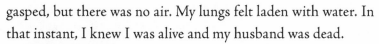

gasped, but there was no air. My lungs felt laden with water. In that instant, I knew I was alive and my husband was dead.

"I want to see Rick."

Flo looked at me, her eyes swollen.

"Yes. First, let's get you cleaned up." She put her arm around me, holding me tight until we got to the apartment. My dad was a mess.

"Chessy. Chessy," I screamed as I ran from room to room.

Flo said she had been hiding.

I didn't even notice Pat standing in the kitchen. Everyone must have thought me mad. Then I heard a *meow*, and Chessy came running to me. I nearly suffocated her, holding her tight, soaking her gray, soft coat with my tears. Her purring instantly calmed my soul.

When I looked up, Pat was holding Flo; Marc, my dad.

What a sight we must have been.

Pat drove us to the funeral home. I remember the looks between Pat and Flo. When we arrived, I jumped out and ran to the front door. Flo caught up to me as I was insisting to see my husband. She grabbed my hand and tried to calm me. She was saying he was not ready yet; they needed to clean him up. I felt my anger swell. I did not know what time it was or what day it was. I just knew I needed to see my husband.

The odor instantly burned my eyes. It was so reminiscent of those nights conducting necropsies of mangy coyotes. Rick would always have dinner ready, and no matter how hungry I was, a shower was first on the menu.

The man in the white coat escorted me into the cold, sterile, bright room. He told me to take my time as he led me to a galvanized metal table draped in white. It was so white. I heard his words but had no comprehension of what he was saying.

All my strength, all my concentration was on one task: to see Rick. The man pulled back the sheet and left the room. He turned and said something like, "Don't remove the sheet."

Rick's wavy, light-brown hair was matted with blood against his forehead. I tried to fix it. It was him, but it was not his face. There was no smile and no dimples. He always smiled. His nose was bent to one side and slashed. He was so still, so quiet. A voice told me not to touch him, not to touch the sheet. I laid my head on his chest, but I could not find his hands to hold. I strained to hear the beat of his heart.

"It should have been me, not you." I kissed his cold lips. I touched his face. My Rick was no longer there. He was in my heart, my soul; he would always be with me. I walked out of the room.

I signed the paperwork for his cremation. In exchange, they gave me an envelope with his ring. As my husband's life ended and our dreams turned to ashes, my life turned into the abyss.

CHAPTER 7

Truth or Dare

I refused to let go of the urn with Rick's ashes in it as we went through the check-in to fly from Anchorage to Seattle. The zombie attitude that possessed my body protected me; people scurried away rather than ask questions.

I understand now the peculiar actions of the parents of my best friend, Pam, after she and her husband Rod had died in a horrific car accident when they were driving from McCall, Idaho.

They were ski racers, who had just been offered coaching positions in Idaho. Her parents requested open coffins, but the funeral-home director insisted the coffins be draped with purple netting. Rick held me back from the viewing; he knew it would haunt me forever. He said, "Remember Pam the way she was the last time you two were together."

The zombie takeover is a survival mechanism. It allows the body to breathe, to move, to maintain, and to survive. Holding the small box near me comforted me. Once we'd landed and walked through the corridor from the plane to the gate area, I glanced up. I saw a familiar, tall figure. I ran to my brother, crying like a baby. I broke through the zombie shield. At least for a few minutes.

When life got difficult during my childhood, I would grab the leash for Jingles, get on my bike, and head for the basalt cliffs outside of town. Nature's silence, with the meadowlarks chirping, red-tailed hawks screeching, catching thermals above, that was my salvation. The simple beauty of the black, smooth columns, thrusting through the ground, reaching to the sky, spattered with mosaics of yellow and orange algae, inspired me.

That is where I wanted to be at that moment. How desperately I wanted to run, to disappear.

Then my mom insisted I needed to buy flowers for Rick. I almost blew up, zombie shield and all. And then, I felt his breath on my neck; he whispered in my ear, "Go fish, Mishie, go fish."

When things were going bad for my mom, she would take it out on her older daughter, me. I learned to do what she said, to keep the peace, fight it out, or run. This behavior started when I refused to take her to the store to buy her beer. I was in the fifth grade.

Rick saw this dynamic between me and my mom, and he remembered a story I'd told him when we were kids in grade school. My mom would let us skip school, and she would take us fishing at the Sun Lakes. She loved to fish. She could sit there for hours, a cigarette in her mouth, patiently waiting for a fish to bite. At least that's what she did when she was manic. She drank when she was depressed. But those manic episodes? The neighborhood kids loved hanging out at my house.

Rick came up with three words to help calm me when she baited me:

"Go fish, Mishie."

We stopped by the flower store, and I bought a vase in the shape of a catcher's mitt, filled with a variety of flowers in white, red, and blue. To this day, I refuse to buy flowers for a memorial or funeral. Flowers wilt and then die.

The day of the service, my brother brought over Matt and Marc. They had flown from San Francisco to Seattle and drove during the night, to my brother's place. Marc still had the cast on; his anguish showed on his face. He was pale and had lost weight. Matt told me he was having a hard time.

The wake was in the small backyard of my parents' home. So strange. The last time I was there, it was for my wedding reception. There were still holdouts of white shasta daisies I had planted for the wedding. *Those damn weeds*, my dad would call them.

My memory of that sad, horrible day is vague, but Kathy, Rick's sister, was so angry at me. She blamed me for Rick's death, but, a few years later, she apologized to me. She was not the only family member who shared those feelings with me, but she was the only person who apologized to me. Pain, as she knew, takes on all kinds of shapes and forms.

If I had never taken the position in Alaska, Rick would still be alive. I knew it was ridiculous to give in to that foolishness, but those words affected me in ways I had never comprehended until recently.

I frequently asked myself, "Was it true? Did I kill my husband through my selfishness?"

Apparently, things were not going so well at work when Dutchman called to see how I was. Then I got a call from Brannen, who replaced me while I was in Washington. They hired him as an agronomist, not a biologist.

"Skippy is a lunatic. I am not going back," he chuckled.

They were thinking of me. And missed me.

Back in Alaska, before he left for California, Marc and I stayed up late, talking into the wee hours of the morning. He told me about the crash, what happened—at least parts of it. Some he could not remember, and some he could not tell me. I knew he was holding back something, and, when I got the entire story, a few months later, I understood why the depth of remorse and survivor's guilt was so raw for him.

He and Rick had planned a day of windsurfing at Big Lake. When they got on the Palmer Hay Flats, the stretch from the Knik River bridge to the "Y" connecting to the Parks Highway, the wind was blowing hard. Rick suddenly pulled off the highway onto the shoulder. He told Marc he wanted to make sure the windsurfer was still secured to the roof of the Chevron vehicle.

Rick was lying down in front of the vehicle, checking the rope. Marc said he was standing on the passenger side, keeping vigil, in case Rick needed him to help. The next thing he knew, he was on the downward side of the embankment.

Marc was shaking, and then he got quiet. I hugged him. The guilt was too much for him. Physically, he suffered a broken clavicle and arm, and scrapes and bruises; mentally, he was in unbearable pain.

Marc and I were two lost souls filled with guilt, wishing it was us who had died and not Rick. Marc and I became kindred spirits in a world neither of us wanted to be in.

When I returned to Anchorage, I moved back into my old apartment, as I had to move out of the Chevron apartment. And a few days after that, I ran away to the field. The wife of a co-worker of Rick's would look in on Chessy. I knew Chessy would be better in her own space.

When I arrived in Nome, I walked over to Bering Air and thanked them for everything they did for me. I got hugs and tears. When my helicopter pilot arrived, we loaded up in the helicopter, and off to Moses we flew.

"You okay?"

"No. But I will be better here than there. Thank you."

"I am so sorry, Michelle."

The Bering Sea was shimmering as the rays of the sun were skipping in the waves. After we landed, my crew surrounded me in a group bear hug.

Ruth let me go. "You are too skinny," she said and walked back to fix dinner.

The field forms were a mess. Kusko came up to see me as I was working on the plot locations.

He was so gloomy.

"What the hell have you been doing? I put you in charge and . . . I bet you ate all the blueberries again, didn't you?"

There it was, his grin. "Yeah." He looked at me. "I will never let Skippy hurt you again."

He was serious. I hugged him and said there was nothing anyone could do.

Then the most amazing thing happened. We had a mechanical problem with the helicopter, keeping us on the ground on a beautiful, warm day. That *never* happens.

We had a picnic on the beach. I stared at the crystal-blue water. The locals had a fishing net draped below the surface from the shore about thirty feet out. It was hot out.

Dutchman said, "I dare you." I looked at him, and into the water I went. It was frigging, freezing cold, but refreshing. I was getting an ice-cream headache, but it felt so good. I was numb, but it felt so different; instead of from the inside, it was from the outside.

Because I keep my eyes open in the water, even in seawater, I saw salmon swimming on a trajectory to the river. I was pink with goosebumps when I ran out of the water. But Dutchman was as red as a lobster!

It was almost the end of August. We packed our gear into the DC-6 and flew back to Nome and, uneventfully, back to Anchorage.

Being back in my same apartment, out of habit, I called Rick. When I heard the recording, "*That number has been disconnected,*" it sent me back down into the abyss. Two weeks later, the police report was ready after I had met with the prosecutor, who recommended I hire an attorney.

Chessy sat on my lap as I opened the police report. I gasped and started shaking, and then the waterfall began. Chessy was meowing and nervously started licking my face. I held her as I read the report.

Two details had sent me into a tailspin. The first was the time of the accident, 2:37 p.m. on the afternoon of the 17th of July 1983. The second took my breath away.

I had asked if Rick had suffered. My brother, who had spoken with the state trooper at the scene of the accident, told me Rick had never regained consciousness. I also knew why Marc was carrying such a burden.

In the accident report, it stated that the victim of the crash, Ricky J. Schuman, was conscious and screaming in pain. He was pinned under the vehicle and dragged.

They cited the driver, a woman, but, after Rick died during surgery, she was cited for vehicular manslaughter. There were several reports from witnesses who called the Crime Stoppers Hotline, stating that a woman had been driving a car erratically from Anchorage. This was the same car and the same woman who was involved in the accident on the Glenn Highway, near mile 32.5.

That night, after reading the police report, I did not think I could go on. The torture was too much. It was as if all the heartache and suffering in my life up to that point had swallowed me whole. I had no energy, no will. The pain was everywhere. I felt his pain. His suffering.

Chessy jumped off my lap. I heard her meowing, but I could not move. She came back, pawed at my hand, and meowed loudly. I looked at my hand. My ring. She disappeared again. Then I heard a thud. I had been lying on the couch. She had jumped onto the dining room table and was playing with something.

I slowly got up. I could barely move. Chessy was now sitting on the floor next to the object that she had knocked off the table. I picked it up. It was my watch. I had taken it off when I'd first arrived from Nome, before going to the funeral home. I remember putting it on the table when I had unpacked in the apartment.

Rick had given me the watch as a wedding present. It had a narrow black leather band and a small, round face. It was a simple watch, with numbers and not Roman numerals. The time said 5:30 a.m. I held it up to my ear; it was ticking. Chessy was meowing, but she was not looking at me. She was looking into the kitchen. She was sitting, her tail swishing across the linoleum floor, meowing, her ears twitching, looking up, looking at something . . . or someone.

I stood there frozen. I did not dare to move. Then she looked at me and meowed. I picked her up, her throat vibrating with her purring.

I held her as I made coffee; then I set her on the couch, while I sauntered into the bathroom and took a shower. I called the office and said I was taking the day off. Then I called my lawyer and a real estate agent. I hugged my cat, put my watch on, and left.

CHAPTER 8

The Spirit of Three

*A*s *I drove to my lawyer's office,* I thought about the last few hours and the last few weeks of my life. *That must have been some wicked pot my computer tech gave me,* I murmured. And the watch? Maybe when Chessy knocked it on the floor, it somehow kick-started it. My watch had stopped at 2:37 pm. That was why I did not know what time it was when Ruth yelled at me to come downstairs.

And then there was the other explanation. I was not alone. I would never be alone. Rick was the only person who knew about the aspirin incident when I was a kid. My parents were screaming, having a knockdown brawl one night. I had convinced myself that with one fewer kid, maybe life for them would be better. I swallowed a half-bottle of aspirin. I wasn't very good at that, either, because all I did was throw it all up. I promised Rick I would never do something so stupid again.

"Life is too valuable," he said.

He was reminding me of my promise. I had three souls to live for now. One taken away from me, one who depended on me, and me.

I gave the police report to my attorney. I had so many questions. Why was Rick tested for alcohol but not the woman who'd killed him? Why wasn't she arrested? What was she doing?

Quietly, he looked at me and asked how much of the report I had read.

"All of it."

As soon as Rick got his official transfer papers, and when I got back from the bush, we were going house hunting. That was the plan, my next task. The real estate agent showed me many places, all depressing, normal houses for families. It took all my control to fight the tears; the reality that someone had ripped away my family from me was too raw. Gone now were the two kids that we had planned, the life we had worked for. We'd hoped to travel around the world!

My life revolved around work, seeing my attorney, and looking at dreadful houses. The crew from the Palmer field office did their best to keep me occupied, at least on most weekends. I almost volunteered for the SPCA again, but thought against it. The previous winter, I witnessed the cruelty of winter on stray dogs and cats. Frozen paws, ears, and tails, especially the cats. Puppy mills were, and still are, prevalent in Alaska, and so is dog fighting.

The realtor called me late one night. "You need to see this one."

The minute we walked inside the house, my heart, for the first time in months, fluttered with excitement instead of sorrow. The clear-story design had an open stairway on the south wall that led to a balcony along the second story. Centered between the two enormous windows was a slate stone fireplace. There was a built-in bin for firewood. The west wall and ceiling were in cedar. The result was a living and dining area that was spacious and open, with a view of the Chugach Mountains.

I loved it. My heart said Rick did, too. The owner was also the builder. They were building a new, larger house in South Anchorage, on the hillside. We negotiated $138,000. I did not make enough income, but I used the meager lump-sum life insurance payout as a down payment. The house was mine. The payments were $800 a month, but I could rent out a room and pay less than my rent at $600 a month. I could do this!

That first night, after we moved in, Chessy and I sat on the stairs in our new home. Even then, I still hoped that the last few months had been only a nightmare and that, once I found a home, Rick would come back. He didn't, but thinking about it helped me settle in.

Thanksgiving came and went, and then it was December.

Christmas was sneaking up. It had been only a year ago when the only person I wanted for Christmas was my husband. This year, not even a phone call, except from Flo, checking on me. We always wrote, but we tried to talk every month. It was a difficult conversation, but we made it work. Crying, laughing, and crying.

I had a handful of ornaments from last Christmas, including the wreath of moose turds. And everyone at work was hinting about a housewarming party, so why not? I bought a tree, put up lights, and had a houseful of laughing people. It felt normal, almost. And then it was quiet. I curled on the couch, Chessy on my lap, and watched the fire.

Rick's co-worker and his wife invited me to their Christmas Eve party.

I split firewood for the wood box, and without thinking, I slammed the door shut before I realized I had left my house key in the house. Damn. The door was locked. I tried everything to get the door unlocked. Even tried my small axe. All I did was scar and chip the wooden door.

I would deal with it when I got home from the party. I arrived to find a raucous group at the Christmas Eve party.

The hostess snuck over to me and whispered, "Don't look, but there is this really cute guy over there," and, of course, I looked. "Quit it," she giggled. "His name is DG. He wants to meet you. He said he is in love." She drawled, emphasizing on the "v."

I don't know why, but I froze. I told her I had this door problem, and it was below zero. I should really go now. She grabbed my arm and dragged me into the back bedroom, where she apologized, as she saw my tears.

"I feel guilty."

And then she lectured me that Rick would not want me to give up.

"He is a nice guy."

And that is exactly what I needed to hear. I promised her I would stay.

DG came over and introduced himself. He was tall, with a muscular build and wavy black hair, and blue eyes full of mischief. He knew of my door problem; he said he could fix it, since he was a carpenter. He was funny and nice and had me laughing within minutes. He said it was good for me to laugh as he yelled at Jon, his boss, to come over.

Jon had brown hair and a silly smile that reminded me of Rick's. He was tall and thin. It was obvious he and DG were good friends, and they also worked together. He explained my dilemma to Jon, as they discussed the options and made a decision.

DG followed me home. As he surveyed the damage and, jokingly, made fun of my tool of choice to fix the locked door, he heard the meows.

"Chessy. My cat."

He got the door open, and I quickly picked up my frantic cat and offered DG a beer. He noticed Rick's guitar in the corner. He asked if it would be okay to play. I said, "Of course," as I set the beer next to him and started a fire. Chessy sat at his feet, mesmerized by the guitar and this guy singing. He would stop, take a sip of his beer, talk to Chessy in this crazy voice, make a joke, wait for me to laugh, and then sing again.

It was the most relaxed I had felt in months. I didn't think I would ever smile again, much less laugh. And then we talked.

He asked me questions most people shied away from. Things like how long were *we* married? How did *we* meet? How did *he* die?

His sincerity was so refreshing, and so was my willingness to have a conversation with him about my husband. People avoid you after a death. To tell someone what Rick was like—not just that he'd died—was wonderful. I had tried therapy, basically paying someone to listen to me talk about Rick, but it felt so cold. DG let me talk about him, tears and all. It felt so natural with him.

And he talked about his family, his four brothers. His dad left his mom and raised them alone. DG was from a small town in Connecticut and had that new England accent; he'd planned a quick visit to see his aunt and her husband in Anchorage. When he met Jon, he decided to stay.

He fixed my door and made me laugh and feel alive for the first time since July 17.

After he left, it seemed so quiet. I crawled into my new bed. And I could still see the red flame of the fire. Chessy curled with her head on my shoulder, lying in the crook of my arm. It was not the best position for my arm, which took many shakes to get it to move in the morning, but it was comforting. This was a behavior that started after Rick died, and I was not about to change it. She needed me as much as I needed her.

As I did every night, I talked with Rick before closing my eyes. I asked him what he thought of DG. I giggled, because I suspected a conspiracy. The locked door? The Christmas Eve party? The carpenter?

Good things like that rarely happen to me. I never lock the door from the garage to the laundry room. Although the door suffered some slight damage, DG was coming over the next day to fix that, on Christmas. I realized my cheeks were already hurting from muscles that had not been used in a very long while.

CHAPTER 9

Blind Justice

Colors sparkled and streaked in the winter sky. Unlike the aurora, these exploded, causing me to flinch. It was New Year's Eve, as DG, Jon, and I cuddled under blankets to keep warm. The fireworks were much more brilliant than in the middle of summer.

Are you watching? I thought, looking at the night sky. A new year. A new beginning?

DG and Jon stopped by in the middle of the dust storm I was making, using a sander to remove the linoleum with the bright yellow-and-orange flowers. The floor store recommended I sand and chip the old linoleum, saving me some money.

I was fortunate that the guys stopped by, because, as they suspected from the dust particles, the floor had asbestos backing. I had begun the sanding just before they arrived, so the damage was minimal to my lungs and my cat's. I'd be lucky if that was my only bad news for the month of January.

The prosecutor who was handling my husband's case called me at work a few days later. He sounded tired and sincere, but it did nothing to subdue my anger.

"I am sorry, Michelle. She is a single mother of two kids with no priors. With our caseload and being understaffed . . ." I did not let him finish.

"And she will continue to have no priors. She ran down my husband."

I hung up. I grabbed my coat and told my secretary I had to leave. Considering she heard the entire conversation, and I saw tears in her eyes, she knew why. Hard to keep a secret in the tiny office of cubicles. She said, "Go."

My lawyer had hoped they would indict the woman who killed Rick, on a charge of vehicular homicide. She should have been indicted, he said. The investigation and the witness reports supported a formal accusation. I let Rick know that Anchorage was worse than the wild, wild west as far as criminals went. Most people had no car insurance, and, if they did, they were underinsured.

The days turned to months. My parents would call to see what was happening with the case, dad somber and mom blaming me for not doing more. Rather than offer support, every conversation with my parents turned into my inadequacies to get justice for Rick. I cherished my conversations with Flo, and her letters were always supportive.

To add to my misery, the only response to my search for a roommate was from males. After one guy who almost burned the place down and always had an excuse not to pay rent, I had to rethink the roommate scene. Being gone for weeks during the field season, I could not take the chance of leaving Chessy and my house with someone I did not know—or trust.

Financially, it was hard, but the constant threats I was receiving from a collection agency put my anxiety over the edge. The medical bills were staggering. Rick died during surgery. I tried to remember the voice and what it had said to me that day at Moses. I saw the name of the surgeon on the reams of paperwork from the hospital. I do not remember a bill from the surgeon, but there were costs from the ambulance, the ER, the surgery itself—the endless pages of what it took to save Rick's life.

My attorney said he would take care of the collection agencies. The lawsuit that was filed against the woman who killed Rick should put a stop to them. I asked him if he knew why the surgeon had not submitted a bill. He, of course, did not. Since we may have needed the surgeon as a witness, I asked him if I could contact him and thank him, especially for spending time with me on the radio. He saw no issue with that.

I called the surgeon's office, and when the receptionist heard my name, she transferred me to the man who'd tried to save my husband. The first words the surgeon said to me were, "I am sorry."

I immediately asked him, "Why? I called to thank you."

His response sent my lips into a quiver, my body shaking; it took every ounce of willpower not to lose it.

"I could not save him. He was so young and fit." He hesitated. "And then I found out his young wife was in the bush. I wanted to keep him alive long enough for you to see him. I couldn't."

We talked some more. I thanked him for his kindness. His receptionist had already told me about the bill. She said, "He refused to charge for his services." That news was that silver lining that everyone refers to.

Jon and DG were coming over to talk to me. And they were bringing food and beer. After my day, I welcomed it.

"We have a proposition for you," DG said in a serious voice.

"And we know you will leave for the field soon," Jon interrupted.

"And you need someone responsible, especially to take care of Chessy," DG added.

We struck a deal. DG and Jon would move in, along with Chester, Jon's Chesapeake retriever.

"Chester stays outside." I looked at Jon as he nodded his head in agreement, a broad smile on his face.

This was not a complete shocker to me. DG had kidded and joked about moving in with me ever since the last roomie had refused to leave. He knew it scared me, not to mention the guilt I felt. He had told me, many times, how he felt about me. And I told him it was too soon. Time was inconsequential to him. And he knew all too well about my guilt.

And as he and Jon reminded me, it was a financial deal. Jon was going out on his own and wanted DG to join him. By renting three ways, the three of us could keep our monthly bills down. DG, always the optimist, chirped about how I would get a twofer. And then he made that funny voice that only Chessy seemed to understand.

Later, as we walked, he squeezed my hand, pulled me close, and whispered in my ear that he loved the way I loved my husband. He said I had enough love in my heart to love two men and that he had enough in his heart to understand that.

In a family of men, four brothers, he astounded me with his overflowing compassion for being such a young man. Later, when I met his mom, I understood.

"He has an old and wise soul," his mom told me.

I theorized that a boy raised by a loving mother, especially as a single parent, no father in the house, might be more at ease in showing love, compassion, and respect for women. DG knew my life was going to get harder for me, and yet it was not he who ran.

When he could, he would go with me to my lawyer's office. My lawyer worried about the lack of anger I had toward the woman who'd killed Rick.

"Why?" he asked. "If I had done what she did, I could not live with myself. I would feel horrible. I would need to say how sorry I was."

My lawyer made it clear to me and to DG that this woman showed no remorse.

"You need to convince her of that," he told DG.

"I need to protect her. You need to get her and Rick justice."

The kick-start for my anger was the first of many depositions, from 1984 through 1985. I remember the first one. At age 27, I certainly did not know what a deposition was. Hell, I was 26 before I had ever been in a car accident, and 41 when I got my first traffic ticket. And 25 when my husband died.

My attorney briefed me on the process of my deposition. I was to keep my answers short, primarily answering with a "Yes" or a "No." He said to keep cool and be honest.

There were no apologies for the death of my husband. There were no questions about the man he was. Or what he believed in, or what he wanted to do in his life. Or what brought him joy or what made him sad. There were no questions about what his future, our future, would have looked like. The kids who would not be born. The life that was taken away from him. Taken away from me. The series of questions, no matter how deep I bury them, haunt me to this day:

"Why were you and your husband living apart?"

"Why did you not have any children?"

"Are you a Christian?"

"Was your husband a Christian?"

"How long were you married?"

"Were you in the accident?"

"What did your husband do?"

"Your husband only worked for two years? Why?"

I answered those questions, but by the third question, a "Yes" or "No" would not be my answer. By the fifth question, my lawyer squeezed my hand. My lawyer finally got his wish.

"What difference does it make what my husband did for a living?"

Her lawyer responded, "He could have been a drunk bum, and we would never pay a dime."

"Do you pay more if the person who died was a Christian? And who makes that decision? You know, if someone is a Christian or not?"

I let go of my lawyer's safe hand. I stood up, anger welling inside me.

"How about your client? What has she done with her life? Other than take my husband's life from him and from me? Every day, I wish to God, that I had been there with him. You said because I wasn't, that I don't suffer? And you dare tell me your settlement offer can be lower because I was not there?"

I was now officially on the record as being angry. I no longer gave a shit about this woman. She does not deserve to be addressed by her Christian name, so I only refer to her by what she is and will *always* be to me—the woman who killed my husband.

Here is what I remember *reading* about the accident. She was driving erratically from Eagle River to Mile 62.5 of the Glenn

Highway. That is where she crossed the shoulder and slammed, without braking, into the back of the car that my husband was under. The impact threw Marc into the ditch at 55 mph. The lower half of my husband's body was crushed.

There were many witness reports, and, because of her erratic driving, Crime Stoppers had offered a reward. The reports suggested she was drunk. Several people had stopped to help my husband and Marc, before the state troopers arrived. The first trooper on scene was green and didn't know how to process the scene. Someone had torn the ticket he'd written by the time the second, more-seasoned trooper showed.

They tested my husband for alcohol—but the woman was not tested. The woman had two kids in the back seat of her car. If one had been injured, they would have prosecuted her.

The woman was single. No one could tell me if she was married or where the father of the two kids was. I was told only that she was a single mother of two small kids. That was one of the three reasons the prosecutor did not prosecute.

A lawyer paid by her church represented the woman. I was told she had connections to the church. I don't know what those connections were or to what church. She was underinsured; that is all I know.

Apparently, she had no money, but she had a house in a pleasant area of town.

One night, we sat in Jon's truck, looking at it. DG said nothing. He held my hand, hugged me close to him.

Jon looked at me with that half-grin and offered, "We could egg her house." I laughed and kissed his cheek; we left.

The legal struggle that consumed my life was no longer about seeking the truth about my husband's fate. It was not about her actions. But it had everything to do with my husband's actions.

Justice failed Rick. I could not. The questions in the depositions were about one thing: money. What is a human life worth?

According to Wikipedia, "the value of life is an economic value used to quantify the benefit of avoiding a fatality. They also refer to it as the cost of life, value of preventing a fatality (VPF), and implied cost of averting a fatality (ICAF)."

In the social and political sciences, it is the marginal cost of death prevention in a certain class of circumstances. In many studies, the value also includes the quality of life, the expected lifetime remaining, and the earning potential of a person, especially for an after-the-fact payment in a wrongful-death claim lawsuit.

In 1982, there was a 1 in 10,000 chance of dying at work. For a company to convince someone to accept that risk, they would have to pay them an additional $300 a year for each employee to work. An economist calculated that the value of an expected death or a statistical life is $3 million, not $300,000, according to the government.

My heart missed a beat. The discussion went on, but I don't remember what it said. I relived that traumatic day in a windowless room, listening to the cold, monotone voice of a lawyer deciding the value of my husband's life. I never knew or understood the numbers or where they came from.

I bounced back to reality when the voice on the radio said, "There was a flaw with putting a value on a life because it doesn't factor in grief, or how or when, a person dies. There are the people who love the person who dies, and their loss."

Sometimes I hid my pain, so DG would not see how upset I was; I know it hurt him to see me in so much pain. I was trying to make my life as normal as it could be. My family comprised two amazing men who protected me; who made me laugh, and who

pissed me off—and who made me feel loved. Then there was the out-of-control Chester, who would knock me down when excited; and my faithful companion, Chessy, always there to comfort me. Soon, Jasper, DG's springer spaniel, joined our home.

The neighbors accepted us, with one exception. After the third phone call and threat to the local pound, Chester had to be secured in the backyard, or else! He was a big dog, friendly, but big. As the Saint Bernard before him, he figured out how to escape the backyard and roam the neighborhood while we were all at work. I think the kids were fine with him; it was the adults who were freaked out. Regardless, Jon and Chester got put on probation.

CHAPTER 10

The Island of Spirits

A*mystery to be solved.* I loved mysteries, especially if they focused my mind on something other than my life, which was hurtling into oblivion.

Despite the underlying issues, I had an opportunity on Nunivak Island to not only do good science but to work with the local people and provide them what they needed.

Nunivak Island is a volcanic island in the Bering Sea about 30 miles offshore from southwest Alaska. The island is a little more than a million acres, which, by contrast, surpasses Rhode Island, with 934,000 acres. It is 47 miles long and 66 miles wide; it was to be my new project for the next two years. I had more questions than answers, but now I knew what questions I needed to ask. And to help me with this project, I had a bubbly assistant by the name of Jules.

A professor from the UAA, whom I will call "Prof," had been assisting me in the identification of lichens. He recommended a young chemistry major for a work-study position that I had advertised. Jules, tall and lean with shoulder-length, wavy, sandy-brown hair, walked into the workroom, a huge grin on her face.

"You must be Michelle. Prof sent me. I need a job."

She was in jeans, a tight T-shirt and braless, with a large bulge in her lower lip. *Oh, yeah,* I thought. *This will shake up this conservative, testosterone-dominated faction.* Although I appreciated her nonconformity in her appearance, I was more interested in her abilities to handle a changing situation.

"What do you know about plant identification? Prof said you are a chem major."

I quickly learned she knew absolutely nothing about plants, but she was energetic and smart, and she could hold her own. And that is what I wanted. I hired her against the human resources (HR) concerns about her dress or lack thereof. Although the rumors promptly went flying around the office about this girl who had tobacco in her mouth and didn't wear a bra, she made my day!

As a downhill ski racer, she had that same cockiness and independence as my best friend, Pam, the ski racer who was killed.

I admired it. She was also friendly, logical, and fun. And those qualities are necessary for a place like Nunivak Island. For the next hour, I explained to her about our project and where we would live for almost three weeks, in a small village called Mekoryuk.

Mekoryuk is the only permanently inhabited village, at the mouth of Shoal Bay on the north shore of Nunivak Island. It is 149 air miles west of Bethel and 553 miles west of Anchorage.

The Nuniwarmiut people, or Cup'ik Eskimos, have inhabited Nunivak Island for 2,000 years. They estimate that 400 people were living in 16 villages on the island when the first outside contact occurred in 1821, by the Russian American Company.

In 1891, Ivan Petroff found 702 Eskimos in 9 villages, including 177 people at a summer camp called Koot, the current site of Mekoryuk. In 1939, the Bureau of Indian Affairs (BIA) built a school, and, in 1940, they opened a post office.

In the 1940s, the women lived in semi-subterranean sod houses, and the men stayed at one or more "kasigi" or men's community houses. They still practiced traditional ceremonies and religious beliefs.

The '50s and '60s brought considerable change to the area, with an airstrip built in 1957, and with the Territorial Guard formed shortly after. Men went to Fort Richardson, near Anchorage, for training. By this time, Mekoryuk was the only permanent community on the island, but, without a high school, many families moved to Bethel, returning during late spring for fishing and sea-mammal hunting. Even with a new high school constructed in 1978, the village was considered "dying." The young people wanted to move to Anchorage and party.

"And that will be our home for three weeks. I hope."

"In the high school?"

"Yes."

I explained the alternative—living in tents—so she thought the high school was an excellent idea!

The crew for this project was Dutchman, Kusko, Jules, and me. As usual, Skippy scheduled to meet us at Mekoryuk, whenever.

The weather was clear as we flew over the Bering Sea toward Nunivak. I could see Roberts Mountain in the distance, a shield volcano that stands guard over the island with a summit just less than 2,000 feet, the highest point on the island. It dominated the surface of the island with broad, thin pahoehoe lava flows, with more than 60 cinder cones and 4 maars.

A maar is a broad, low-relief volcanic crater caused by an explosion that occurs when groundwater encounters hot lava or magma; characteristically, it fills with water to form a shallow crater lake. The names of the four maars on Nunivak are the Nanwaksjiak, Binalik, Ahkiwiksnuk, and one called "385," which is the elevation in feet of the crater lake.

As we walked through town, cherubic, smiling faces welcomed us everywhere we went. We walked the rutted, sandy roads lined with typical BIA wood-frame structures, designs far removed from the subterranean sod homes from years past. Women and many of the young girls wore the traditional kuspuk, long-sleeved, hooded-overshirt with a pocket on the front. It looks like a cross between a sweatshirt and a dress, and always colorful.

It seemed as if we were in a culture caught in a time warp. There were kids riding their bikes, wearing blue jeans, synthetic jackets, and tennis shoes, laughing and playing. But then, there would be a group of women, dressed in their colorful kuspuk, squatting in the dunes, weaving last season's grass into baskets, and speaking a language as foreign as if we were in another country, or in another world.

This was Jules' first introduction to a remote village, and for a moment, she was speechless. As we sat around the work table, a little Bailey's in our hot chocolate, we planned our first day in the field. As we expected, people wandered in throughout the evening from the community. Many stopped by to check us out and chat. And, as they'd warned us, a few brave teenagers asked us if we had any marijuana or alcohol. The village is dry, so we were expecting this question. Because of this, we were very careful to disguise Bailey's in flasks, hidden in the refrigerator.

The next morning, sunlight greeted us and the sound of the "thump, thump" of the helicopter—our transportation had arrived.

The north coast of Nunivak is gently sloping from the interior to the coast, with many bays and haystacks jutting out of the sea. Sea cliffs and bluffs on the west coast rise from the sea to a height of 200 feet.

On the southern coast are miles of sandy beaches fringed with stunning dunes and large saltwater lagoons; to the east are rocky beaches with many coves and bays. The broad tundra is a mosaic of small lakes and wetlands interspersed with low hills. There are more than 70 streams and rivers that dissect the tundra, which surrounds the interior of the island. The interior contains an upland plateau that rises 500 to 800 feet from the tundra, culminating in a mountainous area, underlain with permafrost, the permanently frozen soil.

The helicopter pilot had been flying low so that we could check out the ground cover below us, and then suddenly the ground disappeared as we flew over the crater's edge. We found ourselves in mid-air, hovering over a crystal turquoise-blue lake hundreds of feet below us, one of the several maars. It was thrilling and awe-inspiring, and yet seriously scared the shit out of us.

Jules, who had never flown in a helicopter, screamed, "Holy shit!" and then started laughing.

The pilot, with no warning, had just one-upped us by flying fast and low over the crater's edge, and then over nothing as the ground fell away. This brief episode gave Dutchman an idea as we looked at each other and smiled. Would our pilot play along with us? We both remembered Skippy did not like to fly over water.

Meanwhile, we took in the views from the top of Roberts Mountain and verified my preliminary mapping on the selected imagery. We followed a transect from Roberts Mountain to

Cape Mendenhall, on the southern tip of the island, with hopes to see muskox.

From the summit, we spotted dark-black mounds on the open, dry tundra between us and Cape Mendenhall, and the mounds were moving. Our next series of plots would be our first encounter with the stately, prehistoric-looking muskox.

Our pilot kept us at a safe distance from the grazing animals so as not to disturb them. As we suspected, there were many calves, some hidden beneath their mothers' skirts. We could hear their high-pitched bleat and the roar from an adult or two, or three, in response.

Once on the ground, we kept alert, with the groups snorting and grunting, reminding us that we were guests. The ground vibrated from animals playing and stomping. Although we saw some adult bulls among the groups, it was only July, still outside of the breeding season. But just in case, we kept alert for any bulls. You never knew if or when a bull might show rank by coming after a strange species sitting on the ground, no matter the distance between us and his harem.

We settled into our rhythm on the island. We spent much of our time on the west coast when the weather was clear. Nunivak's seabird rookeries were estimated to be some of the largest in North America. The sea cliffs from Cape Mohican south to Datheekook Point were alive with hundreds, if not thousands, of birds; the noise was deafening once the helicopter shut down. Nesting along the cliffs were Black-legged Kittiwakes, Common Murres, Pelagic Cormorants, and the entertaining, and my favorite, the colorful clowns, the tufted puffins and crested auklets.

Although the magnificent and colorful eiders are often seen on Nunivak, we saw none. The Steller Eider and Spectacled

Eider were both listed in 1991 as a threatened species under the Endangered Species Act and remain threatened today. In many of the lakes, we saw Harlequins, a very colorful and beautiful duck, along with many other waterfowl species.

I am concerned with the threat of climate change, especially in the northern latitudes. We are facing catastrophic effects that we have never seen. Will these prehistoric creatures survive and adapt? Or will the *O. moschatus* join the thousands of species on the Red Flag list of endangered species?

CHAPTER 11

Spirits of Transformation

The cool, salty air and the lush emerald-green hills welcomed us as we exited the plane on Nunivak. It felt as though I was visiting an old friend as we arrived for our second field tour in the summer of 1985.

Familiar, smiling faces greeted us from the village of Mekoryuk.

By the second week, we started getting low on coffee; the weather was cooler than usual. But just in case, I called the state office to leave a message for Skippy to bring coffee—and according to Jules and Kusko, Copenhagen—with him the following week.

The receptionist said he was already on Nunivak. I was speechless for a few seconds and assumed I had confused her. Then I made a second call to confirm what I was told.

"Well, guys, it looks like we may have to barter for coffee if we run out. Skippy, apparently, is already on Nunivak Island."

"Wait a minute," Jules said. "You scheduled Skippy to help the guys on the Hatcher survey this week. Darren made a big f'ing deal about you not being there. And insisted Skippy shows up!"

"Yep. The field manager for the Palmer field office told me Skippy never showed up, because *we* needed him on Nunivak Island. MIA again. For more than a week."

Considering I was completing the manuscript for the Seward Peninsula project, and I was on my second year for Nunivak, I certainly did not need another project. But the *State Soil Scientist* and the *State Engineer* proposed to the *State Conservationist* that I take over the range responsibility of the Hatcher Pass project.

Personally, there were way too many, *State this* and *that* positions. We had no idea what they all did, yet, they were the most important, or so they thought.

Skippy refused to let go of the Hatcher project. He also refused to give me a promotion to a GS-11. I was still a GS-9 Step 2, while my male counterparts had been GS-11s even before I had started as a GS-7, Step 1. Since each full grade is about $10,000, Dutchman was making almost $20,000 more than me. Not that he did not deserve it, but it was not equal pay for each of our duties.

I believe the intention of my supporters was admirable, but at that moment all I got was more work. The State Engineer and State Soil Scientist said they would fix the problem. They told me not to give up.

As Jules and I lay in our cots, surrounded by library books, we talked about Skippy's most-recent escapade. I expressed my doubts about staying with the Agency. I felt so responsible for Rick's death—to lose him for this? If Rick had been alive, I would have applied to veterinary school. His death would all be for nothing if I gave up.

I tossed and turned all night, and finally I went for a walk around the village. I sat on the sand, looking toward Shoal Bay, listening to gulls squawking, as the clouds got thicker and darker, and then I slowly walked back to the school.

Jules took one look at me as I was drinking coffee. "That fucker . . ." she mumbled, and then she grabbed her coffee and spit out her wad of Copenhagen.

"Which one?"

That day, we took advantage of cloudy weather and visited the master artists of ivory carving, basket weaving, and the spirit mask.

After the second basket that Dutchman bought, I let him know the next one was mine.

Our guide took us to an old, small home. He disappeared through the creaky driftwood door with a reindeer hide hung on the inside. We heard some rustling and a woman quietly talking in the local Cup'ik dialect; then our guide opened the door.

Inside, sitting on a bed in her faded blue kuspuk, she greeted us with a large, toothless smile. She was the oldest elder in the village. Her eyes were tiny slits that peered out through her chubby, round cheeks. Her long salt-and-pepper braids hung over her shoulders. She nodded as we quietly entered.

Dutchman introduced us and thanked her for allowing us the time to visit with her, as our guide interpreted for him. Not only was she the oldest person in the village, she was known for her unique, colorful baskets. The guide asked her if she had any baskets for sale. She nodded and held up one finger. She pointed to a shelf, and when I saw it, I looked at Dutchman and mouthed, *mine*.

Dutchman, in his signature chuckle, looked at me and exclaimed, "Hey, this isn't fair."

On the shelf was a basket with a wider weave than the traditional, tight-woven baskets. It was about eight inches tall. The shape was not unlike the silhouette of a very pregnant woman—small at the base, bulging at the middle, and awkwardly tapering at the crown. The opening, about five inches in diameter, came with a removable top, with a small, woven knob.

It was the colors I loved: thick, bright blue, violet stripes alternating with thinner stripes of the natural, tawny color of the ryegrass. There was a single red layer woven in the center of the natural grass stripe. The dye was natural, made from different minerals found on the island. And that basket was mine.

I still have it, along with a photo of the artist, Edna Kalerak, her handwritten scrawl of her Christian name, holding the basket she made. She died a few weeks later. We did not know it, but she had been very sick when we saw her. She insisted on putting on her kuspuk before she welcomed us into her home. Some say she was older than 100; some say she was past 120 years. What a life she must have had! It honored me to be part of it. Every time I see my basket, I think of her; it has faded with time, but it's still full of wonderful memories of Nunivak.

At our next stop, we walked into a house, but the inside was a museum. There were ivory carvings on shelves, tables, and walls. It was an incredible sight, and the four of us just stood there, staring in awe at the glorious carvings. The artist, George Williams, had been carving his entire life. His tools were traditional; we saw no mechanized saws. I regret not having the cash on hand to purchase his art. The carver, lean, with black-rimmed glasses, stood animated among his ivory totems of seal, whale, fish, and walrus. We bowed to him, calling him the Great Ivory Carver of Nunivak. He gave us a glorious, toothless smile.

As we stood on the sloped, wooden porch of the *Great* Mask Carver of Nunivak, Peter Smith, I was holding my beautiful basket, smiling at Dutchman.

Peter smiled, opened the door, and we walked into his small house, littered with shavings of dried wood, and walls covered with brightly colored masks of all sizes. We stood with our mouths open, among the spirits.

In the Nunivak Cup'ik dialect, *agayu* are the dramatic shamanic ritual masks known as Cup'ik masks. The masks vary, but all represent skillful imagination and tradition. The masks are made of driftwood and painted with brilliant colors of blue, red, black, and yellow.

The shamans (*angalkuq*) directed the carvers how to make the masks. Yupik masks could be small, three-inch finger masks, called "dance fans," or as large as a few feet long.

The traditional Nunivak masks link humans to animals, representing the spiritual harmony between the two beings. It is said that the wearer of the mask will have good luck in hunting. During the winter ceremonies, as an act of prayer, the shaman asks that the spirits of animals that are fished or hunted would reincarnate themselves and return in spring to feed the human community.

There are usually two rings in the design. Each ring encircling the mask represents the *ellanguaq* or a *pretend universe* at different levels or dimensions of the universe, including sea and sky worlds where animal spirits dwell. Blue pigment is for animal figures, and red pigment is for humans.

Nuniwarmiut people are deeply superstitious, with patrilineal inherited totems, handed down from father to son. There are usually totems that are more important or sacred than others, especially bird totems. The wearer of such a totem must observe any forbidden practice, such as eating or disrespecting the totem species. The Nuniwarmiut also believed that the designs appearing in the totems and masks give special powers, such as successful hunting. Those designs were found not only in masks, but on kayaks, hunting implements, paddles, amulets, and in songs, dance, and legends.

When Paul Ivanoff, an Inupiaq-speaking trader, visited Nunivak in 1920, he introduced Christianity to the island. The newly adopted religion discouraged the carving of the human image on the masks.

Peter Smith was the first Nunivak Islander who trained as a minister for the new Covenant Church. He started carving a mask using an image of a bird rather than a human.

The new bird masks looked more like wall sculptures than the traditional masks, but soon, other carvers incorporated the bird image into their masks. As the popularity of the bird masks spread among outsiders, the Nuniwarmiut continued to refer to their craft as masks. This compromise allowed the Nunivak Islanders the opportunity to create objects for sale, while honoring the ideologies of their adopted religion.

Peter designed his masks with different animals: the fox, loon, seal, and salmon—and within each, there were small variances. He grew up on the water; his livelihood was from the sea.

Before we left, Dutchman and I each arranged for him to design a mask for us. Doug wanted a yellow loon as his center; I wanted the traditional black, white, and red loon. Normally he made his masks during the winter months, because, during the summer months, he was in his boat on the water. As he walked us out of his home, he looked at the sky and said in a serious voice,

"Hmm, you may have your masks before you leave the island. If you leave the island."

Jules looked a little freaked.

"What did that mean?"

"It's the island of the spirits. Who knows, but he is the master carver of the spirit masks."

For me, it meant *Jules without Copenhagen*—not a pretty sight.

Skippy appeared a week later, with no coffee and no chew. He realized we were aware of his MIA status.

The exhilarating ride over the crater was even more enjoyable when the pilot did a sharp bank on the side Skippy was on. With the helicopter nearly on its side, Skippy was afforded a view looking directly down into the gut of the maar. Our pilot also enjoyed his morning coffee, which was now being rationed.

We joked about it for days, considering it took a year before we had the perfect opportunity.

It was a good thing that he left when he did. Was it the crater? Or the fact we refused to share our rationed coffee with him?

The bad weather grounded us on Nunivak for a week longer. I called the state office and then the Palmer field office to relay the information that I would be late getting back to the Hatcher Pass project. I also let them know that Skippy had spent only a couple days on Nunivak.

The good news was that Dutchman and I got our masks before leaving the island.

Peter knew the weather was going to turn. As we sat at the airstrip every day for a week, hoping and praying for our plane to pick us up, we thought about those words Peter had spoken to us.

Finally, a week later, we heard our plane. The weather was still not the best, but we were leaving. As we boarded, Jules grabbed a newspaper off a seat and said, "Oh, my God! Rock Hudson has AIDS."

The pilot turned around and, with a wide grin, said, "How long have you girls been here?"

Laughing, he shook his head. Unknown to me, that would be my last journey to the Island of the Spirits.

CHAPTER 12

Gold, Glaciers, and Grizzlies

The Talkeetna Mountains are the most spectacular mountains in the world. Bounded by two large valleys, the Matanuska Valley, formed by the glacial-fed Matanuska River to the east, and the Susitna Valley, with its renowned salmon-fishing river, the Susitna, to the west. The Hatcher Pass soil and range investigation, approximately 300,000 acres, included both these valleys, which were distinctively diverse in their climate, soils, and vegetation.

The steep slopes of the Talkeetna mountains, cloaked with blue-tinged glaciers such as the Mint and the Chickaloon, extend their white tentacles, forming the u-shaped valleys. Large, amphitheater-sized circular depressions remain as the glacier recedes, filled with turquoise waters, as the snow and ice melt.

The historic towns of Palmer, Sutton, and Chickaloon, along the Glenn Highway, are tucked between the base of the Talkeetna Mountains and the wide, braided Matanuska River. Palmer, only 12 miles east of Hatcher Pass, is famous for growing gigantic pumpkins and cabbages.

The Hatcher Pass crew consisted of me, from the state office in Anchorage, and the other four, from the Palmer field office. I oversaw the vegetation and range analysis, and Justin was the crew leader and project soil scientist.

With his disheveled, light-brown hair, a Fu Manchu mustache, and glasses, he was strongly independent, smart, and a loner. He had already earned a reputation as the fun-and-crazy guy, known to pull anti-establishment antics.

Darren, a bio-technician, was a range conservationist by education, fastidious, with dark hair and mustache, although, overnight, it seemed his hair turned gray. He had a dry sense of humor; he was stubborn, and, again, an independent guy. Although he had a range science degree, he demanded that Skippy spend a few days with him while I was on Nunivak.

Huntman, the second bio-tech, was a tall, lean, charismatic guy, and a chameleon. He could adapt and become anyone he wanted to pretend to be, a loner or a socialite.

Pooch was a soil scientist on loan from the Fairbanks field office, a slow-moving, slow-talking Oklahoman; he was gentle in spirit and loved to play pranks. You never knew if he was bullshitting or telling the truth.

We met our helicopter pilot at the local Palmer airport. For me, besides the new crew, this project was very different, both logistically and ecologically. The contrast between the snow-capped peaks, blue-colored glaciers, and the deep-green forests and lush, lime-green meadows was extremely distinct—its species were rich and diverse compared to the stunted, open tundra, on permafrost soils.

"It's one helluva an office view," I said into my mic.

"Fucking A, it is that," replied Huntman.

I learned quickly that *the F-Word* is the most common word in his everyday vocabulary.

We had our challenges, as we quickly discovered, while sampling a transect from the alpine area down the slope, through a layer of thick alders.

As Justin and I walked into the dense alder thicket, fighting through the tightly woven branches, looking for a place among the entangled roots to get a spade in, we heard a growl. As we looked toward the noise, we got a glimpse of gold as it streaked past us, crashing through the alders.

The next day, within the same valley, we counted six different grizzlies where we needed to sample. Unanimously, we all agreed to sample another transect in the next valley over. We were shocked to find more grizzlies.

Regardless of what was attracting the bears to this area, we could no longer delay the sampling. We called in the big guns: our pilot.

The pilot planned to first drop a crew off on the upper slope and then fly low over the thick alder shrubs, zigzagging back and forth. If there was a bear within the alders, the noise would scare the bear out of its lair and send it down the slope. Once cleared, the crew could proceed.

However, bears are far from predictable. While half our crew were on the ground, the pilot zigged and zagged over a large alder thicket, a couple hundred feet downslope from the crew. Instantly, a dark-golden body charged out of the alders. As we hovered, the bear ran, but not down the slope. Instead, it ran at the helicopter and then stood up on its massive hind legs, stretching his oversized paws with long, bladed claws toward the helicopter. The massive jaws snapped open and closed with a roar. I swear, if we had been a foot lower, that bear could have snagged a skid.

Pooch, in his slow, southern drawl, snorted, "Well, this could be a problem for the boys," giving a nervous chuckle. "That bear is cranky being woken up."

Quickly, our pilot maneuvered to get between the crew and the bear, now with all four paws on the ground, as it ran back into the alders, and then charged to the uphill side. He stopped, stood up, nose in the air, shook his head, and then galloped down the slope, disappearing into the dense shrubs of the riparian drainage below. It was a warning.

Bears have horrible eyesight. They survive by their nose; their scent of smell is the strongest. When a bear stands with its snout in the air, it is scanning for a scent. When it charged out of the alder thicket and then stood and stuck its nose into the air, it got a scent of Justin and Huntman. It didn't like the smell and took off back downslope. Thankfully, the breeze was blowing in the right direction.

However, this bear charged the helicopter, telling us it was aggressive and less tolerant, which demanded our attention and respect. One of the most dangerous situations—one that should be avoided at all costs—is a sow grizzly with cubs. Fortunately, all our sightings were of males.

I was astonished at the number of grizzly bears we were seeing daily. By the end of the field season, we knew why: Huntman was a walking human bear attractor.

One day, as the pilot was transporting us to our next sample location, Huntman's voice came over the radio. At first, he was calm as he explained he'd spooked a grizzly sow and cubs. She was woofing, so he was slowly walking to an enormous boulder to climb as he gave his location. A few minutes later, he was screaming into the radio that the bear was charging; then there was silence.

As we listened to the screaming on the radio, the pilot went into 'Nam mode. He flew fast and low, and, within minutes, we saw Huntman standing on a boulder, shotgun in his arms. The bear and her cubs were a safe distance away.

It was at that moment we realized he was buck naked except for his face. As we hovered near him, he turned to look at us. What we saw was not the face of Huntman but that of a pig. And then he made these spasmodic-type movements, turning in tight circles, shuffling his feet in what we later coined the "screw dance."

"You are not getting in this helicopter until you cover that damn ass of yours."

Huntman did everything right. He did not want to shoot a sow with cubs. This bear was protecting her cubs, and his response to her was not threatening. If he had run or confronted her, it could have changed the outcome. Sows are very protective of their cubs, as most moms are. Unfortunately, many people who play in bear country do not understand bear behavior and will shoot a bear without cause.

The reason for being naked? He said he'd shit his pants. And the pig face mask? Because he had it in his pack.

The days were never boring with this crew. And, I got to go home every night after the long days in the field. For that reason, I finally convinced my parents to visit. I wanted to show them my home and for them to meet DG. I assumed they would be relieved—that I was attempting to move forward with my life. It was too much to wish for.

CHAPTER 13

Frappes, Grinders, and Packies

My *parents were visiting*, and DG was extremely nervous. He knew, as Rick did, that my mom could be difficult. He heard it in my voice when I spoke with her on the phone.

The first morning, DG had gotten up early and made his specialty, crepes, for breakfast before he took us to the Alaska Railroad train station. I had booked a weekend trip to Denali National Park, including the historic train ride to Denali, and a room for two nights at the lodge.

I apologized to DG for my mom when he dropped us off at the train depot early. My mom made it clear she did not want breakfast. She spent most of her time in the smoking car but eventually joined my dad and me in the sky car.

The only event I remember about that weekend was on the last night. My mom screamed at me, "Maybe you have forgotten Rick, but I haven't."

Not one day, not one minute, has ever escaped without thoughts of my husband. DG understood that. No, not *understood*; he *saw* the consequences of what Rick's death did to me every single day. And he knew I was scared.

I told him the story about when we were herding a group of wild horses in Nevada, about this beautiful, white stallion. He held his head high, and there was defiance in his black eyes, refusing to be forced into the corral by the helicopter above. He would kick his front legs, standing on the back two, with foam spraying from his mouth, as dust whirled. I wanted so badly for him to escape, to be free, not broke. That was my fear—that one day, I would be broken, just like that stallion.

After that event, I could not expect DG to stay with me. I needed to be alone. The truth was, I loved him too much to stay with him; I was afraid. He wanted to get married, have kids, and live this "granola life," as he called it. He gave me such laughter, such genuine love, it scared me to death. What if something bad happened to him because of me? I needed him to be happy, to be with someone normal, to live that *granola life* he so deserved.

It was hard coming home to an empty, quiet house. Chessy, the ever-faithful cat, would wait for me as I walked into the utility room. My heart was heavy with guilt, but, this time, it was me who weighed it down. DG would have a future with his own family someday. That was something I knew I could never give him: I was damaged goods.

Justin and I started spending more time together. It was his attitude that drew me to him; that bad-boy, carefree persona. He defied rules and regulations. Once, when the General Services Administration (GSA), which conducts oversight for general government administration, sent Justin a letter of violation for leaving the doors unlocked in a government vehicle. Justin responded. He stamped the letter with a rubber stamp he'd made with the four letters FOAD and sent it back. The State Conservationist got a call from GSA. Justin got nothing more than a warning. The "F*ck Off and Die" stamp disappeared shortly after.

The rules did not apply to him.

As field season was over, the State Soil Scientist and State Engineer addressed the issue concerning the lack of help from Skippy on the Hatcher Pass project.

I had prepared several items, including the agreed-upon schedule and my involvement with this project. Interestingly, no one from the Hatcher Pass crew was present. I realized there was a distinct separation of sides sitting in the room.

At the end of the meeting, I sat in silence as Skippy told everyone that I had not scheduled him for the Hatcher Pass project. In addition, despite documentation to the contrary, the State Conservationist and the new Deputy Chief blamed me for the lack of state office range assistance to the crew.

I looked at Skippy, his dark beady eyes nervously looking away, his hand twitching, clenching a pencil so hard I thought it would snap. I recalled the moment the pilot had nearly killed him. In that instant, I regretted stopping him from doing so.

The look on my supporters' face was one of disbelief. They had fought to get me a well-deserved promotion; instead, I was getting a warning in my file. And no promotion.

A few days later, I put in for a position on the East Coast, a place called Martha's Vineyard. I called DG, and he came rushing over with a book on New England. We sat on the couch, Chessy next to me, and Jasper next to him, as we looked at the pictures. I knew then that our friendship, nurtured out of the respect and love we had for each other, would never end.

The fallout from that meeting was immediate. Jules submitted her resignation letter. The State Engineer retired. Our database guy quit. And meanwhile, Justin, the project leader, two grades higher than me, and Darren, who had made the complaint, said they knew nothing about the meeting. Justin took off for a month-long vacation, camping in the Grand Canyon, alone.

Before Jules left, the new deputy chief officer called her into his office. He told her if she did not rescind her statement in her resignation letter, that she would be blackballed from ever getting a job in the federal government. She told him to go f** himself.

A few weeks later, I received a cryptic call that I'd gotten the position on Martha's Vineyard. The call came while a hurricane called Gloria was impacting the East Coast.

Meanwhile, the housing market had crashed in Anchorage when the price of oil plummeted. I told my attorney to settle so I could move on. He hated seeing me go, but he understood completely. The settlement would not change; there was no money to go after. As DG took me and Chessy to the airport, I could not help but feel I'd let Rick down.

On arrival in Boston, I ran to the luggage carousel to pick up Chessy, where I found her bright-eyed and quiet. At least I had a little time with her before we boarded a small plane to Cape Cod, where I was to meet my new boss. I had never seen a hurricane or experienced the effects of one, but as we flew to the Cape, the devastation was remarkable. At first, I was not sure what I was seeing. There were endless rows of white-leaved trees, especially along the highways. The chlorophyll had been sucked out of the leaves from the pressure Gloria had caused.

RD, my new boss, reminded me of John Denver except for his dark-black hair. He had round glasses, a warm smile, and an accent, and he seemed especially glad I was there. The next morning, I met the office crew of Cape Cod, who welcomed me with open arms, before RD and I left to catch the ferry to the Vineyard.

As I grabbed my bag and cat, I asked RD what rig we were taking to the island. He looked at me with complete confusion. He asked me what a "rig" was. Not so different from my first time in Alaska, I chuckled.

The island was beautiful, with rich architecture and lovely, rolling green hills surrounded by a stormy blue sea. As we toured the Island, Gloria's remains with debris and large broken trees strewn along the roads, was expected, but it was the boarded shops and the strangely, quiet villages devoid of people that concerned me.

"Where is my hotel?"

RD, explained hesitantly, he did not think reservations would be needed.

I quickly found out that, after the busy summer tourist season is over, everything pretty much closes with the beginning of fall, especially after a hurricane. By the time the last hotel on the island said they had no rooms available, the wind was blowing horizontally, and the rain was coming down in sheets. I drove to the only place I knew.

RD had introduced me to the staff at the Cooperative Extension Service (CES) in Oak Bluffs, so I headed to their office. Chessy was listless, and it worried me. The receptionist, who looked like someone's sweet grandmother, with a head full of beautiful silver hair, was now furious at my boss for abandoning me. She called her sister-in-law, Sal. She smiled with good news: I had a place to stay. Sal owned a beautiful, white, historical house in Vineyard Haven. But she also had a small cabin in her backyard that she used as her weaving studio that I could use.

Sal, my new hostess, was a tall, lean woman with short salt-and-pepper gray hair. She had a hint of Texan accent with a Yankee twist. She was warm and friendly—and would not even discuss rent. She apologized for the coolness, as the cabin did not have heat, but she said she could get an electric heater.

As a gift, for literally rescuing me from sleeping in a jeep for the night, I presented her a pound of qiviut that I had collected while on Nunivak. At the time, the material went for $90 an ounce, and from her expression, she knew that.

Chessy and I settled into this quiet, tiny log cabin on an island in the Atlantic, and there, in the middle of the floor, was a loom and a spinning wheel. I hoped this new island could weave happiness back into my soul.

The first few weeks were chaotic. Like the hotels, most of the service industry and tourist shops were closed for winter. It is a period of rejuvenation for the locals, but very difficult for an off-islander to get a government office up and running.

The small, colonial home on the road to Oak Bluffs now housed a real estate office and my new field office. As I walked through the threshold into the reception area, I stumbled backwards. The onslaught of a bright burgundy red carpet against white-washed walls caused my eyes to blink rapidly. Once I adjusted, my first thought was to get rid of that gaudy carpet. In an old house like this, there must be solid wood-planked floor beneath, which would be much more pleasing to the eye. And yet, as the large moving van pulled up, my attention was diverted to the furniture the hefty crew of two were trying to maneuver into the office.

I called RD, and as politely as I could muster, I asked him how long they had kept the furniture at the bottom of the sea? Considering the cultural divide, I assumed he did not know what I was talking about, since the other end of the phone was quiet.

How could I explain? The two ancient gun-metal gray desks, bookshelves, and file cabinets were covered in a thick slime of black mold and green algae. The only piece of equipment that was usable was the solid wood drafting table, probably built in the 1800s. At five feet long and three feet wide, the drafting table was unwieldy, as it required the strength of two men to wrestle it into the reception area, where it would permanently stay, unless I sawed the legs off to get it into the small adjoining office. Oh, but that would defeat the purpose of having the monstrous piece of furniture in the first place!

RD jumped on the next ferry. I stood back and observed his expression when he saw the office furniture that the state office sent. I let him know that there were three things that I was very allergic to: cigarette smoke, crested wheatgrass, and mold. I put my foot down when the state office replied they expected me to clean the rusted, dented, mildewed office furniture, obviously stored in some forgotten GSA warehouse for half a century. It shocked him. He laughed, but he stopped when he saw my face and body language.

And then I let go.

"Is this some sort of New England initiation for outsiders? First, I get left on an island, after traveling for three days from Alaska, with no place to stay, with a cat, in the middle of a storm!" I was on a roll. "I have no office, but I am asked why I have no numbers to report? Whatever the hell that is! And when furniture finally shows up, it looks like someone found it at the bottom of some damn swamp! And then I am told to clean it? What number does that fall under?"

RD looked like a forlorn puppy, scolded by its owner. I figured I had just broken every New England protocol for well-mannered people. And then, the director of the Cooperative Extension Service walked into the office.

The smell of something like rotten eggs now permeating into the burgundy carpet was quite strong. As his eyes were watering, his face turned brilliant red, almost the color of the carpet. He was pissed off for RD abandoning me on the island, but when he saw the furniture, he let poor RD have it all over again. I felt no empathy.

The state office refused to send or allow any purchase of furniture. They agreed I could hire someone to clean the moldy mess.

The cabin did not have heat, and, by December, it was chilly. I found a two-room apartment in the basement of a beautiful house in the woods, for $1,000 a month. They warned me that, once summer arrived, rents would go for $5,000 a week. The locals rented their homes and camped in tents or went off-island.

I joined a gym with racquetball, so I was feeling a little less anxious. I met a vivacious school teacher who invited me to play ball with her. She was a wealth of information, a local 'chusetts gal from the mainland. She taught during the school year and sold real estate during the summer. We instantly hit it off. She sailed, played tennis, and windsurfed.

The Vineyard, as the locals call the island, is 7 miles off the coast of Cape Cod, Massachusetts, and the only way to get there is by water or by air. The island is shaped like a triangle, with the point facing north toward the Cape and the straight edge facing south. It is about 26 miles long and 9 miles wide. The total land area is 96 square miles, with 125 miles of tidal shoreline, 6 towns, and 3 villages.

As a person who prided myself on reading maps, this little island was a directional challenge. I scheduled to meet a cooperator, which most businesses would refer to as "a client." I told him our new office was in Oak Bluffs, so he gave me directions to a road in Tisbury.

I said, "Oh, Vineyard Haven?" I heard a loud chuckle on the other end of the phone.

That is when I learned about villages and towns—or, more accurately, that there are villages within towns. When you take the ferry from Woods Hole, on the Cape, to the Vineyard, you arrive at the village, Vineyard Haven.

Vineyard Haven, with its quaint shops, is a harbor village within the town of Tisbury. My good friend, Nan, lives in a lovely, three-story house that was once owned by a whaling captain. Or, as she explains it, she lives in half of the original home. The other half is nearby, down the road from her house. The house is a short walk from the village of Vineyard Haven.

Edgartown, with the traditional, elegant, white clapboard homes and black shuttered windows, is on the eastern shore. It includes Katama, where the beautiful long, white-sand Katama Beach is located, and Chappaquiddick, the village made famous, unfortunately, by a political tragedy.

Katama Beach, also known as "South Beach" or "State Beach," is a long, white-sand beach that is open to the public. It is one of the busiest, especially with the younger crowd, for its rolling waves and surfing. We consider it a barrier beach, with its long, narrow stretch of sand that curves to the inlet of Katama Bay. As one of the busiest beaches, the dunes were being affected with human foot traffic causing severe dune erosion. One of my projects, in coordination with many entities, was to transplant a few hundred plants to re-vegetate the eroding beach.

For two weekends, volunteers planted American Beach Grass in the areas that were most damaged. We had the area roped off, but as I witnessed on a weekend, people simply walked over the rope, trampling our newly planted grass!

I knew I needed a little more "pizzazz" to keep people out, so I made a dozen signs and staked them around the perimeter of the planting. It worked!

When I told RD what I had done, he asked, "What did the signs say?"

I responded, "Deer Tick Nesting Area—Beware of Lyme Disease."

A couple weeks later, I was thrilled when the agronomist for the CES invited me to visit one of the Elizabeth Islands. The Elizabeth Islands are a chain of small islands extending southwest from the southern coast of Cape Cod and north of Martha's Vineyard. The Forbes family had purchased all the islands except two, Cuttyhunk and Pennikese. The farm manager needed technical assistance on Nashawena to evaluate some of their pasture land grazed by sheep. It was beautiful, with the green fields against the brilliant blue ocean.

I thought how crazy my life was. A year before, I was evaluating muskox grazing on a remote island in the Bering Sea. Now, here I was, standing on a private island, owned by one of the most wealthy and prominent investors in the world, in the Atlantic Ocean, discussing sheep grazing.

On New Year's Morning, January 1, 1986, the fog was rolling in as I sat on the narrow, sandy beach, the sand pillars lurking in the fog like sentries and conglomerate boulders nested in the gritty sand. The pastel cliffs, veiled in fog, appeared to be dancing into the sea on the western edge of the beach.

This was the place, but I could not explain why. There was no connection here between my husband and me. Not a physical one—but perhaps a mystical one. I had wandered the island beaches all winter. And yet, this is where I found myself. I reached into my backpack and took out the small jar. As I unscrewed the lid, the light breeze carried the ash across the sand and sea.

I remembered the words we wrote below our sketch on the wedding invitations we designed.

I murmured, "You are my happiness, my sorrow, my yesterday, my tomorrow. Be free, my love, be free."

Ironically, while I was visiting the island in July 2004, my friend Nan and I were at a friend of hers who lived in Aquinnah. She had invited us for a beach day with her nephew, on a resident-only private stretch of magnificent sand and surf. It was this beach.

As we lay there, Nan's friend explained the sad event that had killed John Kennedy Junior, his wife, and sister-in-law, a couple of years previously. The debris from the plane crash had washed up on the very beach we were sitting on.

I recalled working on the beautiful estate owned by Jackie O. and felt great sadness at the plane crash of her only son so near to this stretch of beach.

CHAPTER 14

Storms Realign

T*he picturesque island and beaches* are peaceful and accessible, during the winter, I described to Justin for his upcoming visit in January. He was spending six weeks in a soils-training course in Lincoln, Nebraska, but they allowed one trip home, or someplace else, of equivalent cost.

I picked him up at the Cape Cod Airport, where I'd reserved a nice bed-and-breakfast in Hyannis. He learned what a rotary was when I ended up in the wrong spoke, at night with snow. The next day we took the ferry to the Island.

We explored the towns and villages, beachcombed, and sampled the local hangouts like the Black Dog. Justin especially enjoyed the cliffs of Gay Head and looking at boats in the harbors. Just before Justin's departure, we were watching the launching of the Space Shuttle *Challenger* on January 28, 1986, when she disintegrated before our eyes.

Sal, coincidently, had a trip planned to Wellesley, outside of Boston, on the same weekend Justin was leaving, and offered us a ride. As usual, the traffic was congested, and the day was nearly half over when she dropped us off. She made the comment, primarily for Justin's ears, that the traffic was horrendous all the time, especially to the airport. He had been upset with me for not picking him up at the Boston airport and almost canceled his visit. I smiled and winked at her as she looked in the rearview mirror.

The contrast of the historic stone-and-brick remnants among the glass-and-steel buildings along the Freedom Trail was fascinating. We saw the *USS Constitution* and spent time at the Boston Aquarium. It was late, so we looked for a hotel. The next morning, Justin got a cab back to the airport while I paid the hotel bill of $250. It broke my month's budget, so I walked to the bus station and caught the bus back to Woods Hole.

It was quiet after Justin left, but I kept busy with meetings, visiting the numerous small farms, and chatting with locals about conservation concerns. I took long walks and enjoyed the calmness of the beaches around the island.

In March 1986, I flew back to Alaska for a week to complete a hardship sale of my home. As I walked away, it broke my heart, flooding my brain with memories—the happy and the sad.

I kept busy cleaning and working with the carpet installers at Justin's house. It was great timing on his part; he did not have to take a day off from work and went to his sailing class at night. Before I knew it, the week was over, and, as I stepped off the plane on the island, I was greeted with a landscape of green. Spring colors were beautiful, with snowballs of hydrangea in a range of violets and blues, and crystal-clear skies.

"You'd better learn to sail," he demanded. Sailing was his new obsession, as I found out when I was in Alaska.

I thought it would be a simple thing to do, as I was on an island! But I found no sailing courses—none that I could afford, anyway. My friend Nan was an excellent sailor and would frequently crew for a friend of hers, Pat. He was in his 80s and had one of the most colorful histories of anyone that I knew. When she called to ask if I would like to help crew on Pat's Friendship sloop *Erda*, a 23-foot gaff-rigged sailboat, during a race, I was ecstatic! Nan kept Pat on step, as he told endless stories. It was a highlight of my life on the Vineyard, sailing with Nan and Pat.

One lovely summer evening in 1986, Nan invited me to a boat christening at the Gannon & Benjamin Wooden Boatyard in Vineyard Haven. I have no memory of the boat, other than it was a wooden sailboat, or of who the owner was. I was too awestruck at what I was doing, where I was, and who was there. A familiar face, with a bottle of champagne, came up to Nan and me, and asked if we were enjoying ourselves, as he filled our glasses of champagne. I looked at Nan, and said, "Is that . . . ?" "Yep," she said, laughing. Bill Murray and his entourage passed through the crowd, chatting up a storm, pouring champagne into the gathering's glasses.

I may not have learned how to sail that summer, but I got a taste of the sailing world, and I wanted more.

There were growing pains on the island; how could there not be! I always wondered why someone would build a multi-million dollar home next to a working dairy. I met with the owner to address this ongoing problem. As temperatures increased by mid-summer, so did the smell of his dairy.

Our first issue was to design a manure waste lagoon, and our second was to ensure the cows had hay and pasture, both requiring a large contribution of funds to maintain. Seaside Dairy could never overcome the growing financial debt and closed that same year.

In June 1986, Flo visited, and I was so excited to have her. It was obvious she was anxious about me living in this one-room basement apartment. Once she realized I had made many friends, she relaxed and enjoyed herself. And she loved seeing Chessy again.

Flo treated me to a weekend trip on Long Island to visit Rick's "ex" Aunt Jeanne, on his dad's side; a complicated relationship. Flo had kept in touch with Jeanne and her husband, Fred, over the years, and it was quite easy to fly from the Vineyard to Long Island. One day, we took the train to Grand Central Station to visit New York City.

Grand Central was mesmerizing for Flo and me, with arched windows and vaulted ceilings. The chandeliers, sleek marble, and intricate stone carvings of leaves and acorns, and the noise of a working rail station. We wandered through Central Park and Manhattan and laughed at the smells of the city, so new and intriguing to our senses. We said our goodbyes at the airport, with tears and loving words.

August 1986 would be a busy month, with my sister's wedding and moving out of my basement studio into Nan's house, where I was renting a room. To diffuse the belittlement of me being a horrible sister if I missed my sister's wedding, I gave in to my mom's demands. Even with the busy summer season, my boss granted my leave. It was a huge financial burden, with a furlough and no paycheck after October 1986, but it was worth it to keep the peace.

The federal government was furloughing employees in October 1986 and was asking for volunteers first. My boss and I discussed it. The cost of living on the island at a GS-9, with no kind of locality pay, was poverty level. If I stayed, I would need to find a second job, or the Agency would need to help with housing. He agreed to my request for a maximum of a six-month furlough, and in the meantime, he would find a position for me. Justin and I would take the six months to travel—something neither of us had done.

Mentally, I was exhausted. I had taken less than two weeks off when Rick died, but the endless legal fight used up most of my leave. Unlike my male Soil Scientists, who received compensation time for every hour they worked, I only got one hour a day while in the field, regardless of how many hours I worked. It was not unusual for the Soil Scientists to accrue enough "comp time" during the summer field season to take two months off every winter.

In early August, I flew to Spokane, taking a ferry, a bus, and then a long flight from Boston, where I arrived the next day. My cousin picked me and Chessy up at the airport. My mom refused to take care of Chessy while I was traveling, but my lovely cousin said she could.

Being recently divorced and living alone, she was happy to have her. I got Chessy settled in, and then we drove to my parents' home the next morning.

They were leaving for Bellevue the next day to check into their hotel and get ready for the wedding rehearsal and dinner. Apparently, I was not invited to the rehearsal dinner, so my Uncle Danny and Aunt Judy arranged for me to drive with them and my cousins. Wow! I flew across the country, on a very expensive ticket, took a week off from work, because I was expected at my sister's wedding. I guess they meant that literally—*just* the wedding.

Mary, listening to this, responded, "What else is new?"

The wedding was extravagant, including a limo for my sister and her new husband, whom I had met before. When my sister introduced me to her mother-in-law, she said, "Oh, yes: the sister who went to Alaska, and then your husband died? Don't you live on Martha's Vineyard with the rich and famous? That must have been quite a settlement?"

Before I could answer, my sister interrupted and said my job was to collect all the garbage after the reception. She yelled at someone and asked them to show me where the garbage bags were.

My sister's wedding included four bridesmaids in their designer prom-like dresses and fancy shoes. And dozens and dozens of flowers. The groomsmen, their bulging, over-muscled bodies, snug in their penguin tuxedos, sauntered around with smirky alcohol-induced grins.

As the band played, and the catered food and alcohol flowed, I wandered through the reception, feeling terribly alone and out of place. Then my sister's mother-in-law tapped me on my shoulder and reminded me I should start collecting garbage. I smiled, turned away from her, and caught a cab back to the hotel. Mary, the forever party-goer, wandered into the hotel room in the wee hours of the increasing dawn light.

As I flew back to the Vineyard, I thought briefly about how much money my parents had contributed to their youngest daughter's wedding. And then I blew it off. I would take the wedding Rick and I made for ourselves over the fiasco I flew some 4000 miles to attend. A few years later, I realized my sister's in-laws repulsed me even more at my sister's funeral in 2003. She died of a fentanyl overdose in her battle against cancer.

During a phone call to my cousin to see how Chessy was, she informed me that her boyfriend had moved in with his German shepherd and eight pups. I mentioned the situation to Flo. The reason Flo could not take Chessy was that she already had a cat, so you can imagine my surprise when she called me and wanted to go get Chessy in Spokane. She told me her cat had passed and wanted Mary's phone number.

A week later, she drove to Spokane and picked up Chessy. She called me and was so excited to have her at home with her. She later told me about the situation there with all those dogs. They scared my poor cat to death, and she practically jumped into Flo's arms. I felt so guilty and so blessed to have had Flo in my life.

DG arrived on the island while visiting his family in Connecticut. We had so much fun. He removed the moon-roof glass from the Subaru so we could fit his surf fishing poles through the roof. We fished for striped bass, watching the sun set, drinking beer, and eating fish sandwiches on Menemsha Beach. He revealed how much his mom had enjoyed my visit over Thanksgiving. She invited me to her house in Connecticut when she found out I would be alone on the Vineyard. I had an amazing time, as she and her sons treated me as one of her own.

It was not surprising when DG asked me to come as his date to his brother's wedding in September—at his mom's request. The wedding, in Connecticut, would be on the weekend before Justin's arrival on the island. I called to confirm his arrival date and let him know my plans for the weekend before he would arrive. I also disclosed that Nan would be off-island, so we could have the house all to ourselves.

A few days later, he called and said he could get a flight only during the weekend I was going to Connecticut.

DG's disappointment was one thing, but when I explained my situation to his mom, she genuinely wanted me at the wedding. Nan, conveniently, changed her schedule for being off-island for the weekend of Justin's arrival. When she left, I cleaned the house and ordered a special treat from the Black Dog Bakery. Then I called him to confirm his flight the next morning. Now, it was a week later because something had come up. I was speechless. And pissed.

When Nan came back from her off-island excursion, she found out he had changed his plans. She almost called him, but she did not want to ruin our friendship. Years later, I asked her about that event.

"You knew back then, didn't you?" She nodded her head. There was more than friction between the two of them.

It was a beautiful fall day when he arrived in late September 1986, receiving a well-deserved cold shoulder from Nan. A friend offered to teach Justin how to play racquetball so that I could have time at the gym to say goodbye to everyone. Instead, he sat in the car during my goodbyes. He refused to go in and meet my friends, and, specifically, he did not want to play racquetball. I apologized to my friend.

I have thought about that incident for years. One day while Pooch and his wife spent a weekend, we were skiing on the trail behind our home. Justin was always far ahead of us.

Pooch's wife said to me, "You do realize he competes with you? There is no way he will ever accept you, Michelle. You are a threat to him. I see it in his eyes and his demeanor."

I never understood that back then. I do now. He was a loner who kept his thoughts private. I assumed it was because he had no one who cared about him. I thought if I offered him love and companionship, while still giving him his freedom, he would understand what a relationship is about.

As we boarded the ferry that early brisk morning, I anxiously questioned what I was doing. I had always worked. I was the responsible one, and where did that get me? In six months, I would have a choice to make. For now, I needed to take a leap of faith and take a chance.

CHAPTER 15

History Transcended

It was a test for the Subaru and us as we drove north from Cape Cod to Maine, with a carrier on top, and a new mountain bike on the back—just one, since Justin did not bring his, as planned.

I learned quickly not to ride Rick's twelve-speed during the summer on the island, with the crazy tourists. But riding on the bike trails was no easy task, either. After several crashes when the skinny tires hit windblown sand, I knew I needed a different bike. Like everything else, it hurt when a young man loaded it onto the back of his car and drove away.

Rick had kept a scrapbook of that cross-country bike adventure. As he and I were packing one day, he held the faded gray book with a forlorn smile on his face. We sat on the floor while he tentatively opened it. I watched his expressions, pointing at each picture: young comrades, survivors from his platoon, welcoming and cheering him on his ride, or a place he camped on the banks of a river, or a couple who invited him in for a meal, or the cute guy with a head of shaggy brown hair standing in front of his bike with an American flag swaying in the wind.

It was the way he smiled, the fall of a tear, a break of laughter. The trip was a release of those demons from the Vietnam War.

Leaf-peeper time had arrived, and the colors were brilliant. I suppose we were officially now "leaf peepers." I kidded Justin that he could do the driving through Boston, but, as we had with all the major cities, we circumvented Boston completely. We headed to Arcadia National Park, just south of Bar Harbor, Maine, the long way.

This is one of the most scenic and diverse of the national parks in the lower 48, with its rocky coastline, islands, pine forests, and the exposed granitic domes and erratic, large boulders left behind as the glacier had melted. It includes the highest mountains along the Atlantic Coast; Cadillac Mountain has an elevation of 1,500 feet. For us westerners, we would call that a "hill," as I mistakenly did when my boss often referred to the Berkshires as mountains. I reminded him he needed to go on a road trip to the West.

Although the summit of Cadillac Mountain is not that high, the 360-degree view it offers of the harbor, the famous Egg Rock lighthouse, and the dozens of islands shrouded in fog are spectacular. The trail winds and cuts into the granite rock, reminiscent of the glacial-formed landscape in Alaska. We wandered along the rugged shoreline, looking for seals. As gulls squawked overhead, we investigated the smaller creatures in the endless tide pools during low tide.

As amazing as the natural world was, the historic and cultural significance of this park was also fascinating. I'd never *heard* of a "carriage road," much less actually *walked* on one.

John D. Rockefeller, Jr., was an experienced horseman who wanted to travel by horse and carriage on Mount Desert Island without running into any motor vehicles. He duplicated the carriage roads on his family's estate while blending the natural setting of the landscape of the island into the design of the roads. Stone culverts, wide ditches, and many layers of crushed rock were used to divert water from the rainy coastal climate of Maine.

At night, we would amble around the quaint village of Bar Harbor, eating fresh and local delicacies. As it got cooler and cooler with every morning, we knew it was time to stow the tent and continue our road trip, leaving behind this exotic coastline of the eastern seaboard with the hope of one day returning.

It was an uneventful drive until we were at the U.S. side of the border at Sault Ste. Marie, Michigan. As I pulled up to the customs station, the border agent asked me where I lived, as he looked at my passport. Justin handed him his driver's license.

"Well, right now you might say I live in my car," I giggled. I thought it was rather obvious, with the turtle on top, the car loaded, and a bike.

He bent over and took a good, long look at my passenger and then back at the license. Then he told me to pull over. He asked Justin to follow him, but he told me to stay in the car. I don't remember how long I sat there, but Justin came out of the U.S. Customs Office and got into the car. He told me to drive. His face was red, and he told me how stupid I was to tell the officer what I said. He refused to talk or tell me what had happened and slept instead.

We continued to his aunt's house in Iron River, Michigan, in silence. But we did stop and look at Picture Rocks along Lake Superior. I even had a little swim in that frigid water, nearly dying of hypothermia!

It was a delightful visit, but we headed to Iowa to visit Brannen. After our arrival, I explained Justin's moodiness because of the border incident, which I had caused.

"Heck, I've apologized several times."

Brannen reassured me it had nothing to do with my remark. He relayed a story of two incidents while they were driving across the border, in and out of the U.S. and Canada. It convinced him that the border patrol in both countries had red flags on Justin; especially with his Fu Manchu mustache, long shaggy hair, and dark-tinted glasses. And the antics that nearly got Justin strip-searched? Well, as Brannen explained, there is no doubt a file on him.

We then drove south to Badlands National Park, with sharply eroded buttes and pinnacles framed against the background of the largest undisturbed mixed-grass prairie in the United States. The term "badlands" refers to the two geologic processes of deposition and erosion.

The deposition formations underwent a 47-million-year period of spanning three major geologic periods, the Cretaceous, the Late Eocene, and the Oligocene Epochs, resulting in distinct red and white layers of sediment. Once deposited, the material becomes subject to erosional powers of wind and rain, resulting in the dramatic landscape we see today. The noticeable lack of vegetation is no doubt the result of no accumulation of soil on the landforms.

The morning sunrise against the moonscape was even more dramatic as we drank our coffee. I never expected such a sight after my drive, relying on billboards to keep me awake. We spent our days hiking and exploring the geologic treasure chest while searching for clues of the elusive Black-footed ferret.

The Black-footed ferret is the only ferret species native to North America and was almost globally extinct in the 1960s. However, because of the conservation efforts across the continent, these ferrets are slowly making a comeback.

Despite their growing numbers, the Black-footed ferret is still under threat, primarily because of the shrinking numbers of their primary prey: prairie dogs. Black-footed ferrets rely on the presence of prairie dogs for food and for shelter. Because of habitat loss and a strain of prairie-dog plague, the ferrets' primary source of food is dwindling. This is a reason for protection of the mixed-grass prairie, an ecotone between the shortgrass and the tallgrass prairies.

Vast herds of free-ranging bison and pronghorn also littered the short-grass prairie. The prairie was alive with large prairie-dog colonies, deer and elk, and apex predators such as gray wolves and grizzly bears. The carpet of grasses, blue grama, and buffalo grass, with colorful wildflowers, provided habitat for the native bees, butterflies, songbirds, and raptors.

Today, the most common animal on the prairie is domestic cattle. The short-grass prairie adapted to animal grazing, but nature and man have different philosophies about carrying capacity and diversity. Today, the apex predators are gone, replaced by coyotes. The prairie dogs are fewer in number, and the decline of native bees is at a level never seen before in the agricultural industry.

The shortgrass prairie, more common in the western great plains, where soils are shallow and rainfall minimal, has suffered the greatest biological destruction of any major biome in North America. Habitat destruction through extermination of native herbivores and predators, the proliferation of noxious weeds, and altered fire regimes have negatively affected this ecosystem.

The tallgrass prairie extended throughout the American Midwest and small portions of southern and central Canada. We characteristically find them on rich loess soil under moderate rainfall. Natural and anthropogenic fire, and grazing by large mammals, such as bison, were historically agents of periodic disturbance, which also minimized tree encroachment, recycled nutrients to the soil, and promoted seed dispersal and germination processes.

Because of expansive agricultural land use, the tallgrass prairie is only a fraction of what it used to be. For now, the sliver of the mid-grass prairie has some protection, but with the change of climate, it is hard to know what the future will be like, especially for at-risk creatures such as the Black-footed ferret and native bees.

The cooler weather was letting us know we needed to continue west, but we had one more stop: Mount Rushmore.

The four presidential faces carved into the granite symbolize "an accomplishment born, planned, and created in the minds and by the hands of Americans for Americans."

Should we add another president to the faces of granite?

In 2017, at a rally in Ohio, President Trump stated, "I'd ask whether you someday think I will be on Mount Rushmore." He later said it was a joke, and that he was just having fun. We can ponder on that.

Justin suggested we stop at Thermopolis. Suddenly, he was not in a hurry to get to his hometown.

The town of Thermopolis, named from the Greek words for "hot city," is home to natural hot springs, near the northern end of the Wind River Canyon and Wedding of the Waters, where the north-flowing Wind River becomes the Bighorn River.

The acrid sulfur smell, permeating the steam as it rises from the collision of the cool air and the 104-degree water, made my eyes weep, but my muscles melted with joy.

Tentatively, I asked Justin about his parents, particularly why he calls them by their first names. I thought if I could get him to talk, maybe I would have some idea about what was bothering him. At first, he was defensive, as if calling one's parents by their first names was normal.

Then quietly, Justin said his dad could be arrogant and opinionated. He reiterated and said, *very opinionated*. I got that. His son has similar qualities. It was what he said next that shocked me.

"And he told me never to get hooked up with a woman. They only use you."

"When did he tell you that?"

"I was a kid," he shrugged. "He's always told me that. No big deal."

Now I understood. Justin never had a long-term girlfriend. And here he was, coming home with one—one who'd left her job and her home.

When we arrived, the conversation at the house was cordial. I realized a consistent theme of discussion usually included the defective spouses. Although this is not unlike many families, I also noticed there was a complete absence of affection in the family—no hugs or loving words.

When asked if I wanted to go elk hunting, I said yes, but it relieved me when we took a break halfway up the mountain. Justin looked at ease, staring at the spectacular view, sitting on a boulder while sipping hot coffee from the thermos. I watched the steam, and the aroma teased me as I patiently waited for an offering.

Finally, his brother made a wisecrack, and Justin apologized as he handed me the mug. He really was in another place. Unfortunately, I had a small headache, and it was getting worse as we climbed. I was also having a hard time breathing. His brother asked me if I had ever been hiking at 10,000 feet before. With a laugh, I said "No"; I'd lived on an island and, before that, Anchorage!

He looked at Justin and asked him what the hell was he thinking. Justin's dismissive response, an all-too-familiar one now, "She's a big girl."

It was getting late, so we started back down the mountain, which helped ease my throbbing head. That was my first encounter with altitude sickness, and, unfortunately, it would not be my last.

CHAPTER 16

Ancient Beauty

The Movie Ranch was on an isolated stretch of road, outside the small town of Kanab, Utah, just north of the Arizona state line.

Justin found out one cabin was available for rent. He had stayed at the ranch while mapping soils in the four-corner region, along with a large group of whitewater oarsmen for the Grand Canyon.

The setting was breathtaking, the cabins rustic. It was a beautiful place to call home for a month, with the multicolored pink and mauve sandstone escarpments contrasted with the lime-green greasewood and sage scattered on the sandy pavement. It was easy to see Hollywood's fascination with the area.

Once settled, our next visit was to The Coral Pink Sand Dunes Park. As we passed through Kanab, to the Dunes, Justin explained that Kanab, a small, busy town, founded in 1870 by ten families of the Latter-Day Saints, is still a Mormon stronghold.

The Dunes are windblown pink-sand deposits from the erosion of the red Navajo Sandstone found throughout the park. The sweeping coral sand formed wind-swept dunes as tall as 300 feet. At 10,000 to 15,000 years old, they have had centuries to move across the barren landscape.

We spent our days exploring slot canyons, walking through narrow, winding passageways and ribbons of multicolored sandstone. The desolate landscape of olive-green Utah junipers, ponderosa pine, and piñon pine in the overstory must be brilliant in the spring, with muted pink and yellow flowering plants, yucca cactus, and scattered dune grass in the understory, the stabilizers of the dunes and desert pavement.

The cabin was deathly quiet at night, so unlike the stories Justin spoke about when he'd stayed here a couple of years before. Back then, in the late '70s, there were always rotating river guides, and parties were never in short supply. The stars were brilliant white against a dark, midnight-blue sky. As the warmth of the day evaporated into the cool of the desert night, he would pick out and describe various constellations.

One of his friends, who played racquetball, had told him he should learn how to play, since Kanab had a small gym with a court. Justin insisted we should check it out. Considering he showed no interest in the sport while on the island, I was surprised, but I certainly would not dissuade him. That is, until I saw the court.

It was cement. Racquetball is a fast sport, normally played on a hardwood, lacquered floor, much like a basketball court. A cement floor would be a problem, even for a player like myself.

The sport is one of angles, like geometry. A problem with new players, especially men, is that they use power and speed, rather than strategy. Justin had never played a sport on a wood-court surface. Oblivious and defensive toward my instructions, he continued swinging his racquet with an extended arm and running fast, back and forth, across the small court.

As an experienced player, there are two critical safety concerns in racquetball; you do not look at an opponent who is behind you, and you avoid a player with an outstretched arm and racquet. And that is what I did.

He suddenly screamed and fell to the floor, grabbing his calf. He accused me of hitting the back of his leg with a racquet and told me to stay away from him.

It was obvious he was in excruciating pain, but I stood there, frozen. I played soccer, basketball, volleyball, tennis, softball, and racquetball—all team sports—and never had a teammate or player accuse me of intentionally causing them harm.

I explained to him I was on the opposite side of the court and was not near him. I did not hit his leg with my racquet. He refused to believe me. I helped him off the floor, got him into the car, iced his leg, and found a doctor in Kanab. The doctor recommended he see a specialist in Salt Lake, but he refused.

I worried because he was limping terribly, changing his gait. I did not see any improvement. He could ride my bike, which left me alone, as he never brought his. He would take off for hours, leaving me to worry if he was okay. I learned not to ask when he would be back.

We left Utah and entered Arizona.

On the way to Flagstaff, we stopped to visit with another friend of Justin's, who had been in the Baja of Mexico for a month. As we drove from his friend's, he insisted we drive to the Baja. I explained my hesitancy in taking my vehicle into Mexico. I also suggested we get his ankle checked. He said it would be fine with the ACE bandage. I shook my head, as it did not look fine. But, what could I do?

"If you don't want to go, then you can take me to my friends in Montana."

I learned not to argue with him, although, in my mind, I wanted to find a bus station and throw him out. I realized he valued others' opinions more than mine, and, rather than discuss a disagreement, he would shut down. Slowly, over time, his anger would build, at anything I did or said that bothered him, and eventually erupting, directly at me. His behavior was not rational. And neither was mine, as I continued to blame myself, instead of Justin.

To drive my car into Mexico, it would require I get new car insurance and new registration in a state other than my current state of Massachusetts. It was an excellent reason for not driving to the Baja.

Justin's sister, with whom we were staying in Flagstaff, suggested we fly from Flagstaff to Cabo and rent a car. I winked at her, as she was trying to help my cause. She also suggested he get a specialist to look at his ankle. She, too, was concerned.

Although both suggestions seemed reasonable, Justin got defensive. In the end, I applied for a vehicle registration, license, and car insurance for Arizona, using his sister's address. It was an expense I had not planned for, not to mention the unknown consequences of lying about my place of residence—especially after the incident crossing the Canadian border.

The trip was beautiful, and I was glad we went. The San Felipe Desert on the eastern coast of the Baja lies in the rain shadow of the interior mountains, resulting in a very arid desert, with plants I had never seen before. The ocotillo, the multibranched elephant tree, and a palm unique to the area, the blue fan palm, were all new and strange, until I saw the boojum tree.

The boojum does not look like a tree. It is leafless and shaped like a candle, with a wide trunk, narrowing toward the tip. Before heading south to La Paz, we made a side trip back to the east coast to the Bahia de los Angeles. This little bay is full of rock cliffs falling into the sea, with arches along a rocky shoreline. We spent a couple of days there snorkeling in the cool-but-protected waters of the bay, camping on the beach.

Our goal was to watch whales from a place called Magdalena Bay on the Pacific Coast. We pitched our tent on the sand in what appeared to be a broad beach plain. I was hesitant with the soft sand, but Justin had no worries. There were several vehicles scattered along the beach, with other people also intent on spotting the gray whales. We spotted whales in the distance, hiked, and visited the small villages. I made blueberry "muffins," spreading the coals from the fire around the Dutch oven. Hopefully, it would be a delightful treat for breakfast.

There was a loud noise, and then yips and low growls right outside the tent. Justin stepped outside the tent to find coyotes trying to get at the cool muffins. Unfortunately, that was not our only surprise! There must have been a very high tide, because we were slowly being swallowed in water. As I dealt with the tent, Justin gathered driftwood to help get the Subaru out of the wet sand. Slowly, we navigated onto higher ground, honking our horn to alert others.

If it had not been for the coyotes, it might have been too late for the Subaru by the time water reached our tent. To this day, I am cautious of camping on beaches. Two years ago, while camping on a long, wide beach of Padre Island with our camper, a storm was developing, and the rangers warned people of the dangers of high tide. As I was talking to a ranger, he pointed to a line of vehicles leaving the beach, all local anglers. He said that, when the locals leave, it's time to go. So, we did.

As we sat at Border Control on our way out of Mexico, the agent asked me to open the glove box. There, with my stun gun, was a package of cigarettes. I nearly hyperventilated. Justin had given a ride to one guy in La Paz who'd had his van confiscated as the Federales had found a baggy of green herbs.

I hoped that the carton held only cigarettes and not anything else. Fortunately, the agent asked what the stun gun was. I explained it was from my mom, who worked for the police, and she got it for me for protection. He looked at it, curious, but gave it back and let us proceed. Once we got into the U.S., I took a breath.

Finally, when we arrived in Seattle, Justin saw a specialist for his ankle injury. It was a partial tear of the Achilles tendon. At the time, the only recommendation was to cast the ankle to stabilize it and hope the tear repaired itself. They put a plaster cast on, and, the next day, we flew to New Zealand.

CHAPTER 17

Land of the Long White Cloud

"*Waiheke? Where is that?*" Justin inquired of a fellow traveler as we grabbed our backpacks off the carousel.

The flight to Auckland, New Zealand, was our first 22-hour, long-haul flight. The island sounded good to us, so off we went on a shuttle to the ferry dock.

Waiheke Island is approximately 13 miles from Auckland and is the most populated and the second-largest island in the Hauraki Gulf of New Zealand. The hostel consisted of little wooden pods with curtains where people slept. And did we sleep. We disobeyed that standard rule to adapt to the local time zone. Our co-pod roommates feared we might have died, until we finally stirred due to hunger.

The island had everything: beautiful, isolated beaches, amazing hikes among rolling hills, and wine! It would have been easy to just hang on the island for the entire two months.

Meeting people at this hostel did provide us insider information on where to go and what to do in the next two months. We said goodbye to our new friends and continued our adventure as we enjoyed the ferry back to Auckland.

Drivers on the opposite side of the road nearly got me run over when I made the mistake of looking the wrong way for traffic. Justin grabbed my arm and pulled me back, seconds before a vehicle nearly hit me in a busy intersection of downtown Auckland.

Once we got out of the city, we hitchhiked. Astonishingly, the cast was quite the subject of conversation during our many drives with the locals.

Justin would stand along the left side of the highway and stick his hand out. We rarely had to wait very long. Squash is the preferred court sport in New Zealand, and many thought his cast was the result of playing squash. We realized that New Zealanders enjoy meeting travelers and sharing their beautiful country. It would take us a little more time to get from point A to point B, but the side trips were always worth the extra time.

We also learned, when asked where we were from, we would say "Alaska." Consistently, the response was, "Oh, you are Canadian?" And we would nod and answer, "Eh."

For several years, there had been a disagreement between New Zealand and countries such as the U.S., particularly with nuclear-powered navy ships in New Zealand waters. The sinking of the Greenpeace *Rainbow Warrior* in 1985 had exacerbated the anti-nuclear opinion of New Zealanders and resulted in the New Zealand Nuclear-Free Zone Disarmament and Arms Control Act in 1987. The purpose was to promote and encourage an effective process by New Zealand for disarmament and international arms control, at least in their waters.

On the road to Whangarei, our local "guide" took us to a place she and her family loved to visit. As we drove through dense forest scrub, she pulled off onto a small turnaround area. She asked us if we had torches as she got out of her vehicle. We followed her onto a small, somewhat-used path that led us to a rock wall, barely visible. At the base was a small, dark, well-hidden opening. We turned on our "torches" and followed her in as we stooped to get through the opening. We walked about 30 feet in a twisting corridor before stopping in a small cavern. She whispered to us to turn off our light.

Instantly we were engulfed in brilliant flashing lights. The bioluminescence was breathtaking and alive! Our guide giggled and murmured, "Glow worms."

Glow worms, or fireflies, technically referred to as the Lampyridae, are a family of insects in the beetle order Coleoptera, with more than 2,000 described species. They are soft-bodied beetles that are commonly called "fireflies," "glowworms," or "lightning bugs" for their conspicuous use of bioluminescence during twilight to attract mates or prey.

We spent the next week hiking, snorkeling, and camping on remote stretches of sand, overlooking the incredible blue water of the Pacific. We met another local while we were camping who gave us a ride all the way to the tip of the North Island, where the Cape Reinga Lighthouse is located. The last 15 miles was a rough, gravel road, but it didn't faze our driver at all.

We finally made our way south, back to Auckland, where we spent one night in a youth hostel. As we were hitching to the Lake

Taupo region, a man stopped and asked us where we were heading. Then he said, "Get in," as he was driving home to Wellington.

Justin told him about Alaska, and, in that discussion, he asked us if we had any aversion to flying on a small plane. We, of course, said, "No," and, a few minutes later, he pulled into a private airport, where he kept his plane. The next thing we knew, we were flying over the snow and ice of Mt. Ruapehu in the Central Plateau of the North Island. It is in the UNESCO Heritage Tongariro National Park, listed for its cultural and geological significance. Along with having the Whanganui National Park nearby, this area is one of New Zealand's premier outdoor destinations.

Our pilot delivered us safely to the airport and then drove us to one of the premier trout rivers of the North Island, the Tongariro River. We'd planned to stay with him when we reached Wellington but said goodbye as we found a quaint cottage near the river, our new home for a few days.

It was quiet this time of year, bad for catching fish, but good for us, with no reservations. As we walked among the lush vegetation along the river, we saw a group of large black birds with red bills—the black swan.

After a week of exploration, from hot springs to hikes, we caught a bus to Wellington and stayed with our new friend. After a lovely dinner, his girlfriend asked if we would be interested in a private showing at the museum, where she worked. Of course, we accepted, but we had no idea what the exhibit was.

We were shocked when we saw the Terracotta Army, a collection of sculptures depicting the armies of Qin Shi Huang, the first Emperor of China. They buried the army with the emperor in 210–209 BCE with the purpose of protecting him in his afterlife. Local farms discovered them in 1974 outside of Xi'an, Shaanxi,

China. The figures depicted warriors, chariots, and horses, found in three pits and estimated to be 8,000 soldiers, 130 chariots, and 520 horses.

A day later, we were on the ferry from Wellington, on the North Island, to Picton, on the South Island.

The glorious thing about hitching in New Zealand is the flexibility and ease in hitching from campground to campground. The campgrounds are all close or in town, have a large kitchenette, eating area, showers, bathrooms, and nicely groomed grass spots for pitching a tent. One night at a pub, we met a couple; she was Swiss, and he American. After a couple of brews, we found out they both sailed.

The next morning, we found a sailboat charter company for bareboating. I was the only non-certified sailboat skipper, so it was easy to rent a 27-foot monohull for a week.

Marlborough Sounds is an unspoiled maritime oasis. The intricate web of waterways comprises four Sounds—the Queen Charlotte Sound, the Kenepuru Sound, the Pelorus Sound, and the Mahau Sound, nestled among mountains with ancient Rimu trees, lush Punga tree ferns, and the brilliant colors of orchids. The myriad of bays, coves, and bights are perfect for exploring by boat, as evidenced by Captain Cook, who first landed the *Endeavor* in New Zealand in 1770, anchoring in a "... very snug cove ..."—today known as Ship Cove—which would become the base for his Pacific exploration.

About 3 days into our voyage, our mates decided to stay at an island lodge. We enjoyed the endless sailing, fishing, and wildlife opportunities from turtles, seals, dolphins, birds, and flora along the beautiful coastline.

The main channels of the Marlborough Sounds have calm water; however, the notorious Cook Strait is infamous for its strong currents and rough waters, especially when the wind is coming from the south or north. The weather can change quickly, as we witnessed the morning of our departure back to Picton. We saw ships much bigger than our small sailboat heeled completely over amid whitecapped waves. I was very nervous as Justin went to the bow to take down the jib and reef the main, but alas, it was still too strong, as I had the tiller nearly in the water in the winds and sea.

As we were both shaking from "terror," we motored back into the protective cove. We delayed, considering we had to get the boat back, and we decided to motor rather than sail across the Strait. Justin, who was very experienced motoring in seas, got us safely back into the safe harbor of Grove Arm. Sailing was exhilarating—feeling the power of the wind, skimming through smooth, blue water, watching dolphins surfing the bow waves. I was hooked and swore the first thing I would do when I got back to Alaska was to learn to sail.

Bungee-jumping off bridges was the big sport in New Zealand at the time we visited; however, we were more interested in the Shotover, rocky, fast, and clear-blue river cutting through the Shotover Canyon.

But first, one must access the river, which requires a *resistance to fear* and confidence in your driver's ability to maneuver a narrow, winding gravel road constricted by a sheer rock wall soaring to the sky on one side, and a vertical drop hundreds of feet below, on the other, for a nail-biting, breath-holding 17 miles. It should have been a hint to us unsuspecting riders in this old four-wheel-drive van, when the driver repositioned the side mirrors inward, jumped into the driver's seat, and told us to shift our weight to the "cliff" side on the curves.

Skippers Canyon Road, in the southwest of New Zealand's South Island, is today one of New Zealand's better-known scenic roads—and unbelievably scary. Miners carved the road more than 140 years ago. It's a road so dangerous that your rental-car insurance won't be honored if you drive on it.

One of the most famous sections of this road is the Skippers suspension bridge, spanning more than 300 feet long and 300 feet high, above the Shotover River, one of the most spectacular bridges in the world.

It was a beautiful sunny day, but there was a language barrier between the Kiwi, the Koreans, and the Alaskans. Justin and I sat in the raft's bow, and our job was to assist the guide and our fellow paddlers. No matter how many times I showed my fellow paddlers behind me to mimic my "strokes," I failed. I would turn around and receive a big grin, but transferring information never hit home.

The 300-foot tunnel loomed in front of us; the top of the black, half-moon entrance was two feet above the churning water's surface. The guide instructed everyone to get low into the raft. He had Justin lean over the bow to steer. It enveloped us into darkness; the water slapping against the rock, and the smooth rubber of the raft moaning against the rock. As the crescent light grew larger and larger, guiding us to the end, the quietness of the darkness roared, echoing against the walls. The guide was screaming at Justin, "Right, right." And as we looked at the churning water of "Mother-in-Law" rapid on river left, Justin realized the guide meant to *stay right*. A large drop in a narrow channel, with a lot of water, kept us from flipping or being stuck in the hole that was created, and the raft popped out.

In Christchurch, we rented a vehicle to explore the southern half of the South Island. But first, we needed to go to the

Hospital in Christchurch, as Justin's cast had dissolved during the whitewater adventure.

Amazed that he could drive with that monstrous piece of plaster on his foot, we drove to the southern end of the South Island. Along the way, we camped near secluded beaches in emerald bays. We learned the local pub provided the best food, beer, and ambiance. Our goal was to hike the Routeburn Trek, but first, we practiced with short hikes. The cast held firm.

We spent the next four days hiking the Routeburn Track in Fiordland National Park. This track allowed us to camp in "huts" along the way, so we left our tent behind. It was not a loop, but we arranged a shuttle at the end of the hike to take us back to our rental car. Alpine vistas, waterfalls, cirque lakes, a swing bridge, wetlands, open meadows, steep cliffs, and Harris Saddle, the summit, near 5,000 feet elevation. Staying in the "hut" allowed for a warm place at night and the opportunity to chat with other hikers.

The shuttle worked effortlessly and we were overjoyed to find the windshield wipers intact. Kea birds have a reputation for destroying weatherstripping around windows and stealing windshield wipers.

After a day in Queenstown, we drove to Wanaka, capturing the views with many "*Wows!*" and the desire to stop and hike. But we needed to return the rental car and catch our flight from Christchurch to the U.S.

It felt strange to drive the Subaru from Bellevue to Seattle to catch the ferry to Haines, Alaska. Our only desire once in the States was to find the spiciest Mexican restaurant there was!

Once we boarded the ferry, we climbed to the solar deck on the top floor and grabbed two chaise loungers and spread out our sleeping bags. We watched the snow-covered mountains disappear into darkness as we sailed through Queen Charlotte Sound.

This was my first ferry through the Sound, and it was a rough one. It was night, so we could not see the size of the waves, but the sound was deafening as they slammed the port side of the ferry.

There would be a sonic boom as a wave hit, followed by sea spray over the bow and onto the foredeck. The engine was stuttering as it sunk in the trough, and it chugged as it climbed another wave. I could taste salt on my lips and feel the moist crust on my chilled face as the spray hit me.

Seas calmed as daylight welcomed us to breathtaking mountain views amid towering Sitka Spruce forests. Seabirds chattering amid morning fog, hovering between water and land. Unfortunately, we had to remain onboard as passengers debarked in Petersburg, Ketchikan, and Juneau. A few hours later, we arrived in the winter wonderland of Haines, Alaska.

And the next leg of the journey, 700 miles on the Alaska-Canada Highway (ALCAN), would take us through Canada before entering Alaska. At least it was getting lighter, with longer days for driving.

Caribou, licking salt on the snow-free highway, might be a concern at a normal speed, but the undulating frost heaves, from the freeze-thaw of permafrost beneath the highway, prevent speeds of more than 35 mph. After a nerve-wracking, bladder-slamming drive, with grandiose views of the Chugach Mountains and the Matanuska Glacier glimmering in the distance, we arrived home. After six months of travel and more than 12,000 miles on my 1984 Subaru, traversing the United States, Canada, Mexico, and New Zealand, I was home, in Alaska.

CHAPTER 18

Mountain Highs
and Lows

T*en-foot snow berms* hid the turn onto the narrow road off the Glenn Highway. At least the mile of mountain road was plowed; although the Subaru had front-wheel drive, we chained up.

The winding road or "trail," as some people called it, is notched into the side of a 1,000-foot-prominent ridge, the remnants of a glacial moraine. Once you make the sharp left turn onto the road at the base of the ridge, there is no turning back!

The three-story, 1500-square-foot cedar house with a chocolate-brown metal roof stood among the lingering snow. A narrow tunnel of snow led to the stairs of the front deck and to the entrance. Without an arctic entry, we walked into the dining area of the house with our snow-covered boots on. I stood, shocked at what I saw, as I quickly took my boots off. Justin grabbed an armful of wood stacked on the back deck, and soon a fire in the large wood stove was warming the cool air. I focused on finding food.

"I know. The house is a mess," he said. That was an understatement.

Not surprisingly, the parquet flooring that covered the dining area, especially in front of the door, had molded and peeled. Wood pieces of the parquet, from being wet for long periods of time, had swollen and broken.

In need of the bathroom, I walked through the living room and entered the bathroom at the base of the stairs to the top floor. I turned the light on and gasped. Justin's sister, when she lived in the house with her three kids and husband, had painted the walls a dark brownish-red—it was as if I had walked into a small cave. Large brownish-red blobs splattered the beige linoleum on the floor. The color made the brown bathtub look like an enormous sarcophagus, while the toilet and marble-like sink, in shades of white and beige, were like beacons, guiding me to my goal.

When finished, I walked into the living area. The redwood wainscoting that lined the lower half of the walls of the small living area had been "carved" by a very sharp object in several places. Petroglyphs of multi-colors from crayons and permanent sharpie ink stamped every beige wall above the redwood. I noticed burn marks in various locations on the brand-new carpet that, a year earlier, I'd spent three days helping to install.

I asked Justin what had happened. He shrugged his shoulders and said the youngest of the three kids had a fire fetish. Wow! *Okay*, I thought as I shook my head in disbelief.

Justin agreed that everything would need painting. I said, "Yes" and that I could help. He looked at me and said, "Well, I thought you could paint because I have to work."

I bought paint, ladders, brushes, rollers, sandpaper, and ten gallons of polyurethane for the floor. Male privilege had always been part of my life—as a small child, as an athlete, and as a female in my profession. And I continue to allow it, a flaw I recognize in myself. But how do others know that about me? Is there an *undercurrent* I project?

When I asked for help, Justin was always busy on the weekends, and he did work during the week.

The value of one's time—*my* time—was never a consideration or of any importance.

It reminded me of when I was a kid, listening to my dad's angry words, fueled by alcohol, how he worked all day to put food on the table, and he deserved dinner and a clean house when he got home. Typical of that generation, my *mom did not work.* How often we all heard those words. No wonder she was depressed and drank!

A career was my path to freedom—not to be *undervalued* and subservient to a man. Justin's repetitive response triggered the fear of what I never wanted. But he never subsidized me. It was our decision for me to resign and move in with him, but I knew I needed to find a job—and soon.

Is *male privilege* a learned behavior? Or is it in the DNA? *It is both*, I thought as I scraped and sanded and painted.

As a previous homeowner, I took pride in the skills I'd learned, although they were nothing compared to the competencies gained on the mountain. Over the next few months, I learned to lay tile in the shower; measure, cut, and stain trim; hang wallpaper; mud and texture sheetrock, patch carpet; and resurface parquet floor.

My behavior, in response to him, set the tone for the rest of our relationship. If I complained, he would yell and take off— sometimes for hours or for days without a phone call.

I was Italian and Irish—yelling did not bother me; it was in my genes. But the lack of communication? That scared me. That, too, created a behavior. I studied and practiced animal behavior, yet, I failed to recognize that *I* was the dog in Pavlov's theory.

Although Justin worked in Palmer, he rarely got the mail or brought home groceries. I asked why, considering he worked across the street. His answer, which I became familiar with over the years, "It was good for me to get off *the mountain*." If we needed a gallon of milk, I drove to town.

One day, I needed his truck to haul the garbage to the landfill and realized where all the mail had gone. I found long-forgotten rotten food mixed in with government envelopes—paychecks that were never deposited. Astounded, I also found envelopes from the local telephone and electric companies, stamped in bright red letters "Overdue Payment Required."

As a responsible adult, it shocked me when I found unpaid electric and telephone bills in the mail, so I paid them all, apologizing for the lateness. I deposited the half-dozen paychecks in Justin's account and changed the post office from Palmer to Sutton, closer for me to get the mail.

Most importantly, I was thrilled to be working again with a large, well-known environmental consulting company. The project was an environmental assessment of wetlands for a proposed gas line from Valdez to the North Slope. The team from the Colorado office was led by Dr. H, well-known in wetland science, a hydrologist, and me. We would spend a month delineating wetlands and conducting a wetland functional assessment, from the Arctic Plain on the Northern edge of Alaska to Valdez in Prince William Sound, following the Trans-Alaska Pipeline System or TAPs.

"Wow! Thank you, Skippy," I murmured, never thinking I would ever say those three words in one sentence.

I was first introduced to wetland science in 1983 while working for USDA. Skippy assigned me the task of assigning a wetland indicator to each plant species I identified on Seward Peninsula. He was part of an interagency group in the development of the wetland plant list for Alaska. He gave me a month to provide him a list, with very little information on how I was to do this task. Considering I did not know what a wetland indicator was, I called Fish and Wildlife Service (FWS) for more information.

I did not have a computer with a correlational database, but I had experience after mapping nineteen million acres of plant communities. To expedite, I cross-referenced the plant communities I had developed with the classification of wetland types FWS had developed.

Then I enlisted my computer technician to generate a list using soils data and other features we collected in the field. After several dozen iterations, we could assign wetland categories to a few hundred plant species, guesstimating on the statistical frequency with which we found them.

Skippy had his list in a month, and he presented it to the team, who were impressed not only by the large number of species but by the associated site information. However, Skippy did not know how this list was developed, so FWS called me. Impressed with the work we had done, FWS strongly recommended I represent the Agency on the wetland team for Alaska.

And that was the introduction to my expertise in wetland science and, no doubt, the reason I got the job four years later in 1987.

The "art of science" is never truer anywhere as it is in wetland science—a field that requires expertise in soil science, plant ecology, and hydrology, bound with years of applied local and regional field experience. For me, the process of wetland identification was like reading a good murder mystery.

The pipeline is an oil-transportation system spanning Alaska, including the pipeline, 11 pump stations, several hundred miles of feeder pipelines, and the Valdez Marine Terminal. It is one of the world's largest pipeline systems, conveying crude oil 800 miles from Prudhoe Bay to Valdez, with a pipe diameter of 48 inches.

Because most of the pipeline is above permafrost, each of the stanchions holding up the raised sections of pipeline contained a sealed tube of ammonia. As the permafrost below the pipeline warms, the ammonia absorbs the heat and rises to a radiator on top of each stanchion. The outside air cools the ammonia, condenses, and falls back to the bottom of the tube, where the process repeats itself.

It was a sunny day as we sat eating our lunch near the Trans-Alaska Pipeline System (TAPs) or, as Alaskans call it, the Pipeline, when we heard the thump-thump of a helicopter. It came in fast, and, before we knew it, two Alyeska pipeline-security police jumped out and had us in their sights. It was obvious we were not carrying a weapon, but we were not sure if we should stand up or hold our hands up. Apparently, our firm did not inform Alyeska that three field scientists would be within the Pipeline corridor. They knew we were harmless because they had seen us on the security cameras, sitting there, eating our lunch.

Despite all the government legislation, policies, and programs, wetlands will not be protected if the regulations are not enforced.

If the public does not recognize the benefits of wetland preservation, wetlands will not be preserved.

Since implementation of the Clean Water Act in 1972, the Environmental Performance Index developed by Yale University estimates that greater than 60% of the wetlands have been destroyed in the United States. For sensitive and highly affected wetlands, including estuarine wetlands, the loss is much greater. This percent does not include permafrost wetlands.

After nearly a month on the road, I invited my team in for a cup of coffee when they dropped me off at the house. The newly constructed entry was unchanged, but the interior of the house hit me in the gut. I apologized for the mess as I made my way to the kitchen.

The hydrologist looked at me with pity on his face and said, "If my wife came home to this, she would kick me out of the house. And she has the summers off as a teacher."

Although embarrassed, I was angry too, as there was no excuse for Justin to leave me a mess like this. For a month, my peers treated me with respect, as an equal, while we had fun with banter and professionalism. That was a message from my new friend, the hydrologist. It scared me, because I knew it was true. Justin had left for his two-week tour in the field, and he'd left me with his mess.

Unfortunately, I was female, responsible, and preferred to live in a clean, organized environment. I did not have the luxury for such indulgence.

CHAPTER 19

Sail Away
Serenity

The breeze was cool, and the maples glimmered like diamonds in the sun's rays, as autumn embraced San Juan Island. What better place to learn to sail? At mean high-tide, the archipelago of 400 islands lies within the rain shadow of the Olympic Mountains to the southwest. They receive less rain than Seattle, 65 miles to the south.

After a filling breakfast at my B&B, I strolled through Friday Harbor, window shopping. I walked by a pier, remembering that lovely weekend Rick and I had had there, collecting tubularia, the puffy white hydroids, for his research project at WSU as an undergrad.

I found our 47-foot sailboat, with a bright-pink flag on the stern, stamped *Womenship*, as it flapped in the breeze. A lean, salt-and-pepper-haired woman was on the bow.

"I am Michelle, and I believe this is my boat."

"Ah, Alaska? Joan, I am your instructor."

There were two captains and five students, all women. We were from Colorado, Michigan, Annapolis, Alaska, and Friday Harbor, for five days of sailing and instruction. I admit, I was apprehensive of being on a sailboat for almost a week with all women—something totally foreign to me. And it was fabulous. There was no yelling. There was no ego. We were all there to learn and enjoy sailing in one of the most beautiful places on Earth.

Shallow inlets and deep harbors, tranquil coves with a mixture of slate-colored sand and glistening rocky beaches provided many spots to anchor and explore. Gnarled, ochre-colored madrona trees hugged the shoreline, while Douglas fir, hemlock, and red cedar loomed in the background—a landscape reminiscent of New Zealand.

We spent the days raising and trimming sails, practicing points of sail, anchoring, piloting, and plotting a fresh course every day. And at night, we sipped wine, tasted smooth brie on crisp multigrain crackers, and listened to classical music while discussing our day.

At the end of the week, as we said our goodbyes, I felt lucky to have hooked up with such a fun group of women and competent instructors. I felt confident in my newly gained skills and looked forward to my next sail.

Snow arrived in mid-October, requiring me to leave my Subaru at the bottom of the hill. Justin's Chevy 4x4 truck usually would have no problem climbing the mountain—but not always. I filled my days with shoveling snow, skiing, and working for the consulting company, although I worked fewer hours. I could work from home most days, which was helpful.

The darkest months are November through mid-February. By January, sun, surf, and beach are a necessary requirement for mental health! I booked an Offshore Navigation sailing course with a reputable school in the Virgin Islands for us. Although, *Womenship* does offer courses for both genders, I knew there was no way Justin would agree to that.

As I stepped off the small plane on St. Thomas, humid, warm air filled my lungs, and my alveoli screamed with happiness. The air in Alaska during winter can be extremely dry.

After we got settled in our small bungalow, we wandered to the principal center of Charlotte Amalie. Out of habit, I grabbed Justin's hand to hold. A nasty habit, as I was reprimanded, months ago, by him to not to do that. He would shake his hand away, like I had leprosy.

"I don't do that," he scolded one day when we went for a walk by the house. Instead, he would put an arm around my neck and lean in, at least for a few minutes. A compromise, I suspected. I took what he could give.

Our boat was a 47-foot single-hull, like the one I'd sailed in the San Juan Islands. As expected, I was the only female, and I was intimidated. The captain, grumpy and on his 364th day of instruction, was looking forward to this last sail before going home to Saba. I listened to the introductions.

Two middle-aged men each bragged about their lengthy sailing experience on the Great Lakes and owning their own sailboats. There also was a young, good-looking and fit, recently ex-Navy guy from San Diego, with sailing experience, but not a braggart. Justin chatted about his experience, and then there was me, the least experienced and most brutally honest.

They gave us the stateroom in the stern, a full-size bed and a head, so that was a plus. With no introduction to the boat, we set sail east for St. John Island. A welcoming contrast to St. Thomas, most of St. John is a national park. We dropped anchor and, over dinner, discussed our strategy for sailing at night to St. Croix. Until then, we had the late afternoon to snorkel in the warm turquoise waters in a luscious Caribbean landscape.

We saw multitudes of striking yellow and blue darting fish, and my favorite, the blue-and-yellow parrotfish, while a turtle lazily swam and fed, paying no attention to us.

That night, we set sail into the darkness and followed the course to St. Croix. The stars soon disappeared as clouds blew in, along with stronger winds. Although we could not see the churning of the sea, we felt its power. Rollers slammed the bow, spraying us in the cockpit. All had a chance at the wheel, except me. Piloting, especially in rough seas, helps minimize sea sickness. Each male sailor spent some time with their head over the rail, except for the captain.

Finally, I was grateful to see light shimmering on the horizon. The buoy lights, disappearing and reappearing with each swell, marked the entrance to the channel into Christiansted. This is one of the most challenging of channels to navigate, as it divides in two a hundred yards from shore.

If you miss the critical turn, the chances of smashing into round reef are high. We did not plot using a GPS, so we hoped our calculations were spot on.

Once we entered the channel, we saw the buoys. With calmer water and the squall past us, the captain ordered us to lower the sails so we could proceed under power. The next thing we knew, the self-furling jib jammed. I don't really know what happened, but the captain had us going in circles, trying to give us time to bring the sails in. Everyone knew that if we missed the port turn, we could end up on the reef, like so many other cruisers had done.

No one said a word until we passed the second buoy and went hard to port. The boat responded, and soon we were in the boat slip. At that moment, I threw up.

When something goes wrong, whether it is flying or sailing or diving, it is never just one thing, but a series of errors. Most likely, if we had learned the boat before heading out, furling the jib might have gone smoothly. In our favor, there were many eyes and hands to deal with the sails. This allowed the captain to focus on the buoys and the entrance. There are many stories where a crew of one or even a crew of two have missed the second buoy and turned into the jaws of round reef. All it takes is a few seconds of distraction.

While Justin took a quick siesta, I walked through the town of Christiansted. "Navy," which is what I called the young, handsome co-sailor, saw me and asked if I would like to go out to dinner with him, just the two of us?

Although flattered, I kindly declined and said, "Justin might not take that well."

He responded with a surprised look. "At first, I assumed you were with him, but when you sat by him, or got close, he would leave. So, I figured you guys were just friends." Then he shocked me and said as he walked away, with a teasing smile, "When you tire of that, let me know."

Most days were clear sailing. Flying fish would go suicidal and fly out of the water onto the boat. And in response, I would run around gathering them and throw them back into the water.

Spinner dolphins rode the bow wave, while brown booby birds followed the stern and frigates soared above until they plummeted into the sea. We had been following weather reports and, late one morning, spotted a water spout not too far off on the horizon.

We changed course and headed to the Spanish Virgin Islands, specifically Culebra, known by sailors as a safe harbor to find during a hurricane, referred to as a 'hurricane hole.'

Culebra and its sister island, Vieques, belong to Puerto Rico. Culebra was closer to St. Thomas than Puerto Rico, but the weather was calm and sunny, as they reported several squalls in the U.S. Virgins. We headed to Culebra.

We stopped by a local dive shop in our boat and rented tanks. There was no checking of dive certifications, so Justin was going diving! His first time.

You could see the anchor at 50 feet down. Crystal-clear water. Giant barracuda greeted us as we slowly descended along the anchor line. Brilliant purple and red fan corals swayed in the current. I stayed near Justin, checking his gauges, but he acted like a seasoned diver.

I'd gotten my PADI certification at WSU, and it was difficult. In those days, in the pool, the instructor would sneak up behind a trainee and turn the air off. There was a 50% dropout rate by mid-semester.

In exploring the crevices and sunken ledges, Justin fixated on two long antennae extending from below a brilliant-yellow brain coral, almost buried in the sand. Leery, he peered in, trying to maintain his buoyancy, as the antennae disappeared deeper into the coral. Spiny lobster soon would become a compulsion of this new diver.

He was hooked, and I saw his grin when we surfaced. We were diving in an aquarium. The place was incredible, and we made plans to return as we sailed back to St. Thomas. This time, I raced to the bow, helped with the jib, and went to the port side to hang the bumper rather than wait for the captain to tell me what I could not do.

Noticing that my shipmate from Michigan was having a tough time getting a bowline ready to throw over a piling, I grabbed the line, tied the bowline knot, and secured the line.

Apparently, I thought, *all that sailing experience did not include knots.* I smiled and looked at the captain as I grabbed my duffel. I was grateful that we'd learned and practiced sailing knots at night with Womenship. Our skipper, from Annapolis, had shown us gals a quick and easy way to tie a bowline.

As we had no desire to stay on St. Thomas, Justin and I caught the ferry to Tortola, one of the many British Virgin Islands. From there, we caught a taxi to Cane Bay Campground for two nights. We snorkeled during the day in a small crescent-shaped bay. There was a gradual sandy bottom from the reef system to shore, causing the water to become murky in places, with current and swell.

Suddenly, two large, shiny silver objects streamed by me, causing me to swallow a snorkel full of seawater. No dorsal tail was showing. Then I saw Justin do the same thing I did. Again, a flash of silver, this time close. Justin looked at me and yelled, "Tarpon," before diving underwater. This time, we could see the hard, metal-like plates covering the fish like armor. They were feeding on schools of skad and jacks, small, fast, silver fish.

At night, an open shuttle with a yellow canvas roof and tassels dangling from the edges would take campers to the Jimmy Buffett Bar, where we could drink $1 piña coladas all night. Great food and, of course, Buffett music. For the next three nights, we moved to a hotel on the pier and scheduled two days of diving. Justin never got asked for a dive card. We were diving the *RMS Rhone*, a mail ship that had gone down in 1867 during a hurricane.

On the first dive, we descended the anchor line, being watched by a dozen glaring eyes with jaws snapping. The anchor was at least 100 feet down, but you could see the anchor hooked into the sandy bottom, along with the remains of the *RMS Rhone* herself. We started at the bow at 80 feet and swam the length of the immense driveshaft. Our second dive was shallower, at 60 feet, and near the stern, where we encountered the enormous propeller. I was astounded at all the artifacts still scattered throughout the wreckage and—even more so—all the fish that now inhabited this artificial reef.

The next day we dove with turtles and sharks, and discovered octopus and spiny lobsters hidden safely in their protective coral habitat. The third day, we took the ferry to Virgin Gorda to snorkel the Baths.

The Baths are unlike any other beach in the Caribbean. It features white sandy beaches framed by gigantic granite boulders, some of these with diameters reaching 40 feet. Geologists believe that these outstanding sculptures formed from volcanoes, with caves and grottoes created by these irregular boulders. Entranced, and with Justin searching for spiny lobster, we completely forgot about time. We missed the last ferry back to Tortola.

There was a boat harbor within walking distance, so we took the chance in hopes of finding a shower and a bite to eat. We could always camp on the beach once it got dark.

Luckily, there were showers in the bathroom. I quickly noticed a woman curling her hair, wearing a pink shirt that caught my eye. She said she was sailing with Womenship and let me know what slip the boat was in. Justin and I found the sailboat, and then I saw Joan. It thrilled her when I asked if I could come aboard! In fact, they invited us to sleep on the cushions that lined the cockpit. Her students took off to the bar, leaving the three of us to chat.

After telling her of our sailing adventure, she looked at me and said, "And let me guess, did you receive the same treatment as your . . . sailing mates?"

Joan mentioned to me that the current students were more intent on looking for men than they were tying knots. We laughed, but I let her know that my time in the San Juans meant even more to me after sailing the Caribbean. We thanked her and caught the ferry back to Tortola.

Crazy at it was, I bought seven bottles of local rum for $5.00 each and wrapped them in my duffel bag. As we picked up our luggage at the Anchorage Airport, I could smell rum. I laughed when I discovered that five out of the seven were still intact.

When we finally made it home, warmed by the wood stove, I poured two shots of rum to toast our trip. The Cruzan rum was not as smooth as I remembered it to be on the Islands. It is strange how the ambiance of a place can enhance the taste of food and the sip of a drink. I closed my eyes and thought of the tartness of lime and mango, and the sweet scent of coconut, as the golden liquid slithered down my throat. Adventures are great, but so is home, and this one, I had created for us.

CHAPTER 20

Earth's Blood:
Tundra to Desert

Rapids churning, haystacks bucking the raft like a bull, and then calm. Whitewater rafting was our glue, whether a day trip down the Matanuska or Chickaloon rivers or our annual ten-day July 4 Alaska wild water adventure.

Over the years, we'd explored a few dozen rivers in roadless, wilderness areas of Alaska. By the second or third "fly-in," we had the "gear" organization down. Darren maintained and organized the "kitchen," and I did the menu and camp gear. For the remote fly-in trips, weight was critical. If there were four of us, we needed two rafts, not only for safety but for sharing the cost of the charter.

An example was the Tlikakila river. We used the scales at the Kenai Landfill, a requirement by the charter company for the trip. The landings were short and on water, so we could not go over our weight restriction. With the scale tipping slightly over our target, Debbie asked, "The booze or the 12-gauge shotgun and ammo?" We left the gun.

Debbie, Darren's girlfriend, a tall, athletic, white-skinned blonde, worked with us. She joined the three of us on several excursions before she got married and left the state. She was quite a few years younger than Darren and tired of the non-commitment issues.

Another crucial element, the availability of a reputable air charter with the right plane and a pilot familiar with the location and knowledge of the river we wanted to float. What we learned from this little-known river in the Lake Clark National Park and Preserve laid the foundation for future wilderness trips.

The Tlikakila river is in a geographically unique area, where the Alaska Range ends and the Aleutian Range begins. Glacier-shrouded mountains, vertical granite cliffs, caves, waterfalls, and Class III and IV rapids made this river a challenge. Our plan was to fly from Kenai to Summit Lake, where the river originated, according to our topographic quad sheets. The pilot we chartered with let us know the river had recently changed and that we might have to walk our gear to a side channel.

The weather was clear, so the pilot flew low and then circled over our "planned" put-in location. Our river was no longer connected to the lake because of changes in the glacial landscape; the pilot had been correct. The landing spot went from water to land, as our river started in one of the many glacier-fed streams about ½ mile from the lake.

After unloading, Justin, grinning with dimpled cheeks, confirmed with our pilot that our pickup location would still be on the river.

Laughing, the pilot waved goodbye and wished Debbie and me "good luck." Every plane that flew overhead would circle and buzz us—as we carried our rafts on our shoulders to the river—not once, but twice. We must have looked like a large desert tortoise from above.

Most days, however, were without incident, as we lazily floated downriver, fishing and taking breaks to hike. As always, the wildlife was remarkable: large caribou herds, bald eagles soaring, and grizzly signs on the sandbars. Camping requires due diligence in bear country. The coolers are kept far away from tents and rafts. A shredded boat can be a disaster.

As we approached our designated departure location a week later, the weather had transformed. We packed most of our gear; however, we kept our tent out, just in case we were spending the night. As we waited, another group appeared, who had floated a different fork. Justin hinted to them their charter might not show because of weather. They were not pleased, as they planned to be at work the next day. We shrugged our shoulders, whispered "Texans," and settled in. Weather or a mechanical malfunction made the ultimate decision as to when a remote trip was over.

We heard the plane, and our boater friends, relieved, were shouting for joy. As we watched the plane descend on the straight stretch of the river, the wind was at its tail. Darren, with a calm but sarcastic voice, yelled at the boaters to get out of the way. They did not know that the plane was coming in too fast for such a short landing. Lucky for them, they ran just as their charter ended up on the beach where they had been standing.

Sheepishly, one boater looked at us and said, "You want to trade charters?" Nervously, the passengers boarded the plane as we wished them good luck.

When our charter arrived, the expertise of our pilot was obvious. First, the plane landed into the wind, and second, our pilot changed our departure method. Because of the winds and the minimum length of "the runway," he preferred to be lighter. Although it took three trips to shuttle half the gear and people to a nearby lake, he preferred the longer approach the lake offered.

Soon all four of us and our gear headed for Lake Clark Pass, the next challenge with this weather. Debbie, who gets airsick, her face whiter than normal, kept her eyes closed as we bounced up and down and side to side as the pilot flew through the Pass.

Sitting in the plane's rear with the gear, my hands numb from hanging on to the seat, I clicked my mic on and squeaked, "Don't we get enough of this excitement at work?" Everyone quietly chuckled, except Debbie.

River travel provides an opportunity to see wildlife up close, passing through the waters like a ghost ship, without threat or intrusion. A few times, we floated a little too close, not wanting to grab an oar in fear of making too much noise. Once, on the Kobuk, a large boar nearly ended up in the raft with us, and, on a lazy float on the meandering Gulkana, a large herd of caribou enveloped our rafts as they charged into the river on a crossing.

While on the Marsh Fork, our raft hugging close to shore, a large female wolf, black as night, stood watch over her two pups as they played. The balls of fur quickly stopped as she signaled them with a low bark, and they huddled close to mom, their small ears twitching with curiosity. Mama wolf never moved, but we felt the intensity of her golden eyes as we drifted by.

In the wilds of Alaska, you plan for the unexpected. The Tatshenshini or "Tat," our 1989 adventure, is the ultimate wilderness float trip in North America. It involved a drive of 715 miles from Palmer to Haines, Alaska, passing through Canada. The access to the Tat is Dalton Post, in the Yukon, 617 miles from Palmer or 100 miles north of Haines. Justin and Debbie dropped Darren at the access with the gear, including the shotgun, and continued to Haines, where I met them. I was in Haines in response to an oil spill, another chapter. We spent the night in a hotel room, and, early the next morning, we dropped off a vehicle at the flight charter office, scheduled to pick us up 10 days later in Dry Bay. We headed back to Dalton Post.

In 1989, NPS required no permits for the Tat, and pre-9/11, it was easier to take a 12-gauge shotgun across the Canadian Border. The upper half of the 150 miles of the river is in the Yukon Territory, and the lower half in Alaska, ending in the shadows of the Fairweather Mountains in Glacier Bay National Park and Preserve. The take-out is near the mouth of Dry Bay, in the Gulf of Alaska; if you miss it, you end up in the Gulf.

The first 30 minutes downriver requires maneuvering a jungle of sweepers in the shallow channels. And 15 minutes later, the Tat welcomed us to five miles of churning whitewater in the 14-mile canyon. This is where the upper Tat flows north and then turns 120 degrees on itself to start its southward run to the ocean, crossing four major tectonic fault lines. We made camp on a sandy beach littered with grizzly tracks. We gave up trying to find camping sites without the massive footprints, distinctively showing the outstretched claws.

This area has the largest concentration of grizzly bears in North America and is where the habitat of the interior Dall's Sheep overlaps with the coastal Mountain Goat. Hiking through the alpine meadows, sprinkled with purples and yellows of lupine and mastodon flowers, among towering, rugged, ice-covered peaks, was breathtaking. We were the only humans within a hundred miles of nature's glory.

Where the Tat joins the lower Alsek River, it widens into what we called Alsek Lake, before its final giant crescendo of force, dumping volumes of water—more than 100,000 cubic feet per second—into the Gulf. In silence, we were in awe as Justin guided the raft into a world of white and blue. The thunder and crash of ice, calving from one of the seven glaciers, brought us out of our hypnotic state. Icebergs bobbed in the cold, milky blue water.

As we waited for Darren and Debbie, we noticed a small cavern in an iceberg the size of a basketball court, rising 60 feet above the surface of the water. Justin rowed close to the small opening as we peered inside the gut of the berg. We looked at each other. The cavern was just wide enough for the raft to enter.

"What the hell?" Justin said as he turned the raft, the stern at the entrance; with a powerful pull on the oars, he stowed them as we slid into the iridescent blue ice.

I listened to her creaking and groaning, as if she were alive, telling us her story. No doubt we were the first humans she had ever met. The blue ice was thousands of years old. Who knows what secrets she holds? She traveled for centuries, slithering from the mountain peaks, gathering whatever lay in her path, into the fractures of the ice, and then shedding her mysteries as the ice crashed into the river, and then into the sea.

We knew the danger of being inside this berg, so after a few pictures, our gloved hands against the cold, blue ice, we pushed the raft through the opening.

Darren and Debbie were looking for us and our boat. Suddenly, there we were, popping out of the ice. We could see the white of Darren's eyes as he yelled, "I can't believe you guys did that!"

Large blocks of ice breaking away from a glacier, known as "calving," can create waves 100 feet away, and have submerged many unsuspected boaters venturing too close to the face of the glacier. The irregular shape of an iceberg can cause it to flip, or "turtle," as gravity prefers most of the mass hidden beneath the water's surface. We hoped this berg was happy and stable.

This unfamiliar landscape, recently uncovered by glacial ice, is as close to the Pleistocene Era as you can get, with some visible remains of the mammoth steppes, a mega-continental ecosystem that spanned northern Eurasia, Alaska, and Canada. The woolly mammoth, horse, and bison coexisted with a variety of mammalian megafauna, rich in species diversity, with little niche overlap.

Our last night, we watched two dark grizzly youngsters playing on the icefield. They tumbled down the ice and then ran back up to do it again. As we sat on the sandy beach, red flames warming the cool night, we listened to the glaciers creaking and moaning.

It was difficult to navigate through the braided channels, and, to our surprise, a Park Service ranger helped us from shore. He said the river had changed her course, making the take-out difficult to find. He also mentioned that several of the big bergs were flipping and wanted to know what we had witnessed. We kept quiet about our little adventure, but Justin talked technicalities about glaciology with him while we packed gear.

Soon we were flying back to Haines over some of the most spectacular and rugged coastline. Over the years, our river explorations took us from the northern ends of Alaska to the South.

We explored rivers in the far north in the Gates of the Arctic Wilderness Area and the Kobuk River, with challenging Class IV rapids; the Marsh Fork of the Canning River from the Brooks

Range to the Arctic National Wildlife Refuge; and the clear waters of the Charley into the fast, broad Yukon River.

While working for the local rafting company, NOVA River Runners, *AVON* spelled backwards, the most popular raft in the '80s; we spent three days of excitement with 15 miles of Class IV to V in the Canyon on the Talkeetna River, my second trip with them. An outstanding, thrilling adventure of whitewater, bears, and wilderness.

One of the most remote and famous rivers is the mighty Copper River, known for its red salmon. It is 80 miles of fast-moving, glacial river with 15-foot standing waves in the canyon.

We were entertained with seals, popping their gray-spotted heads above the river, while chasing the world-famous red salmon from the Copper River Delta, 40 miles from their saltwater home.

What will happen to these rivers and all the life they support when the glaciers are gone? What will the effects be on man-made structures, like roads, from glacier rebound?

In the fall of 1988, we headed to the desert, specifically to raft the Grand Canyon on a private permit. Ten people, strangers except for Justin and Richard, who had the permit, traveled from three states to a magical place for 22 days. We hiked among the echoes of the forgotten. We conquered the holes of Lava, House Rock, and Crystal, and rode the waves of Hermit, Hance, and the Horn. In the heat of the day, we challenged the rapids and hiked, but in the night's cool, we shared stories by the fire's light as strangers became friends.

The Colorado, one of the great wonders of America, her waters overdrawn and over-allocated, is drying up. A rare event, not observed since 2009, for a few weeks in the spring of 2014, was the Colorado River reaching the Pacific Ocean. Scientists estimate that by 2050, the Colorado will lose about one-fourth of its flow because of overuse and climate change.

And it is not just the Colorado that is disappearing. In January 1995, Justin and I flew to Santiago, Chile, to raft the Bio Bio River, one of the world's pristine whitewater rivers and, unfortunately, endangered, and now disappeared into cement. The Bio Bio had been on our bucket list for years, but time had run out; we could no longer delay. Endesa, a Chilean power company, was proposing seven dams along the Bio Bio River for power in the growing city of Santiago. It would displace more than 2,000 indigenous people, flooding their villages, destroying their livelihood.

The river is the second largest in Chile, with monster holes, face-ripping ledges, and Class V water. I booked our trip with Bio Bio Expeditions, not only experts in whitewater but leaders in river conservation around the world. After spending ten days with the three owners of Bio Bio Expeditions, the river was not just their namesake; it was their passion.

Included in this trip was a two-day hike to summit an active volcano at 11,000 feet. We camped in a forest of monkey pod trees, and, in the early morning, with headlights, we started our ascent in ice and snow. I felt my tongue swell, a sign of altitude sickness. On the summit, the chill of the wind numbed my cheeks, as I twirled in a circle and saw only blue sky and the endless white spires of the Andes. It was then time to make the descent. Sliding on our asses with an ice axe as a brake, we flew down the mountain.

Our last day of whitewater ended in sadness as One-Eyed Jack, our next rapid, was gone. The Bio Bio, for centuries, had nurtured, protected, and provided life to a myriad of species. Once powerful and free, all that remained of this beautiful river was a trickle of her lifeblood.

As a child familiar with our anthropogenic need to destroy a resource for our own gain, I thought of the iceberg. Mother Nature always strives for stability, and a dam made of cement by man is no match for a mountain range of active volcanos.

We said farewell to our new friends at Bio Bio Expeditions and continued our adventure south to Puerto Montt. Our next adventure was the Lake Crossing, a passage that starts from Puerto Varas on the shores of Lake Llanquihue in Chile, to Bariloche on Nahuel Huapi Lake in Argentina. Originally, this was a trade route worn down by the indigenous people of the region. Now travelers like us, using a combination of buses and boats, traverse the national park, crossing three lakes and eventually ending in the beautiful village of Bariloche.

Although the rest of our travels were memorable, the death of the Bio Bio lingered in my heart. On my return to Alaska, I joined the non-profit International Rivers Network and Project Raft, a group Bio Bio Expeditions recommended.

The following September, I joined Bio Bio Expeditions on a three-week expedition to Zimbabwe, specifically to raft and kayak the Zambezi River and be part of the Project Raft whitewater river racing event, with proceeds for saving the Zambezi River from a proposed dam between Zambia and the Zimbabwe governments.

CHAPTER 21

Black Death

Greed, *I whispered*, as tears flowed down my smudged cheeks. The rage and disgust curdled my stomach. For months, I breathed the pungent benzene. My tastebuds lost the ability to discern anything except the bitter, acrid taste of oil. Every pore of my skin exuded the contaminate.

My "coasty" comrade and I watched the river otters in silence. After weeks on the Green Islands, which we nicknamed "Quail," after our then-vice president, all we saw was black crude, in the water and on the rocky shoreline. One otter ran back and forth, back and forth, back and forth, on the rocky shore, frantic, as her mate shadowed her in the water. He could not find an opening through the thick, slimy, black poison to reach his mate.

During the summer of '88, Justin was furious with his new supervisor, who had the nerve to insist he turn in a leave slip prior to taking leave. I took that as an opportunity for a career and life change.

I had never been to Southeast Alaska except on the ferry, so when a position with the Alaska Department of Environmental Conservation (ADEC) came open in the regional office in Juneau, I applied. I never dreamed of getting the position and was speechless when it was offered.

Juneau, the capital, is a quaint and quiet town between the end of the legislative session and before the summer tourists arrive. There are no roads to the capital. Access is only by ferry or plane.

There were several opportunities in Juneau for someone of Justin's caliber in soils science. The Pacific Northwest Research Station in Juneau, a branch of the USFS, is the hub for soils research in Alaska. Also enticing, Juneau is home to the University of Southeast Alaska. There is also a marine-technology school, as the Gastineau Channel is the gateway to sailing and boating among the hundreds of islands.

Justin drove with me to Haines, and eventually we landed by ferry in Juneau amid a winter blizzard. He flew back home while I settled into my new position as an oil-spill and hazardous-waste ecologist, something I knew nothing about.

As my supervisor suspected, despite my lack of confidence, I learned quickly about oil-spill containment and the laws that regulate the business of producing and transporting hazardous materials. While attending a week of oil-spill training in Texas, the reality of a large-scale disaster in Alaskan waters hit me full force. It was not a question of "if," but "when." The inadequacy of enforcement, because of the political influence Big Oil has in the state, was blatant.

After an oil spill by a tanker in the Cook Inlet, ADEC made a request to fill 10 oil-spill regulatory positions. The state legislature approved the budget for one. That was the position I held for the southeast region.

Oil-spill prevention, control, and countermeasure (SPCC) plans ensure facilities establish sufficient containment and applicable countermeasures to reduce the potential for oil spills to reach navigable waters. However, oil spills typically result from accidents or human error, which can occur at any place, time, or location. And that is the reason for oil-spill contingency plans (OSCP). The plans address response measures to be taken after a spill has occurred.

Once there is a spill, the best approach for containing and controlling it is to respond quickly and in a well-organized manner. The contingency plan, through a series of scenarios, addresses what could go wrong and identifies the resources and strategies to assist in the response to a spill.

One of my many responsibilities was to review the plans to ensure that a facility had complied. A "spill plan," depending on the complexity of the facility, could contain volumes. Imagine a state like Alaska—one that depends on oil development—and the number of oil-spill plans under review. And with limited resources to do so.

I likened these OSCPs to the National Environmental Policy Act (NEPA). NEPA requires an Environmental Impact Statement (EIS) to analyze if a proposed project is damaging a resource. The EIS does not prevent a project; the EIS documents the process of analysis for the project. Many times, the decision to develop the project is the same after the EIS as it was before the EIS.

Overall, this is a battle of money and time—a poorly paid regulator working for an under-funded public agency versus a team of lawyers working for an oil company? Or a mining company? To minimize the threat from a regulatory agency, all an industry must do is pressure congress to cut the budget of that agency. Follow the money and the vote; a continuing resolution is one strong-arm method to accomplish this in the federal government.

I realized several of the plans before me were nothing more than a template developed by a business specializing in developing spill plans. So, I focused on the details of the plan—the scenarios, emergency contacts, resources affected, and the equipment required. I encountered what I thought were harmless typographical errors for several plans under review. After years of complacency, I suspect, the "typo errors" went by without challenge. As the new Ecologist, I sent not letters of approval, but letters requesting corrections. These letters apparently caused mayhem at the top of the food chain.

The battle had begun, and when my supervisor called me into his office, I showed him why I did not approve two plans. After I presented my evidence, he sat in his chair, a grin on his face, and said, "Bingo." I had the authority to approve plans, but that didn't last long. *They* later changed the approval process to someone higher than me.

Justin visited in March for an interview at the research station. He had recently taken up hang-gliding and was flying when one of his buddies reminded him that he had a plane to catch.

When I saw him at the gate, I asked, "What happened?" His hair looked like a bird's nest entwined with hair, twigs, and grass. His face was filthy and his clothes encrusted with dirt.

He grinned and said he was lucky he was even there! If it hadn't been for the guys, he would still be hang-gliding. I, however, had bought a new outfit, gotten my hair done, and had planned a romantic dinner. At least his interview was the next day—although, later, he told me he did not want to move to Juneau and, in his animated way, referred to his new sport of hang-gliding as better than sex. He was in love! Not surprising, I concluded, as Justin had been on the college sky-diving team and an instructor. I have a feeling he canceled the interview, if it ever even existed.

Two days later, we enjoyed skiing at Eagle Crest, a community-owned ski resort on Douglas Island. The alpine conditions had fresh powder, with T-bars and lots of sun. I had not downhill-skied since Christmas of 1982 with Rick.

After skiing, we went into the small gathering room to eat. We noticed a few people intently listening around a radio. When we asked what was going on, the cook said a tanker had crashed into Bligh Reef and was spilling oil. There was no phone at the lodge. Although Valdez was not in my region, we headed to my office in Juneau.

The news was grim, and the place was chaos. My incredible and supportive boss said that the *Exxon Valdez*, a fully loaded tanker of oil, had struck Bligh Reef. Reports were vague and spotty. He recommended I go home, pack a bag, and hold tight. He said that Dan had been one of the first to board the tanker.

Dan was the Valdez supervisor for ADEC, and, for years, he'd reported to his superiors that Alyeska was not capable of responding to an oil spill in Prince William Sound. The industry considered Dan a crackpot and had him on their radar for removal. To me, he was a hero—he was who I called when I found conflicting information in the oil-spill contingency plans that I was "expected" to approve.

Alyeska Pipeline is the oil-industry consortium that was hired by Exxon and a conglomerate of oil companies to manage the pipeline.

Shortly after midnight on March 24, 1989, the 987-foot oil tanker *Exxon Valdez*, piloted by the ship's third mate, ran aground on Bligh Reef in Prince William Sound, Alaska, spilling nearly 11 million gallons of tar-like crude oil and creating America's biggest environmental disaster in history.

Two days later, with no other way to quickly get to Valdez, I joined Justin on an Alaska Airlines flight from Juneau to Anchorage. Flying over Prince William Sound, the pilot circled, diverging from the normal flight path. Below, we saw the shimmering rainbow of colors spreading from the tanker, 27,000 feet below us. The pristine, calm, and productive waters of Prince William Sound, with not a boat or yellow boom in sight for miles, were unprotected from the assault.

Once on the ground in Anchorage, Justin took me to the National Guard compound, where I found my next flight, to Valdez; I walked up the rear ramp of a C-130 loaded with skimming equipment. After takeoff, I visited with the pilots in the cockpit until they gave me the word to strap in tight. The big ox of a plane was already bucking, the wings bouncing up and down, rolling the C-130 from side to side. A wind warning was in place for Valdez.

As I walked out the ramp, I saw planes flipped, cables swinging. I whispered *Mother Nature is one angry lady today.*

Dan was holding meetings in a makeshift incident-command center in the Valdez Courthouse. He knew I had expertise in soil, plants, and wildlife. He assigned me to the beach-assessment team to document the damage.

The priority was identification of the "seal-pupping areas" and deploying booms. This was the critical time for seals to give birth to pups in the upper limits of the beach. But you couldn't deploy a boom if you did not have one!

Then someone yelled, "Hey, you!" I turned toward him as he rushed up to me, and he handed me a plastic bag of jars. He told me to get to the harbor. A shrimper was coming in loaded. *Say what?* I thought, as I looked at the gentleman and then at the baggy. He noted my confusion; I did not know even where the harbor was. He quietly explained what I needed to do and the importance of the task. I found out later he was the Attorney General.

I boarded the shrimp boat and nearly broke down when I saw the nets and the shrimp. The shrimp, called spots, is one of the largest shrimps in the world, found in the deeper waters of Prince William Sound. Their body is normally a reddish brown with white horizontal bars on the carapace. They have distinctive white spots on their abdomen. I saw nothing but blackened bodies. Everything the shrimper had—his net, his boat, his livelihood— was coated with black slime. The smell made me nauseous.

Shaking, I recorded the information and took samples, carefully placing them in the containers, apologizing for what happened.

That night, I dragged my duffel and my sleeping bag to the courtroom to catch some sleep. While the oil spread along Alaska's pristine coastline, locals waited. The first three days of the spill had not a breath of wind, and the seas were unusually calm. Days went by while corporate and government officials bickered. Meanwhile, the spill, 25 miles from Valdez, polluted more than 1,000 miles of beaches and killed more than 36,000 migratory birds; thousands of sea mammals and bald eagles were dead.

Sleep evaded everyone in the room. At morning light, I headed to the airport to meet with the pilot who would fly me and my crew to assess beaches. The United States Coast Guard (USCG) is the lead agency for oil spills on water. They were scrambling to locate spill equipment, coordinating with Exxon and agency heads to contain the oil. Calculations of wind speed, tides, and currents—the factors that determined the direction of the oil— were made. The calculations suggested the crude oil would go out to sea, away from shorelines. They were wrong.

The devastation of what we encountered was only the beginning. For each beach, we ran transects from the forest edge to the water, and for every beach we inventoried, it was Armageddon. March is a busy time in the natural realm, especially in one of the most productive marine ecosystems on the planet. The oceanographic spring is a time when the marine production cycle is escalating, with migratory seabirds, marine mammals, and herring all returning to the Sound to reproduce or use it as a stop for migrating further north.

Normally, the noise in the fjord-carved bays is deafening, with the squawking of Black-legged Kittiwakes, Pigeon guillemots, murrelets, terns, Glaucous-Winged Gulls, and the Common Murre. It was as if the world had gone silent. I stood in a foot of ooze, staring into a sea of nothing. No noise. No bird acrobatics. Not even an eagle screeching.

Murres, the pudgy white-and-black seabirds, were the hardest hit by the spill. They usually gather in large pre-breeding aggregations and lay just one egg at a time. Their feathers protect them like a down coat, while they use their beaks to rearrange their feathers, to provide insulation. Feather-trapped air also provides buoyancy, helping seabirds like murres float when they are on water. Oil interferes with that process.

As we ran our transects, making note of the substrate for every beach, what appeared to be rocks were not. They were murres, hundreds—oiled and dead.

Before I left the command room, I asked, "How will I treat survivors?" No one answered. Dan shook his head. Later, as I walked the beaches, I didn't need to worry about that; there were no survivors.

The best estimate of the number of animals that died from the spill was nothing more than that; initially, there was a rough estimate of 250,000 seabirds and 250 bald eagles that had died. There is no way to measure the number of deaths, either current or projected. What about those animals that were rescued? All we could do was hope.

Dish soap removed crude oil from feathers, but it also removed the natural oils produced by birds' bodies to maintain feathers and "waterproofing." How many times have you witnessed a bird preening? Preening is an instinctual response birds perform to clean their feathers. Losing insulation and buoyancy caused by an oiled coat is death to a bird.

Dawn gave the public false hope. Were they so naïve that they believed that a soap detergent would make them feel good about themselves during an environmental crisis? If only it were that easy.

Oil is toxic. As a bird preens itself, it ingests the oil. The result is respiratory inflammation, irritation, or pneumonia. It causes ulcers, bleeding, diarrhea, and digestive complications. Absorption through the skin can damage the liver and kidneys, suppress the immune system, and result in death.

The days and nights rolled into one. I slept when I could, but, mostly, I didn't. After a long, depressing day, documenting more dead animals, as I was walking back to the truck, I heard yelling. I noticed a group of men gathered around a Blackhawk helicopter. I recognized two guys from ADEC. A guy dressed in an Alyeska coat was in the face of a state employee, yelling at him as they were toe to toe.

I asked what the problem was. Alyeska said the generator was theirs; ADEC said it wasn't. Tensions were high, but the toll on Prince William Sound was growing every day. And this type of behavior was why.

Alaska state law holds Alyeska Pipeline Company responsible for cleaning up Prince William Sound, while federal law holds the shipper, Exxon, responsible. I walked away, disgusted. I felt the politicians were ultimately responsible.

When the president of Exxon Shipping Company contacted Alyeska about their emergency response to the spill, Alyeska responded that it was Exxon's responsibility. When Dan Lawn boarded the *Exxon Valdez*, around 3:30 a.m. on March 25, there was no containment around the tanker. He stated, "Alyeska's only containment barge was in repair as a wave of thick, black crude was flowing from the Exxon into the night." He said the crude was 2½ feet higher than the surface of the water.

After my first rotation in Valdez, I returned to Juneau. Short-staffed, the receptionist forwarded a call to the only body in the office—me. When I answered, a landowner yelled at me about how *incompetent* I was. He had a water-quality complaint. With as much control as I could muster, I took the man's name just before he hung up on me. A few minutes later, I got a call from some senator complaining that I did not respond fast enough to a constituent who was reporting a smell in a creek by his house. I hung up on him. After what I had witnessed for a month, it was better to hang up. Then my boss walked into my office. He said a call just came in, and then I cut him off.

"Well, that was fast. If that asshole senator actually . . . ?"

He stared, with a half-cocked grin, and cut me off, "Do you want the Ketchikan Pulp chemical spill or the spill by a fancy yacht in Sitka?"

I demurely chose the spill in Sitka. The charter flight from Juneau soothed my mind as I looked at the beautiful blue water with flocks of birds on the surface.

As we circled the forest-shrouded bay on the eastern side of Baranof Island, I saw the sheen in the violet-blue water. As I walked up the boardwalk, I saw the familiar, good-looking, dark-haired ADEC supervisor out of Sitka.

Uh, oh, I thought, when I saw his arms crossed on his chest and that pissed-off look I had learned to understand. Next to him was a hefty man with tawny-gray hair, whom I recognized. I called him Rambo, my nickname for the owner of a dive salvage operation, whom I had met on a previous spill.

It was not a good day; the owner of the yacht and one of the largest hotel chains was an ass and would not allow us on his half-drowned yacht. He should have been nicer—although, the fine was pennies to someone like that. My companion smiled and gave me a small package before I flew off.

When I finally made it to the house I shared with my friend Jules, who had worked for me, and her boyfriend, I took the package out of my pack. Inside was a blue T-shirt, and it made me grin:

WE DON'T CARE

WE DON'T HAVE TO CARE

WE'RE

EXXON

HERE AT EXXON, WE ARE PART OF THE PROBLEM

On my second tour, they assigned me to one of the Resource Assessment Teams, or what we called "RAT." This was a multi-agency team representing USFS, USCG, Environmental Protection Agency (EPA), and ADEC, whose task it was to assess cleanup techniques.

Considering the hundreds of workers walking on greasy, slick-covered rocky beaches, and the heavy support equipment, skimmers on barges, the number of boats on the water, and aircraft in the air, there were very few accidents involving humans.

As RAT members, our job was to assess cleanup techniques on the water and on the shoreline. Most controversial was using scalding water in high-pressure sprayers. The least was using soap, absorbent pads, and scooping the oil into buckets. The most hazardous was using chemical surfactants, known to cause cancer. The work on shore was dangerous—no doubt about it.

While the oil spread, Big Oil argued with agencies about whose responsibility the cleanup was, and locals finally could watch no more. People armed with nothing more than buckets began scooping the toxic substance by hand. Bucket by bucket. I was shielded with heavy-weight gloves, rubber boots, and a full survival flotation suit. Even then, I could taste benzene after two weeks on the spill.

By now, Exxon was overseeing the cleanup. They assigned us to Green Island and Little Green Island, south and southeast of Bligh Reef, between Montague Island and Knight Island. Exxon used the USS Juneau as an incident command center near Green Island. The Juneau also housed the cleanup crews. It was a war zone, complete with a navy ship.

Every day was combat. What many people did not know is that we had lost the war within the first few days of the spill.

Containment equipment such as skimmers—which skim the oil off the surface before the oil is squeezed into holding tanks—and booms, floating barriers that keep oil away from an area or keep oil in an area, work efficiently only in calm conditions, with waves of less than a foot.

For the first three days, the *Exxon Valdez* spilled oil with no containment system. A representative for Exxon had made a statement explaining that there was no containment because vapors would condense around the *Exxon Valdez,* causing a hazard. The truth was that there was no spill-containment equipment available, although the OSCP said there was.

Another problem in Alaskan waters is the four tidal changes in one cycle, two high and two low. For booms to protect a shoreline such as Green Island, a skiff must man the boom, especially at tidal changes. And a human must man the skiff.

In this madness, pregnant seals, driven by instinct, were in desperate need to find a place to give birth. They would maneuver between skimmers, skiffs, booms, and people, and drag their swollen, blackened bodies along the oil-contaminated shore, to give birth. If they survived the birth, pups had no choice but to suckle on toxic milk and teats.

Watching this horror, it reminded me of what Cy would say to me after I euthanized an animal: "You get used to it—you have to. You can't save every life."

The toxin did not discriminate. We observed seals and sea lions, birds, otters, eagles, and fish, and watched orcas and humpbacks surface in the oil. I never got used to it. I refused to get used to it.

From the air, I observed herring balls within the multicolored water; herring form these as they swarm in a tightly packed spherical formation around a common center. It is a last-ditch survival mechanism they use when threatened by larger predators such as whales.

I saw bubble nets envelop the balls; bubble nets are a feeding technique by humpback whales, where they group up and swim in a circle, blowing bubbles below a school of prey fish. Forage fish, fearful of large bubbles, form a tighter circle or cluster, easy prey for a whale to swallow. Killer whales have a similar hunting technique, called "carousel feeding," which we also observed.

One afternoon, as we were assessing Green Island, a black Zodiac approached us at a high speed, with several military-looking guys on board, all dressed in black. The Secret Service ordered us to leave the area. We ignored them. We noticed a group of the cleanup crews spending their time building a ramp, and then taking it down. This became a daily event, along with another group, sitting on the rocks near the ramp, "polishing" a small section of the beach near the ramp.

I asked several workers what they were doing. The response: "We were told to make the shore look like there was no oil on the rocks."

They were polishing the rocks.

One afternoon we saw a commotion, and the ramp was on the beach. The black Zodiacs were zigzagging back and forth. The radio crackled with a message that we needed to go to the beach. Something was up—was it some big wig?

We stood there as Vice President Dan Quayle shook hands with some of us and said what an outstanding job we were doing; then he left.

And yes, the rocks were clean, but my clam spade, however, was not. I dug it into those polished rocks, and it came out dripping with coagulated black crude.

The next morning, the smell of crude was intense. I went on top and stood in terror as I saw the beach completely covered in oil. Our boat was in oil.

We went to the *USS Juneau*. And it was a firestorm. Because the crews had worked double time to ensure that the beach was clean for Vice President Quayle, we learned the crew had the day off. There was no one manning the boom. A few days later, Exxon informed us they were moving on to another beach. Our Coast Guard leader said they were not moving on until the RAT gave approval that the beach was clean.

That night, we wrote our report, signed by each member, which we submitted the next day.

While sitting on the rocks early in the morning, we watched two otters as the *USS Juneau* departed. I went back to Juneau and requested another assignment.

They sent me to Seward, to lead the beach-assessment teams. There were only a few ADEC people in the command center in Seward. We started noticing clicking noises on the phones during our phone conversations. Were we getting paranoid?

One late afternoon, after a day scouting beaches, I got a message about my T-shirt. How in the world would anyone know about that? The Exxon T-shirt was under layers of clothing. There were two employees in the office when I had removed the layers, and one of them was me. After that, we assumed our office was not secure.

The next day, I went back to Juneau. I had an oil-spill exercise to conduct in Petersburg. And I had a proposal to make to my boss, a daring proposal, but one that desperately needed to be done. *How can he refuse?* I thought, as I walked into his office and shut the door.

He accepted my proposal. I then sent a letter informing the oil company and the contractor. This time, both of us got called into the commissioner's office. Complaints about my request had gone to the top of the food chain and back down to us.

We made our case, and we got the approval to conduct a hands-on exercise. Even the USCG complained that this was not the protocol. We flew to Petersburg and got some beer and a lot of popcorn. The next morning, I had set up displays around the room with a few dozen pictures I had taken from the Exxon oil spill. I felt the tension as I looked at the faces staring at me. My boss felt it as well. Then he looked at me and raised his eyebrows; an alarm went off on his watch.

He announced to the room that there was a spill. He gave them information they would normally know if this was a real spill. And that was it. The popcorn, unsalted and unbuttered, floated in the water, acting as the "oil." And then we watched the chaos and confusion as the mock oil contaminated a high-value estuary. No one could find the boom or the weights for the boom. The skiffs were equipped with motors, but they did not work, and no one knew where the emergency-contact list was.

As we watched, I looked at the manager of the operation and said, "I believe we just saved your company a couple million bucks."

"I believe you did. And I owe you an apology."

The energy in the classroom changed. Everyone was talking. I was no longer the center of attention. Adrenaline filled the room. I'd earned my right to be in the room, and everyone knew it. My boss was grinning, and, when he looked at me and nodded, I mouthed, "Bingo."

The manager suggested a second oil-spill exercise at their facility in Haines during the Haines State Fair. They invited me. There were no complaints about getting the boom into the water.

One of my last jobs for ADEC in Juneau was to inspect the transfer of mining waste at a mine on Admiralty Island.

The next morning, I flew to the mine, one of the largest and lowest-cost silver mines in the world. When I arrived to inspect the transfer of material to the barge, the manager informed me they'd done the transfer during the night. He apologized with a smirk and said it was too bad I'd wasted my time. Policy requires ADEC to give notice when visiting a facility, which I did. They'd loaded it under the cover of darkness, with no regulatory eyes watching.

As I was leaving, I noticed several workers who were lingering near my discussion with the manager. I went over and talked with them.

I located the manager and asked to see the transfer belt they'd used to make the transfer. He stared at me, dumbfounded, but showed it to me. I thanked the manager for his time and left. I submitted my report, along with the maximum amount in fines—pennies for an operation as large as theirs.

It would not be my last visit to the mine on Admiralty Island.

Before I transferred to ADEC in Anchorage, I asked Justin for a commitment. I loved Juneau and the place I worked. He said we could get married the following spring.

It was fall, and my drive was breathtaking, with golden leaves of aspen among a patchwork of brilliant shades of red. *Fall in Alaska is one of the most beautiful seasons*, I thought as I drove the buckled asphalt, among taiga and tundra, toward home.

CHAPTER 22

All Creatures Great and Small

Books. *They have always formed the underpinning* of who I am. Some kids liked toys for gifts. Me? It was books. My mom's love of reading, like her love of all creatures, is in my DNA. A childhood without the comfort of a book is as unfathomable to me as a world without nature

The *Book of Knowledge* opened the world to me. In it, I could escape to Morocco or Bali or Africa by simply turning a page. There were so many dog-eared pages that my mom said the book would start barking!

The *Nancy Drew Mysteries* stimulated my inquisitive nature to ask questions and seek answers. *White Fang* and *Call of the Wild* taught me humility and empathy. As a child, I understood the cruelty of the natural world—the instinctual need for creatures to survive.

However, the ease of obliteration of creatures by the human species—considered the most dangerous animal in the world—is what I have never understood.

Justin and I settled into a routine. Once I understood the rules of that routine, then our relationship was compatible, and the world became our book. I likened my relationship with Justin to a chemical reaction, like the reaction when you add vinegar to baking soda. The more vinegar that is added, the hotter and faster the reaction becomes. I am the vinegar, the catalyst; Justin is the soda or the buffer, taking his time until he wants something to happen.

I was busy working for three consulting companies and converting the "garage"—which never could be used as a garage—into an office. The condition of the sheetrock persuaded me to choose wallpaper rather than mud. One late afternoon, I stopped by the Agency to show Justin some samples of wallpaper. He wasn't around, but Darren was there, so I showed him the samples. He asked me, "Why the rush?" So, I told him.

Darren looked at me and laughed, saying, in his sarcastic tone, "He ain't never going to marry you. Marriage? Where did you get that crazy idea?"

Stunned, I walked away. Apparently, Justin had not told him or anyone else about our spring marriage plans.

Rather than talk with him about Darren's comments, I planned our trip to Australia and Rarotonga. I learned early in our relationship that there is a time and a place to discuss things. The tone of my voice could set him off, especially if the subject did not appeal to him. I would wait; I tried to be the soda rather than the vinegar.

We were planning a dive trip to Cairns, so Justin could get certified in scuba diving. Cairns is the point of departure for diving the Great Barrier Reef (GBR). However, our plan to leave in mid-January got put on hold when a call from my mom said to come home immediately.

"Your father is sick. You need to come home now. He might not make it," she said.

I bought a plane ticket and flew to Seattle, where my brother-in-law met me at the airport. In his braggart swag, he informed me of his current situation. I confronted my sis as we drove to the hospital in Wenatchee. Rather than being upset at the situation, she was mad at her husband for telling me their secret. I kept my sister's secret with conditions.

As I walked into his hospital room, my dad's eyes grew wide. His mouth opened, but no words came out. His hands shook. With me being home, he thought death was near. I saw syringes on the floor. I saw the look of complete helplessness on my dad's face. I buzzed the nurse. Nothing. I buzzed again. Nothing. I assured him he was fine and stepped out briefly to see Flo.

My sister had errands, so when I came back to his room, I asked him what the hell he thought he was doing. Lying around in a hospital bed? He grinned.

At that moment, Flo knocked on the door, and, with her beautiful smile, she warmly asked my dad how he was feeling, as she grabbed his hand and held it. She looked around the room, and then we made eye contact. She arranged an appointment with the hospital director the next morning, and my mom was furious.

Dad had gangrene in his arm from an IV. There was an open wound, an inch wide from his shoulder to his wrist, where the doctor had removed the poisoned vein. Although that was not the initial reason for him being in the hospital, he thought he was dying. By the third day, I told him we were going outside.

"Susie, I don't think I should."

"Why not? Sun and air will be good. Do you want to walk or the wheelchair?"

Outside, his pallid complexion glowed with sun and fresh air. Flo would stop by every day to see him. My mom sulked, and my sister went back to Seattle.

As I walked down the dim, dreary hall to my dad's room, it horrified me to see patients in their beds as thin and gray as my dad was. "What the hell?" I whispered as the disinfectant of death made my eyes water. We live in the greatest country in the world, and yet basic medical care in a clean environment was unattainable.

Considering I was expecting to be at a funeral, I was happy we were taking him home. My brother stopped by every night after work and changed his dressing. His mood was mechanical, avoiding interaction, especially with our mom. It was later that I found out why. I do not understand the need for family secrets. It serves no purpose.

After three weeks, I flew home. My dad's health had improved, so we flew to the land of Oz. After Justin's two days of pool instruction, we spent four amazing days on a live-aboard dive boat. While Justin was in class, I dove with a couple from the States.

Giant clams, three feet across, covered with velvet-like glimmering algae of deep purples and turquoises, lived among the coral. The bright colors of circles on the clam's flesh are iridophores, which direct sunlight onto its mantle. If the giant clam senses there's not enough light filtering through to the algae, it extends the fleshy mantle out of its shell and reduces the color pigmentation to offer it more. The encrusted grooves and ridges of the shell define the giant clam, which can live to be 100 years old. The mollusk breathes in and out through the siphon, a hole in the flesh, luring plankton and divers.

Unfortunately, the flesh of this ancient creature is considered a delicacy by the Chinese. Hence, they are listed as endangered.

Sea snakes, classified as threatened, are a marvel to watch, with their sleek, red-ringed body, slithering skillfully through the water; luckily for me, this little guy was slithering *away* from me.

When diving in Australia, you learn to touch nothing. You keep your hands clasped across your chest or by your side. This prevents divers from killing coral and the ecosystem they provide, but also protects the diver. Sea snakes are extremely venomous.

A Potato cod, six feet in length, swam lazily next to me, like an old, faithful golden retriever. They have massive jaws but are the friendliest fish in the sea. They are bluish, with large, dark-brown blotches that give the grouper their name. Because they are so friendly, they are easy to spear; they are rarely seen now outside of protected Australian waters.

There was so much life; I was dizzy, twirling in the water, trying to see everything. The orange-striped clownfish were darting through brain corals, and lemon-yellow trumpet fish were hanging, motionless, upside down.

Several species of psychedelic-colored wrasse and vibrant-blue parrotfish darted through the swaying branches of blues, oranges, and yellows of soft coral. Mesmerized by the colors of life, I did not notice the large shark coming toward us. There must have been an invisible wall, because it suddenly veered away. We were expelling air bubbles rapidly while levitating in the water as still as we could.

We said our goodbyes to our new dive mates and crew, but we were not ready to say goodbye to the GBR. Instead, we booked a catamaran sail and dive charter from Cairns to Cape Tribulation.

As of April 2020, the GBR had suffered three major bleaching events on all portions of the great reef in the last five years. The water temperatures recorded by the documentary crew of the film *Chasing Coral* had risen as high as 80 degrees Fahrenheit. This event alone sent a clear warning to everyone that our Earth is in crisis.

Have we listened to her call?

We made our way south from Cape Tribulation to a campground nestled beneath the overstory of exotic trees in the Daintree Rainforest. This rainforest is one of Australia's most beautiful natural wonders and one of the oldest and diverse ecosystems in the world. A large variety of plants came from the ancient stock of Gondwana, the supercontinent that broke apart 180 million years ago.

The most famous plant, and one reason we wanted to visit this forest, is the idiot fruit. It is one of the rarest and most primitive of the flowering plants, with a lineage spanning 110 million years. The plant was discovered after a small group of cattle were found dead below the canopy. The huge towering trees hold large brown fruits, and the seed is highly poisonous. For this reason, the only method of seed dispersal is gravity, limiting the trees to isolated pockets of lowland tropical rainforest. Life in the understory can be unpredictable.

Colorful bird species swoop below the lush, green canopies of mahogany, tulip oaks, and, of course, the stinging tree, a plant that can kill you. The diversity of plants, king ferns, flowering epiphytes, gingers, and fan palms sustain a variety of creatures in the understory, including the endangered Cassowary. Camouflaged and difficult to see, this large, black bird, which looks like a cross between a turkey and an emu, is flightless. It has a thick, bony "helmet," like an Egyptian warrior's, mounted on a bright-blue naked head. And we were lucky to see it on an early-morning walk.

Oz was an adventure on land and in the sea. We got up one morning to find a spider with brilliant orange legs quietly sleeping, in its golden web, woven across the top quarter of the door of our wall tent. Luckily, these orb spiders are harmless, but we took no chances as we snuck out the bottom part of the door, not to disturb its masterpiece.

We explored as much country as we could; we took a bus to Darwin and a rental car to Brisbane. We camped and hiked; we watched kangaroos and 14-foot crocodiles. We had sun and rain—even a monsoon—and, for two days, when the road was closed due to flooding, we were "forced" to stay in a wonderful hotel in the forest, a treat after camping for a week.

"Oz, we will return," I whispered as we caught our flight to the island of Rarotonga, the largest of the Cook Islands. Fortunately, a representative of the tourist board greeted us and assigned us lodging, a requirement before leaving the airport. For budgetary reasons, we scored a thatched hut at a place called Tom's. We hiked the volcanic peak—the tallest on the island—did some snorkeling, and toured the island, but we had plans for a quieter adventure.

Two days later, we jumped an Air New Zealand plane for a 50-minute flight to Aitutaki, a smaller, laid-back Island. There was only one hotel, so, the first night, we enjoyed the nightlife. This was a younger, free-spirited crowd, from all over the globe.

The next day, we went to the only known dive shop on the island. The gear was outdated, and we left, accepting the fact that snorkeling might be our only choice. As we walked through the tiny village, inquiring about a place to stay, we heard about a new dive operation called Mike's. Yes, there is a theme on the Cooks with first names for the owners of their business. We loved Tom's, so we headed to Mike's.

Mike was a friendly expat and retired Navy diver, and we were his first inquiry about scuba diving. Unfortunately, his boat had a hole in the hull, but it would be like new in a day or two, he assured us. His gear was all top-notch and new. Being his first clients, *he* asked *us* how much we would pay for a two-tank dive. With slight apprehension, we settled on a price, including a few days of two-tank dives.

We found a room to rent from a Mormon family whose brood now lived in the States, with an outdoor shower and kitchen. Our next stop was finding a moped and touring the island. As we proceeded to the highest point, we saw a thin, barefoot, black-headed boy spray-painting graffiti on an abandoned brick building. Justin asked him what it said.

Justin laughed at his response and told the kid, "We have a term for that: *Shit happens.*" The kid repeated the phrase and smiled.

On our way back down the hill, the boy was gone, but he'd left his mark. On the wall in red paint were the words, "Shit happens."

"You might have just changed the culture on this very Mormon Island," I said. Justin laughed.

The barrier reef defines the outer limits of Aitutaki, which is roughly the shape of an equilateral triangle, with each side approximately 7.5 miles. The fertile volcanic soil provides tropical fruits and vegetables, which we enjoyed immensely.

For the first of our dives, we stayed inside the reef system and spent lunchtime at the lagoon. Here, we enjoyed snorkeling with large manta rays, their wings blocking the sun as they swam over us. The shallow lagoon was full of fish and mollusks.

Outside of the barrier reef, we dove water so clear that I kept my gauge in my hand, so as not to go deeper than 85 feet. And then I saw the exotic lionfish, a highly venomous creature, considered invasive in many areas now, characterized by conspicuous warning coloration, with red, white, creamy, or black bands. With showy pectoral fins, reminiscent of a woman's feathered hat, I noticed the hidden and highly toxic spiky fin rays. I kept my distance as I admired it.

After a glorious week, we checked into the Air New Zealand ticket counter. Not understanding what the problem was, someone quickly guided us to a back office. I found out my father had passed away. Air New Zealand put us in first class, with endless glasses of champagne. With a changed itinerary, we flew to Washington.

We arrived a few minutes before the memorial service started. My brother was livid! *How could anyone go to a place where you can fly out only once a week?* He had been trying to get ahold of us for days.

Dad had suffered a massive stroke. He survived but unexpectedly died right after my sister visited, before they had time to move him to the rehab facility. They had diagnosed the clot in my dad's brain at the hospital in Wenatchee, which, I learned, was the reason for his stay when I visited. My brother wanted to transfer him to Spokane. My mom did not. It was a very sad situation—one that haunted and fractured our family forever.

Before we flew back to Alaska, we stopped at Flo's and got Chessy, who was coming back to Alaska with us. Flo was terribly upset. She'd had to move out of her rental house and could only find a small apartment that did not allow cats. Chessy missed her terribly, but she settled in with us. After all, she was an Alaskan cat. I frequently sent pictures to Flo, and, when we talked on the phone, Chessy, cocking her ears, would sit on my lap while Flo talked to her.

Almost a year later, we headed to Belize. With an abundance of terrestrial and marine species, as well as its diversity of ecosystems, it was on our list to sail, dive, and hike.

Although we were disappointed that we couldn't find a sailboat to rent, luckily, we met a couple with a multihull catamaran. We spent the next two weeks sailing with them. The snorkeling was amazing, but it was time to do some terrestrial exploration.

Our shipmates said they would store our gear, as they dropped us off in Placentia, a low-key fishing village where we found many Canadian expats. Our goal was to take a bus to Belmopan and then north to Tikal, the ruins in Guatemala.

After an eventful trek to the jungles of Guatemala, we spent the next three nights in the campground at Tikal. The cacophony of howler monkeys roaring and "laughing" as they dropped large seed pods on the top of our tiny orange tent left us with little sleep. Every morning at 5 a.m., with headlamps, we strolled deep into the jungle and sat.

One morning, in the dark, there was a rustle in the dense, lush understory. Our awareness was on alert, but we dared not turn the headlights on. In the shadows, we saw an enormous cat, with its familiar rosette markings, appear on the trail. Holding our breath, the jaguar disappeared into the jungle. There are fewer than 15,000 of these beautiful, large cats left, because of deforestation and poaching.

As light filtered through the thick forest canopy, it came alive with the barking and croaking of brightly colored toucans and the screeching of ruby-red parrots. On two occasions, we glimpsed a slight flash of reddish-brown hair as the sleek, long-bodied golden-eyed Jaguarundi slinked off into the dense understory.

The "coati" made their presence known as we walked throughout the ruins. They are very similar to a raccoon, with a long ringed tail that they hold straight up, grunting and chirping, using their long nose, sniffing for lizards, snakes, and insects in the thick litter.

All this natural beauty existed among one of the largest archaeological urban centers of the pre-Columbian Maya civilization ever discovered. Tikal is growing as more structures buried under the ground are excavated. At the center lies the Grand Plaza, bordered by two temple-pyramids, the North Acropolis and the Central Acropolis. At the center is the Temple of the Great Jaguar and the Temple of the Masks. The most alluring is Temple IV, thought to be the tallest edifice erected by the ancient Maya.

We crawled to the peak of Temple IV to watch the sunset, grabbing roots and branches, spreading across the stone, like a spiderweb. Standing at 65 meters tall, we saw the endless green of the Guatemalan jungle, fractured by the other temples of Tikal rising above the treetops. As the jungle swallowed the brilliant orange, it exploded with howls and screams—and then there was silence. As we carefully made our way down the hand-carved, ancient stone and wandered back to camp, I could only imagine what secrets were still hidden in the understory.

After a near-life-threatening incident leaving the border, we made our way back to Ambergris Cay, where we visited our friends and grabbed our gear, for our next adventure, diving with the "Reef Rammer" for three days.

Our first dive on the second day was the Blue Hole. A nearly perfect circular body of water, the Hole is a "karst-eroded sinkhole," surrounded by the Lighthouse Reef atoll. Measuring 984 feet across and 400 feet down, it is the largest sea hole in the world.

Because of the complexity and depth of the dive, only experienced divers can explore the thousands of stalactites and stalagmites in one of the top-ten dive sites, according to Jacques Cousteau. As divers descend into the Hole, the dark sapphire-blue waters become clear, allowing for an impressive view of the flooded cave network that is home to a variety of marine life, including a few elusive hammerhead sharks.

As a recreational diver, to do this dive to 140 feet, which is the maximum one can dive as a recreational diver, requires around 8 minutes from the beginning of the descent to reaching the surface on ascent. This dive goes against everything a diver learns. You rapidly descend; there is no time for ear compensation. The clear blue water, filled with an abundance of barracuda, angelfish, and groupers darting along the reef, quickly fades to a dark, sapphire blue with only a few large gray bodies darting quickly by. I did not want to know what species they were. Lemon, hammerhead, reef . . . those are fine. But bull sharks? No, thanks.

My regulator was registering a depth of 147 feet, the deepest of all my dives. The blue melted into a creamy white. It is a wild feeling staring at nothing but blackness below and the milky sky above—all the while, feeling totally drunk!

On the ascent, I slowly released air from my buoyancy compensator (BC) as I pondered the fact that more than 15,000 years ago, this cave was on the surface of the planet. The giant stalactites I was swimming around had formed at the ceiling of the cave. It was mind-exploding. Literally!

Although we saw little bleaching of the coral in 1991, we did witness sedimentation from the agricultural area of Belmopan, slowly suffocating the coral. Belize became the first country in the world to ban bottom trawling, in 2010. In December 2015, they banned offshore oil drilling within one km of the barrier reef and all its seven World Heritage sites.

Despite these measures, the reef remains under threat from pollution, uncontrolled tourism, shipping, and overfishing. Hurricanes and the increased ocean temperatures have bleached more than 40% of Belize's coral reef since 1998.

When we arrived back in the States, I learned my Aunt Judy had passed. They had diagnosed her with pancreatic cancer. How would my uncle Danny make it? First his twin and, now, ten months later, his wife.

"Two trips, two deaths. Is it me?" I whispered to myself.

I was not ready to close the chapter on this book of adventures. There were too many endangered ecosystems, too many habitats to explore.

One of the most mystical and spectacular diving excursions was in Micronesia, on the volcanic islands of Yap and Palau. There, 2 out of 600 islands, nestled in the middle of the Pacific Ocean, offer an aquatic biodiversity I have never seen before.

Arriving on the tiny Micronesian island of Yap, the western world is nonexistent. Women still wear the traditional hibiscus skirts and nothing else. We quickly settled into our small, thatched hut in the dense forest and booked a dive trip for the next day, recommended to us by our new neighbor from Germany.

We hooked up with her for a kayak-paddling tour through the mangroves. That was also our introduction to the huge circular stones, called "Rai stones," still used locally as currency. These have been a part of the Yapese culture for hundreds of years. Obviously, they are permanent fixtures around the island and passed between families as payment. Their new ownership is an oral history.

The next day, we dove into the Mi'il Channel, a well-known manta-ray-cleaning station. Sightings of manta rays are "mostly guaranteed," and we were not disappointed. These graceful creatures visit Mi'il Channel with such frequency that many even have names!

Waiting for our second dive, we were chatting with a Peace Corps volunteer. We learned that the island was transporting villagers from a nearby sister atoll to Yap. Saltwater intrusion from the rising ocean had made the island uninhabitable for growing food. The volunteer, a teacher, was frantically trying to preserve medicinal and traditional plants before the island was under the sea.

As our flight departed Yap, I looked down on the endless coral reefs in pristine blue water and wondered, *Will Yap survive, or will she, too, disappear where the currents from the Indian, the Pacific, and the Philippine Seas converge?*

Palau is called the "underwater Serengeti" because of its diversity of huge schools of reef fish, dugongs, sharks, rays, and living, healthy coral. The Blue Corner in Palau is one of the best dive sites in the world, our next dive adventure.

You drift along a wall of coral with brilliant purple anemones and then hook yourself into the top edge of the reef wall. Suspended in the strong current, a highway of sharks, jacks, and manta rays pass you by. As we were lazily watching the world swim by, our German friend had a different encounter.

A large green eel had made an appearance below her, and, with a flash of gray in a turbulent swirl of sediment, she found herself in the middle of a feeding frenzy between two sharks. All we could do was watch. And then, as quickly as it started, it was over. And luckily for our friend, she still had all her body parts. As an expert diver, she remained calm throughout the entire frenzy.

We explored the caverns and the blue hole, a diminutive version of the one in Belize, but no less spectacular, with its ambient light at 95 feet. Colorful gorgonian fans, tubular sponges, and butterfly fish paid no attention to sharks, tuna, and grouper. At shallower depths, turtles and the large birdlike manta feed on a very, very healthy reef. We saw no signs of bleaching or sedimentation.

Off the coast of Koror, the main village on Palau, the Rock Islands contain about 70 marine lakes. One of these is home to the Mastigias jellyfish, which are large, beautiful, orange creatures that are completely harmless. Snorkeling among these delicate beings was mesmerizing and spiritual.

The privilege to swim with the Mastigias requires swimmers not to kick or use their arms except for short, gentle dog paddling. I grabbed several snorkelers who did not understand this rule, as they had killed several jellyfish with their fins or outstretched arms. The slender, fragile bodies are easily killed with a strike from a fin or a hand. How ignorant we can be? In 2018, this lake was closed due to increased stress on the dwindling jellyfish population from droughts and tourists.

A few days later, as we watched the documentary *Chasing Coral*, an overwhelming grief took hold of my heart. Some of these creatures of the sea are more than a century old. The ocean supports all life. All creatures great and small. It moderates our weather and our climate. And yet, we have treated it like a garbage dump.

Over the next two decades, our diving adventures took us to Bonaire, the Bay of the Islands of Honduras, Tobago, Mauritius, Hawaii, the Ningaloo reef, and the deep undersea canyons in

southwest Australia. All are unique systems with a variety of life, and all are showing signs of death. My last underwater exploration in 2009 was Yap and Palau.

What is the future of our oceans? The sea is the understory of all life, and, without the sea, humans will cease to exist.

CHAPTER 23

Seasons of Him

*I*ce-*fishing and hang gliding,* I contemplated, *and somewhere in between is me. At least he ain't sitting on the couch, drinking beer, and eating chips.*

It is also the season to tend to the gardens and landscaping, stain the cedar siding, and repair and paint the decks. It marks the end of ice-fishing and the beginning of hang gliding. In the early years, I accepted the fact that flying season, like everything else in Alaska, is constrained. It truly was Justin's genuine love.

Justin would monitor the winds compulsively, and if cumulus were forming over the mountains, he was flying.

The "airheads," as I would refer to his buddies, could sit for hours, patiently, on a mountain ridge, hooked into their wings, observing the air. In a split second, a thermal would form, and one by one, they ran off the edge and soared into sky. My heart would always miss a beat as I watched Justin launch, and it wasn't just me.

On his last annual summer visit, Justin's dad and I sat on the back deck, scoping the guys with their easily seen orange, pink, and purple wings.

"Why do you let him do that?" his dad demanded.

I got up, reached into the cooler for a beer, and gave him one as I opened mine. "He's your son. You raised him to do what he wants. Free, with no commitment," I said, swallowing the cold brew. It had taken me many years to get up the courage to say those words, as I remembered that "first summer" in '88, when he came up for a month.

"Hang gliding is dangerous, Michelle. If I don't keep up my skills, I could crash. Your choice? But maybe you should try to find some friends and not be so needy."

That was Justin's response when I asked for help around the house or if I suggested we go do something together, in between field tours.

In the fall of 1991, the Northern Latitude Soil Scientists group invited Justin to speak at a Cryopedology conference in Pushchino, Soviet Union. As a member of the Alaska Yukon Soil Scientists, I was also invited to attend. It was an opportunity of a lifetime.

This was a time of transitional change for the Soviet Union. We grew up with the nuclear threat from the Soviet Union. Sirens would sound, sending us under our desks, thinking we were safe from a nuclear fallout. The Soviet Union reminded me of one of the many third-world countries I had visited—not one of the world's most powerful.

We saw Stalin's body in the Mausoleum in the Red Square and St. Basil's Cathedral. As I drank coffee in the Café Pushkin,

I swear I could hear whispers among the walls. I was with a group from the conference as we got a private viewing of the gemstones and jewelry of Catherine the Great.

The exception is the Moscow subway system, reminiscent of a once powerful country, opened in 1935. It is like a living piece of art, gold leaf glittering in the lights, elaborate murals everywhere. Our tour guide and Russian soil scientist told us to keep close as he darted in and out of the crowds, hopping one subway car to another. He was our mother hen and we, his ducklings! A subway is foreign to us Alaskans, but a bigger challenge? ВЫХОД В ГОРОД means in Russian, "Exit to the city." We looked at the metro station board, written in Cyrillic. We clung to our mother hen!

It was midnight in Moscow as we boarded the local train to the newly "renamed" city, St. Petersburg. Our guide hustled the four of us quickly into our berth—a soil scientist from Canada, a soil chemist from Palmer, Justin, and me. He told us to go to bed and not to answer the door. Fifteen minutes later, there was a knock. The knock got louder, and the porter was asking us something!

"Maybe he wants money?" our Canadian friend whispered.

"Give him some rubles," someone whispered back.

He opened the door and gave the porter rubles. Shortly after, someone was pounding on the door. This time it was our Russian guide.

He was yelling at us, and, we assumed, from his gestures, it was not pleasant.

Annoyed, he had to pay more rubles for us, and, although scorned, we were grateful no one threw us off the train.

Following the trip to the Soviet Union, we flew to Harare, Zimbabwe, in January 1992.

It took us a few days to find a car to rent for three weeks, but a guy who knew a guy at a hotel scored an old beater Mazda for us. We threw our packs in and headed to Hwange National Park. Justin became a natural at driving on the left side of the road, and, once we got out of the capital, it was easy driving—our first trip to Africa.

Our small thatched hut with a mini-fridge on the screened porch was $5 a day. Since the gate to the park opened at 6 a.m. and closed at dark, we had time for a drive.

Justin was trying to avoid these large black mounds scattered across the narrow, two-lane road. Steam was rising, even in the warm air. After nearly high-centering the Mazda, we stopped. I opened the door and saw dung beetles rolling small, round balls from the mounds.

At that moment, we felt the ground shake. The trumpeting was deafening as a herd of elephants engulfed us—one of the most powerful and magnificent mammals on the planet. I don't think we breathed as our view became "gray" from the massive animals. They were that close. I saw beautiful, long black eyelashes as a large matriarch walked by the front of the car. I looked right into her eyes and saw humanity.

Back at the hut, we sat at the picnic table and drank a cold beer. It seemed the nightly entertainment had begun.

The rangers warned visitors to lock their doors, and we soon found out why, as a troop of baboons sauntered by. They work in pairs, with one as a sentry and the other checking the screen doors on the huts. If the occupant leaves a door unlocked, the thieves help themselves to any item, including beer, from the small refrigerator.

Night after night, baboons provided entertainment as they investigated the metal garbage cans. One large male grasped the lid of the garbage can while he searched for delicious items. When finished, he carefully put the lid back on the can.

Meercats, with sleek, tawny bodies and black patches around their eyes, would sit upward on their haunches, looking around, chattering, and barking with each other, always on the go. The warthogs were also comical. One morning, we saw a tent surrounded by a family of warthogs, sound asleep. The owner of the tent was afraid to do anything until the heat made his decision for him. Rather than die of heat exhaustion, he took his chance waking the tusked, whiskered family away from his tent.

For a month, we traveled this country, hiked the tallest mountain, and fell in love with Zimbabwe. On our last day, before departing to Mauritius, the military police were stopping cars on a major road into Harare. Justin looked at me. We expected the worst after our travels through Mexico and Central America. The officer asked Justin for his license. We were there for 30 minutes as every officer wanted to meet the couple from Alaska! They asked us about igloos and snow. Justin asked what the stop was for. The officer said, "It is a car safety check."

We left this beautiful country, with the warmest, friendliest people, for a week in Mauritius and then back to the States. It was four years later when I returned with Bio Bio Expeditions for the Project Raft whitewater competition. Within that short period of time, the country was in the beginning of a drought, and civil unrest was peaking. President Mugabe had become power hungry, and the country had spun into turmoil. Wildlife died of starvation and were slaughtered. Farmers who were white, and lucky, were evicted from their farms; others, unlucky, killed.

A few years later, we planned a month's road trip from Cape Town, South Africa, along the Skeleton Coast to Etosha National

Park in Namibia. Locals warned us not to attempt the Caprivi Strip area because of unrest in Zimbabwe. Instead, we spent some time in Botswana. We heard story after story from locals of murder and complete wildlife devastation in the parks of the land, the people, the wildlife we had loved. For what? Vanity?

That's the problem in Africa. A country is stable for a few years, and then it is not.

CHAPTER 24

The Season of Me

Traveling with him was incredible. And creating a home, among one of the most picturesque landscapes on earth? Well, I knew it was a risky decision, but one I had to make.

After twelve years, sacrificing my career and putting too much distance between me and my friends, I had done enough to prove my commitment to him. Now I required reciprocation and commitment from him.

After I watched him crash his hang glider for the third time, I got the courage to demand a change.

"It's time we add my name to this property." No response.

"There never seems to be a good time to get married. If something happens to you, I need to be protected after putting everything I have into this home."

I handed him a quit-claim deed. He looked at it, and, without any more discussion, he said, "Fine." The next day, we stopped by the Sutton Library. The librarian, who later would become a neighbor and friend, was a notary. Justin had left his wallet in the truck and asked me to fetch it while he completed the form. When I came back, the librarian stared at me with a puzzled expression; her white eyebrows arched, and her eyes were questioning. Justin quickly folded the notarized document and sealed it in an envelope.

It was a month later when I found out why she'd looked at me so strangely. While he diverted me to "fetch" his wallet, Justin had crossed out "equal ownership" on the deed and wrote "one-fifth" next to my name.

"Is that how you value me? After twelve years?"

"You blow everything out of proportion. It's not a big deal."

"Nothing is," I muttered as he walked away.

In early spring of 1998, my mom was diagnosed with lung cancer. She called me and asked if I could visit. My cousin picked me up, and we drove to my mom's house.

She was still smoking, so before I left, I got a prescription for an emergency inhaler from my doctor. And I needed it.

At her request, I sat in the smoke-filled, cluttered, filthy living room, taking notes for her. The grand-girls would get everything "girlish," including the beautiful beaded purse I'd adored since I was a child. The rest would go to my sister, but I could have the large cement lawn ornaments. I looked at Mary; we both knew it was because Tish did not want them.

"Pat, how the hell is she going to get those to Alaska?"

"It's okay, Mary, you can have them. They would look much better in your front yard."

Some things never change, even when death is near. She had a will, so why were we having this discussion?

After my dad died, my mom took a trip to Kenya and Tanzania. I was ecstatic that she finally was going on safari. It was near the end of her trip when I got a call early in the morning, from my sister. Mom had had an accident in her hotel room and was in the hospital in Nairobi. Tish told me she could not deal with it because she had two kids. And since I had been to Africa, I would know what to do, she said, and then hung up.

After many calls to Kenya, I found out my mom had a fractured femur at the hip joint and needed surgery. Because she could not smoke in the hospital, she wanted to go home. She was a handful, the embassy representative articulated, trying to be diplomatic.

After many long-distance phone conversations with the trip leader and the State Department, she could be released after surgery. However, someone would have to fly with her. They could not let her fly alone.

It was a crucial time in consulting. I could not lose my job and take care of the expenses. I gave my sister $10,000 to bring our mom back from Kenya to Seattle. The agreement, between us, was for mom to stay with her in Seattle until she was healthy enough to go home. Instead, my sister took her home and left her alone.

A couple of years later, she bragged about the money she got when the travel insurance reimbursed my mom for all her expenses. No one paid me back.

My mom died in May 1998, but at least she was not alone; my sister had just left her room. Tish had her cremated her even before I found out she had passed. I had talked with the doctor two days prior to discuss the next phase of medical bills and prognosis. He said the state would be taking over financial responsibility.

There was a small memorial at mom's house, which was now my sister's. She gave me three days' notice over Memorial Day weekend. I could not attend.

I was on a committee to organize the Society of Wetland Scientists National Conference in Anchorage—a gigantic task for a group of five of us to pull off. I held many roles: speaker, field trip organizer, a field trip leader, and fundraiser. It started the same day as my mom's memorial in Washington. Considering Justin's dad had been at the house for a month and was leaving that same day, I was overwhelmed, but grateful to be busy.

In June, I barely had a moment to catch my breath. A friend who I worked with at a consulting company had started her own company and offered me a partnership. I said I would consider it after a few months working with her. She had strategically taken a client, a mining corporation, we had both worked with, when she left the consulting firm.

The gold mine, in the interior of Alaska, was accessible by air from Delta Junction. When we landed near the camp, we found out several black bears had been shot and killed in the area. It did not take long to understand why.

Crews were eating food in tents, garbage was scattered, and there was no camp policy to minimize bear and human contact. At other mining operations, the first day was always a safety briefing. This includes ATV operation, bear protection, helicopter briefings, firearm safety, and meeting the EMTs.

A year before, the Mining, Safety, and Health Administration (MSHA), the agency that oversaw safety regulations for mining, was forced to close in Alaska due to budget cuts by congress. The closest office was now in Montana. The result of that action was obvious.

The helicopter pilots we met were from the deep south, not experienced in mountain country. They were flying large, heavy-lift transport helicopters for hauling large loads such as mining equipment. With a lot of ground to cover, we worked alone on most of our transects. Miles from the camp center, we found garbage and a solid network of bear trails leading to and from the camp.

After two weeks, more black bears were shot and killed. The workers carried an array of firearms. There were three helicopters that flew around the clock. During that first tour, there were two near-collisions because one pilot refused to talk on the radio.

One day, a sling broke, dropping a load of live dynamite near the camp center. Slinging gear from a helicopter takes skill, not only of a pilot but a certified slinger. I witnessed more violations in two weeks than in my entire career in Alaska.

I did not plan to return for the next tour. A consulting company out of Fairbanks offered me a position on a contract for Denali National Park. I informed my associate of my decision.

Her response, somewhat shocking, said I was breaking my contract with her. If she could not find a replacement, she might have to take legal action. Instead, she offered to buy medical equipment to relieve some of my worry about the absence of safety procedures. Being certified as an Emergency Technician (ETT), I had every reason to be concerned.

I had those unsettled feelings in the pit of my gut when we were back in the mining camp. The first day, we each had a representative from the mining corporation from Japan. It was a long day of field work. While I was eating dinner, she asked me if I would take the GPS equipment to the upper camp. I gave in, walked to the helicopter, and climbed up to the passenger seat. The pilot was new, and he had no idea where the upper camp was.

We landed, but he did not shut down, since he was simply dropping me off. I carefully opened the door, so I could see the tiny step that was a couple of feet below. Suddenly, the door flew open and I went flying. The next thing I knew, I was on the ground. A young man helped me up, but I screamed in pain. I could not stand; it was like my legs were jelly.

Rule number 1: If the helicopter is not shutting down, no one approaches a live helicopter—meaning the blades and rotor are moving—until the pilot nods his head. This means there is always eye contact between people on the ground outside the helicopter and the pilot. The pilot will nod his head only when the people in the helicopter have safely exited.

Rule number 2: If the helicopter is shutting down, no one approaches a live helicopter until the pilot nods his head. You sit in the helicopter until the blades quit turning. Even then, you depart only when the pilot tells you to.

There were no helicopter safety briefings. However, for someone like myself, who had been flying in helicopters since 1982, the rules are the same. I expected no one to open my door. The seat in the helicopter was several feet off the ground, and I never saw the young kid who grabbed the door that I had my hand on—a basic violation of helicopter safety.

I knew my injuries were severe. The pilot knew there was a problem and shut down the helicopter. Now, there were two people on the ground as those blades lost momentum above our heads. I had to grab the kid and force him to drag me to the skids, stay low, and not to move. I also knew I was going into shock.

With the bird shut down, I looked up at a group of wide-eyed young men, frozen and staring at me. I yelled at them to go find something to immobilize both my legs—two by fours, towels, whatever—and get the EMT. I hoped one existed, but I could not depend on that unknown.

I had fallen several feet, landing hard on my left foot but not on solid ground. My foot rolled because it had landed on a circular, rough rock about the size of a grapefruit. That caused the leg to roll sharply, sideways.

Everyone heard the loud "pop" as my knee exploded and the "thump" of the rotors slowed down.

My right foot had caught the tiny, three-inch "pedal," or step. But when the door flew open, the force bent my right leg backwards and sideways. It was a bloody mess.

One guy returned, but without an EMT, and gave me an air splint. I knew I needed to stay conscious. I had blood on my right knee, but there was no major arterial bleeding. I needed to be immobilized from the hip to the ankle. I did not need to shut down the blood supply to my leg.

Finally, a young lady approached. She knelt beside me and whispered her name. She was an EMT. I finally let my body do what it needed to do—I passed out from shock.

The crew carried me down to another helicopter, the same type as the one I'd been flung out of.

To get me up and into the back seat was difficult and worrisome enough, but I had to sit up in the back seat with my legs stretched as we flew to Delta Junction. We landed at the local airport, where an ambulance was waiting. However, due to the height difference, there was no way to get me from the helicopter to the ambulance. And then a group of burly guys in yellow shirts and green pants asked if we needed help—the wildland fire crew!

During this entire time, I thought I was going to Fairbanks, to the hospital, not a small clinic a hundred miles from anywhere.

I insisted to be flown to Anchorage or to Fairbanks. I found out later that someone from the mine had said it was not life threatening, so they refused to fly me to a hospital.

How did they know it was not life-threatening? I could have broken my neck or my back! The volunteer EMT with the ambulance asked us what the hell was going on at that mine. I was one of many accidents they had responded to.

The X-ray technician, who, I believe, was also the bartender at the local bar, took X-rays of my legs. I asked where the doctor was. They did not have one. However, one was on call from Greely, a military base nearby. He held the X-ray up to the fluorescent lights on the ceiling.

"What the fuck is that sticking out of my knee?"

At the same time, the EMT who'd flown with me, yelled, "What the fuck?"

Slowly, the technician unrolled the towels and boards away from my left knee. Inside a roll in the towel, was a reddish-brown rock the shape of an overstretched arrowhead, about three inches long, an inch or two in width, narrowing into a point at one end. A fear of mine, and the EMT, was a compound fracture! I don't think any of us breathed until we found that rock.

The doctor finally showed up. As he looked at the X-rays, I asked if I could still work.

"Honey, you'll have a long recovery. You have destroyed both your knees. In this type of accident, I normally see broken necks and/or broken backs, along with the damage to the legs."

At that point, I should have insisted on an ambulance to a hospital. He had no equipment to evaluate any other damage other than I could move my toes. I called Justin from the helicopter operations hangar, where I would sleep on the cement floor. He had just gotten home from his two-week tour at Denali National Park, his current soil survey project.

"Hi," I whispered, in tears, but struggling not to cry.

"What's up?" he asked, bluntly.

I told him what happened and that I would be home tomorrow.

"I will need to see an orthopedic specialist." Before leaving for the field, I ran into a friend of mine who was in a full knee brace. He told me his surgeon's name.

"There is a good surgeon in Anchorage. Can you make an appointment immediately?"

"Don't expect me to stay," he said. "I am going to Wyoming in two days." He hung up.

It's July. It was his *season. Not* our *season,* I thought, as the EMT helped me to the cement floor, my bed for the night. She apologized for not helping me sooner, and explained why. She was an engineer and was tired of responding to accidents at previous operations. She never told anyone she was an EMT, until she heard what happened to me.

Justin's voice was harsh and the words cruel. I knew the pain in my legs would heal, but would my heart? His inadequacy to have empathy or love was his, not mine. He was a lost pup I just could not fix. I felt sorry for him, and while his words stung, they also made me more determined to be who I knew I was, a survivor.

CHAPTER 25

A Time to Heal

Sharp, consistent pain was searing through my legs as I sat on the back seat of the truck. It was difficult, as my associate did her best to maneuver the rough road from Delta Junction toward Sutton, Alaska, through the construction traffic.

"I'm glad we went back for the pain meds," she said, with concern on her face.

After a grueling nine hours, the last mile was excruciating, with washboards and gullies a foot across, zigzagging the rocky road up to the house. Justin was in the garage as I hobbled on the used crutches someone had donated to the clinic, from the truck, up the many stairs, to the front door.

I lay on the couch, both knees swollen. The open slashes on my right leg were caked with dried blood. Dirt stained my hands where I had lain on the ground, clenching the soil, trying to stay conscious. Chessy jumped on my lap, meowing.

"I'm OK, Chessy," I whispered as she licked my face.

Justin finally came in and asked what I did. I explained the situation to him. He told me he was packing for his vacation, but he made a doctor appointment in Wasilla.

The next morning, the nurse asked Justin to come in with me to see the doctor, but he preferred to stay in the waiting room. A few minutes later, the doctor insisted he join us, but the nurse found the reception area empty; he had already left.

The doctor reviewed the X-rays. My left knee was destroyed. The ACL had completely ruptured. He suspected the meniscus had torn, as well as the collateral ligaments.

The right knee, bent backwards and sideways, caused the bones to shift. He suspected damage to the meniscus, but the ACL looked intact. However, until the swelling went down on both knees, he could not be sure. He ordered an MRI and fitted me with two titanium braces that provided support and a suitable set of crutches. He set me up with a physical therapist. Surgery would be next.

I was too embarrassed to tell him my partner was leaving on vacation.

"Will I be able to drive with the braces on? I live 40 miles from Wasilla."

"No," he said sternly. "Your husband needs to hear this. You have a long recovery ahead of you," he lectured.

I sat in the waiting room. By the time Justin returned, the doctor was busy.

Instead of going back to the office, we got groceries and went home.

He moved my computer to the dining-room table and brought up a foldable foam mattress that would be my bed for the next 10 months, on the floor of the living room. He left the next morning for his vacation in Wyoming.

I called a physical therapist and explained my predicament. She gave me exercises until I could physically come see her. I diligently did my PT two to three times a day. The phone rang during one of my killer sessions.

It was the voice of a man talking, but my brain was not comprehending what he said. *This cannot be real. I must be delirious.*

When Justin had his torn Achilles tendon reattached, he was on a machine that pumped morphine. For five nights, I curled up in a chair in his hospital room, listening to the "beep" when the pump forced the narcotic into his arm. *Maybe I'm in a hospital, and I'm only dreaming that I'm alone at home.*

Chessy jumped on my lap as I held the phone to my ear. It was an agent for my workers' compensation claim. I vaguely remembered that the doctor in Delta Junction had said he would file the claim within ten days.

"You are accusing me of joyriding in a helicopter?"

The idiot on the line was quiet. Well, of course—what else would I be doing at 7 p.m. but joyriding in a helicopter?

"Yes. I was still working," I said. The conversation was unbelievable.

Frustrated and angry, I called the State of Alaska Workers Compensation Department. It was a mind-blowing conversation about a subject I knew nothing about. I had been working in the field since I was 19 years old, the last 17 in Alaska, living and working in hazardous conditions. I had never had an accident.

The agreeable gentlemen on the line explained that the insurance carrier, my agent, was a freelance subcontractor who had a reputation for being an asshole.

"What do I do?"

"Get a lawyer in workers' compensation law. You have an advocate in this office."

I dialed the only attorney listed for workers compensation. I had talked with him at social events and knew him to be a fair, quiet, intellectual thinker.

"I need your help," I said when he picked up. I explained the situation. His soft-spoken voice calmed me immediately.

For the next couple of weeks, I educated myself about workers' compensation, associated laws, and the rich history in Alaska on this subject. Workers' compensation claims had skyrocketed in the state as hundreds of people came from all parts of the U.S. to make money building the oil pipeline—not unlike the gold-rush days.

Injury claims and the associated dollar figure were staggering, and, considering how little oversight was being applied, it broke the system. In response, employers lobbied for strict regulation, and the pendulum swung to the opposite end of the spectrum. Unknown to me, my boss had hired me not through the mine but through a personnel agency offering the lowest insurance coverage available. I got stuck with the bottom of the barrel, as they denied everything, accusing me of fraud.

Justin came home for the night, bringing food and prescriptions. It was nice having human company, but he took off for the field the next morning. My days became a blur of monotony: exercises, ice, write. I was having difficulty ignoring the self-doubt and anxiety about my future.

I worked hard. In less than two years, I finished graduate school in environmental policy and wetland science and restoration. And shortly after, I applied and received my Professional Wetland Scientist Certification in 1994.

The questions never stopped in my head. Will I ever be able to work in the field again? Field work is the bread and butter of a field scientist in Alaska. Will I ever be able to walk normally again? What will I do?

Friends from Anchorage called frequently. To ease the anxiety of my predicament, I focused on writing. Friends suggested I write about workers' comp and the influence that fossil-fuel development corporations have on our congressional representatives.

Those subjects were too depressing. I needed mental time away from my reality, fighting with doctors and weasels in the insurance game.

I remembered listening to a mining CEO brag about a mine collapse in a country in the northern region of South America, killing many of the local miners. He joked there was another 200 waiting in line, willing to risk their lives for a couple of bucks a week.

At that point, I knew what I was going to write about. The research took me to the jungles of French Guiana, where I learned about the threat that mining posed to a small indigenous tribe and the medicinal plants that they relied upon. It was fascinating, and it led me to a field botanist in Montana who'd developed a taxonomy guide of the flora of French Guiana, along with a vegetation map.

Soon, a plot and characters developed. Every night I worked with a vengeance, with a cat on my lap and my computer screen as my only companions.

After six months, I completed *Jaguar Moon* and submitted it for an e-book contest—where I won free publishing! Writing relieved me of the reality of pain, unhappiness, and anxiety; I enjoyed the experience tremendously.

With delays in scheduling the surgery and my complete dependence on Justin's field schedule, the word "needy" kept popping into my brain. Enlisting the aid of two friends in Anchorage to take care of me, my angst grew. Finally, in September, there was a date for surgery that would accommodate both Justin dropping me off at the surgery center, and Coug picking me up. He told me he could not change the helicopter schedule. And then his partner from the National Park Service (NPS) called, trying to reach him.

He was shocked when I told him why I was home and not in the field. Justin hadn't said a word to him. He got the helicopter departure delayed one day.

And then a day before my surgery date, the insurance company attempted to delay the surgery *again*. This time, my attorney was in charge, but a fight with Justin left me red-eyed with a sleepless night. Justin was angry about the one-day delay of his field schedule, requiring him to wait until my surgery was over to take me to Coug's. To make it worse, the surgery took longer because the meniscus, torn in quite a few places, had folded over and remolded. Justin dropped me off and left, only after he told me he had no means of communication where he was going and not to expect a call.

A few hours after Coug came home from work, the headache started, and, by 9 p.m., Coug called the surgical nurse. She was ready to take me to the ER! The nurse told her to make me some coffee. Easy fix, except for one problem: Coug was not a coffee drinker. Her husband, a coffee connoisseur, had equipped his kitchen with an espresso contraption.

While she was figuring out how to make coffee, I was of little help, because I was strapped into the continuous-passive-motion machine, a device that helps improve circulation and decrease swelling. With my head throbbing, as I tried to help her, we were soon laughing so hard I had tears, not from pain but hysterics. Well, maybe both.

The sludge she concocted worked, and my headache disappeared.

Later in the week, I found out that Justin had a phone where he was staying in Denali. His partner called his wife every night. She called me and, unknowingly, told me this. She was furious with Justin for telling me there was no communication from the field.

The next morning, I called Justin's supervisor, Joseph. I informed him of what had happened to me and the coordination it required for surgery because Justin could not take time off from the Denali Soil Project. He was quiet.

"I had no idea. If I had known, Michelle, I would have found a replacement. He never said a thing."

Justin had not told anyone about my accident. I thought no one cared; instead, the truth was that no one knew. Except his family; they knew, because he went home.

The next day, Coug and her husband dropped me off at Jules', who would take care of me the second week. I was so grateful to have such caring and loving friends. Jules took me to see my surgeon, and, after two weeks, Justin picked me up and took me home.

To feel so helpless and vulnerable was a difficult situation for me. I did not dare say a word to him about what I'd found out. There would be no benefit; it was not worth the risk. He would likely only get angry. My goal was to get my body strong; mentally, writing was my salvation.

The following spring, I had the surgery on my right knee. This time, I knew to have the anti-nausea medicine in my IV. Justin took me to the surgery, waited, and took me to Coug's, where we both stayed the night.

The insurance agency, as required, sent me to a "specialist" in Seattle to be evaluated for a disability rating. The hotel was in the red-light quarter; it had a push-button lock that rarely worked, judging from the scrapes on the door. You could rent a room by the hour or the day!

Normally, I was a strong person. But, now, I had two full leg braces, I kept a light on, put a chair against the door, and stayed in my clothes. All night.

Finally, after two years, I was ready for a different surgeon. A friend in the rafting business recommended another surgeon to me.

He is not only a wonderful human being with a bedside manner that reflects his culture but also a superb orthopedic surgeon. He looked at my X-rays and commented that the bone loss from the staph infection in my left knee was healing. I thought, *So, it was an infection, just as my PT had suggested.* The surgeon, however, said the pain and stiffness were a result of me not doing my exercises.

In 1999, when the director of the Plant Material Center in Palmer, Alaska, asked if I was interested in developing a native plant-restoration program, I said, "Yes!"

The job required developing protocols for propagating and cultivating native plants for restoration. The director was particularly interested in propagating wetland plants—a challenge I was excited to take on.

Another challenge was addressing the ease of abandonment by Justin after my accident. After a year of therapy, the therapist strongly recommended I leave. She said his behavior would not get better but, very likely, worse.

I applied to two positions and got an offer for both. One was in Bend, Oregon, as the Eastern Director for Wetland Restoration. The other one was in Anchorage, Alaska, for the Agency as a field manager.

It was incomprehensible to me why Justin treated me the way he did. I drew up a new quit-claim deed to transfer my one-fifth back to Justin. My plan was to load what I could in my car and drive to Oregon with my faithful and elderly cat. I wanted nothing to do with the house—*or* the man.

When Justin came back from the field, I sat with him on the front deck and told him about the two job offers. It astonished me when his eyes welled with tears as he told me not to leave. I told him I didn't want to work in Anchorage for the Agency. He could transfer to Oregon. Of course, that would not work for him.

"We will make it work—whatever you need," he said.

The truth was, emotionally, it would have been easier to walk away from him. But, all things considered, it would be more difficult for me, considering the accident, worker's compensation, and my need for some normalcy.

I desperately needed normalcy, especially for Chessy. I was not ready to run simply because Justin had no ability to communicate.

While the warnings from the therapist pounded in my brain, all I could think about was how sincere Justin was. His eyes watered! Logic went out the door. Maybe he really cared?

Chessy was so weak and fragile. I could not uproot her again, but I kept the deed as a reminder.

I decided to accept the offer as the field manager for the Anchorage and the Juneau field offices. It required renting an apartment in Anchorage and commuting every weekend. Life at home went back to status quo.

In 2003, I was offered the State Range Conservationist position, a lateral move, without a promotion—but the position was in Palmer. No more commute! I was excited and expected Justin to be as well. He was not and didn't want me to accept it. I did anyway.

A few weeks later, I got a call from the State Conservationist informing me to apply for the position when the announcement came out. She apologized for the confusion and encouraged me to apply.

It was odd. I asked the human resources person in the administrative office when I could expect to be transferred to Palmer. She replied that the paperwork was being processed and that they would let me know within the next week or two.

"If you want to back out, it's too late," the voice on the phone said. I had known her for years.

When word got out about the vacancy announcement, I received several phone calls encouraging me not to apply for the job, all from other agencies and nonprofits. They all made me smile and feel valued.

I did not apply for the State Range Conservationist position. I do not understand why; maybe I was pissed because it was originally an actual offer—not just a notice of a job opening. I felt manipulated. Had someone convinced the State Conservationist differently? It was not a promotion, so a vacancy announcement was not required, so why would she change her mind? Or was it a *who* and not a *why*?

Deep down, maybe I was not ready to leave the projects and the people I was working with.

And one of those projects was training employees from consulting companies, agencies, and our own employees, in wetland science.

It was during one of the sessions that I got a call from a neighbor. She told me I should come home. Although I had been gone only three days, Chessy was very thin and wobbly. I held her all night and through the morning, calling every vet I knew. No one would come out to Sutton. The thought of taking her to town was devastating for me. She went to town only when she went to the vet. She hated it.

I told her she could go; I would be fine. And then, Huntman showed up. He looked at me holding Chessy.

"It's time, Michelle."

We got in his truck and went to the emergency clinic in Wasilla. Huntman did the paperwork, but he, too, was crying; he'd known Chessy since I'd gotten her in 1982. I held her in my arms as she passed. When we got home, Huntman dug a hole in front of the house—a place with a view, where we sat, cried, drank beer, and said goodbye.

I called Justin that night, who was at Denali, working.

"She was fine when I left," he said quietly, his voice breaking.

But she wasn't, as they had to take her out of my arms to insert the IV because her veins had already collapsed. Then I had to call Flo. And then DG.

Chessy was 22.

In 2004, Nigel "offered" me the field-manager position for the Palmer office and the statewide toolkit coordinator position for the Agency. Again, it was a lateral transfer, not requiring a vacancy announcement because it was not a promotion.

The same person who had offered me the range job also said I should apply for the toolkit position. He supervised both positions, but when he found out one had been added as a collateral position, with Nigel supervising the position, he transferred out of state a few months later.

Both positions should have been in Palmer, but Nigel required me to be in the Wasilla field office at least three days a week. And still, I accepted it. At least I could be home every night!

Nigel, always devious, had proposed the toolkit coordinator position, which should have been a stand-alone position, as a *collateral position* in the position description. If, at any time, the statewide-toolkit position, a GS-12, was offered to someone else, it would leave me with a field-manager position, normally a GS-12, but without supervisory duties. Nigel could, theoretically, demote me to a GS-11.

Rather than sign the acceptance of the above position as dictated by Nigel, I only accepted the position as a GS-12 statewide toolkit coordinator with a collateral position as the field manager for Palmer.

Apparently, this pissed off certain individuals in the state office, especially Nigel, and the target on my back just got bigger.

CHAPTER 26

A New Beginning

A marriage proposal? After all these years? I was curious, but there was usually a reason when Justin did something so astounding!

My patience had been tested these last few years, and I had struggled about my decision to return to the Agency. The proposal followed a turbulent beginning with them.

On my first day, in August 2001, the State Conservationist (the head of the Agency in Alaska) directed me to discipline my "young" employee, whom I had never met. Young? He was in his late 30s, and a single dad with a young daughter with fetal alcohol syndrome (FAS)—a rampant birth defect in indigenous villages. He also wore a very large chip on his shoulder. He was caught using a government credit card for personal business, two years prior.

Then on New Year's in 2002, my employee took the government vehicle for his own use, which required me to begin the suspension process. This was after I had given him a raise; he was smart, but he was in a no-win situation with the Agency. I also approved a two-week vacation, so he could take his daughter to Disneyland.

In February, he went AWOL, never returning to work after his vacation. I tried to find him, so I called his sister. She said he was very angry, and, tentatively, she was worried for my safety. She explained her brother had expected the field-manager position and blamed me for taking it away from him. I told her I wished to God he had gotten it and not me.

I called Federal Protection. Luckily, he resigned, and, for the first time since I'd taken the job, I felt a sense of relief. However, it was short-lived as a series of consequences soon followed.

The State Conservationist quickly transferred back to the state he'd come from. He was replaced by a State Conservationist who'd been pressured to leave her state after a cryptic disagreement with the State Resource Board. As fate would have it, she was the one who'd promoted Nigel to the state office, which was a shock to all of us. None of us remembered seeing a vacancy announcement for the position, usually required when promoting an employee to a new position.

In early spring of 2002, I received a call from the chair of the Anchorage resource area. He was also on the state and national board of the organization, as he made his importance clear to me. He inquired about a wetland determination for his property, which had been done by Kenny in the summer of 2001.

"You should have gotten a copy from Kenny right after the determination was completed. Why are you waiting until now?"

"You need to fix it. I hired you, and now I own your ass," he chuckled.

"The only person who owns this ass is me. And you did not hire me. Now that I am aware of the determination, I assure you, I most definitely will look in your casefile right after I hang up on you."

Shocked at what I read in the report, I called the State Soil Scientist. Joseph became silent.

"You knew about this?"

"Everyone knew about it, including management staff from the regional office in Spokane. We had a program review at his property. We were told to avoid it."

Joseph explained what had happened. It made sense now; my professional wetland certification was highlighted on the State Conservationist's copy of my resume. No wonder he'd transferred to another state so quickly.

"I can feel the crosshairs on my neck," Joseph commented.

"Yeah—me, too."

I had previously relayed to him what my new employee said when she was at the landowner's property. He had made quite a spectacle about showing her his arsenal. Then, he implied what would happen to me if I got involved with his wetland determination report.

This action prompted a second call to Federal Protection.

That night, as I studied the nuances of the Food Security Act, I contemplated that fateful day when I'd declined the position in Oregon.

All for a GS-11? What the hell was I thinking? I mused as I drank my second cup of coffee at midnight. The next morning, I called the State of Oregon, just in case the position they'd offered me was still open. It was not.

Not one person in the Agency lost their job or were suspended over the collusion to cover up the wetland violation. The one person who *should* have been held accountable received not one but *many* performance awards, including merit awards, for excellence. How naïve I was! He told me later that he was doing what he was told to do; in exchange, he was rewarded for that loyalty.

Our new State Conservationist recommended an outside audit of books for the Anchorage resource area—and she was promptly transferred out of Alaska. Coincidently, the resource chair left for Panama.

A few months later, a man with a long career with the Agency who had submitted his retirement papers, asked for and got the position in Alaska. His retirement papers were torn up, and the Agency went from unbelievable to dysfunctional distress.

It was during this transition in 2004 that I was transferred to the Wasilla office and Justin asked me to marry him. When he opened the small, velvet box, I was stunned. I was standing in the kitchen, my hands dripping soapy water on the floor, staring at the most beautiful rings. This was not a man who strolls into a jewelry store and buys a ring—much less an engagement and wedding ring. He was giddy!

After all his years of indecision and lack of commitment? Hell, the lack of emotional connection to me? Was this real?

The accident—I must be in a coma, I thought. It was the only logical thing that made sense. I was dizzy from trying to keep up with him—the Russian Roulette of Justin.

Then he said, "My dream job will soon be open! The guy is finally retiring. If I want it, he'll make sure I get it."

"In Lincoln?"

"Yeah."

Was he asking me to marry him because of a job? Of course, he was! It was Justin.

"Yes. I will marry you."

CHAPTER 27

Down the Road, Again

The future of agriculture in the Palmer area was under threat. What were once fields of hay, with the most important soils in the state, were now covered with houses. Farmers, after working the ground in a harsh environment, were selling their land for more money than they could ever make at farming.

For a handful of us, it became our goal to protect the quickly disappearing farmland in Palmer. I teamed up with an outgoing employee for the Palmer resource office and with an entity whose director wanted to expand into agricultural easements, later known as The Alaska Farmland Trust. The borough assembly, for the first time, were receptive to protecting farmland.

Joseph and I tried for a year to get agricultural soils of importance listed for the state, only to fail each time. An inside person and friend within the Division of Agriculture showed me a copy of our proposal, with defensive comments: ". . . this is an attempt to lock up land from development."

And then LeRoi walked through the Palmer field office door. He had the passion, the courage, and the vision to protect his forty acres of farmland for future generations. Eventually, Alaska had its first conservation easement in the Farmland and Ranchland Protection Program.

Life in the field offices was tumultuous. The several field office managers across the state received a memorandum, requiring us to keep track of our time in fifteen-minute increments and file a report each Friday with what we had accomplished for the week. We were the only group of employees who had received such a memorandum.

I met with the State Conservationist to discuss his memorandum. He was from Alabama, and he played his role like a well-seasoned actor—his southern charm rolled up with more than forty-five years with the Agency. I asked him how I could improve. He looked confused as I showed him the memorandum he'd signed, which had been sent only to his field office managers, the bread and butter for the Agency.

He glanced at it and threw it on the floor.

"You want me to ignore a memorandum from you?"

He told me he never saw the memorandum—although he'd signed it.

A week later, at a meeting, he informed us that he would supervise the field managers.

The target on my back got bigger with that decision.

It was all show. Nigel was never far from the management decisions over the field offices.

During a performance review, Nigel told me I was too passionate about my job.

Nigel had been a field office manager for many years in Delta. It made me wonder.

This would be one of many memoranda from the State Conservationist.

One late Friday afternoon, as I was leaving, I received a phone call from Nigel demanding I send a list of my workload for the next month, before the end of the day! He apparently had received a request from the field manager in Delta saying that she needed help, and he was going to send me!

I called the chair of the Palmer resource board and let him know that the state office was sending me to Delta for a month. I mentioned to him that I would not be available for any field-office help, including assistance with the planning database, which two of his employees were learning.

And then I made a call to Delta to find out what kind of help the field manager was requesting. She knew nothing about a request. A young, dynamic, assertive, and smart woman with a master's degree, she always stood her ground. And so, she, too, had a target on her back.

I never went to Delta.

A couple of years later, she resigned after her hair started falling out from the years of harassment. The nail in the coffin, after spending hours and hours of time, one of many administrative assistants had been tasked with going through the Delta field office gas receipts.

Their goal was to accuse the manager of using the government vehicle credit card for purchasing fuel for her personal vehicle. When they accused her and the State Conservationist was ready to fire her, she responded with one small detail that the toadies had failed to address: her vehicle was a diesel truck. The vehicles in her command were not diesel.

Around 2006, Nigel told me a new employee had been hired who would take over my duties as the toolkit coordinator. They had transferred him, his "stay-at-home" wife, and his two home-schooled daughters, from Saipan to Alaska.

They closed the Palmer field office and reassigned me to the Wasilla field office, 39 miles from my home. A reassignment of more than 40 miles required an official reassignment.

What's next? I wondered.

Then I received an amazing phone call from the State Resource Conservationist (SRC) a couple of weeks later. He had a proposition for me.

The Soil Program Manager, Joseph, whom the State Conservationist had promoted to a GS-14 (and Justin to a GS-13 regional soil scientist), found himself in a difficult situation. After 25 years of neglect, a new mandate required every soil survey to include interpretations for ecological sites.

The dilemma for Joseph? It was the responsibility of the resource specialists under the SRC to develop the interpretations. This is the primary responsibility of the State Range Conservationist—it was why I'd been asked to take a lateral move into the position by the previous SRC.

I listened to the SRC's summary of the regional ecologist duties.

"Let me get this right," I said, trying to choose my words carefully. "You want me to take over the ecological-site duties of the range conservationist, the biologist, the agronomist, the forester, and the resource soil scientist?"

Then I added, not waiting for an answer, "At the same pay grade, even though the regional soil scientist position is a GS-13?"

I shook my head in amazement, but I said, "Yes."

I found out later that Joseph and the SRC had made a deal that half the salary would come out of the soil program's budget. This was not unique, because someone always transferred money between and among programs every year in the battle of the budget game.

Although I had to develop a program that previously failed to succeed in the Agency, I was excited because the regional ecologist position would be the culmination of my 30 years of field expertise and educational degrees.

By the summer of 2008, I'd developed an ecological-site training program for soil scientists and plant ecologists. Protocols and procedures, more than 100 documents, were written and posted; equipment was ordered, and implementation was started for the five soil surveys across the state. I accomplished this in less than 6 months.

Joseph called me into his office one morning. He said, "I would like you to prepare and present a strategy on ecological sites for the Western Soils Conference in Spokane."

It was the first time in my career with the Agency that they had given me a chance like that. I responded, "I assume you discussed this with my supervisor?"

Joseph nodded "Yes," but then he got quiet, and looked down at his desk. I knew this look all too well.

He explained that the regional soil scientist was not thrilled that *I* was going to the conference and *he* wasn't.

"So, send Justin. I have no problem with that. He is the regional soil scientist, at a GS-13," I smirked.

Joseph said he was only sending one person for this meeting.

"He'll get over it," he said.

In 2009, after a technical review by the national soil program leaders from DC, they were so impressed at what we accomplished in the ecological-site program that they proposed and then implemented it throughout the United States. There was continued resistance from the range science—the same resistance I'd encountered between 1982 and 1986.

To assist the national effort in this transition, Joseph submitted the 100 technical reports, white papers, and support documentation I developed. He also sent my position description, along with a copy of a proposed multi-relational database we had been working on for correlating soils, vegetation, and wetland interpretations.

During my performance review, my boss said he'd nominated me for a Merit Award, one of the highest at a local level. As he looked away, he somberly told me that Nigel had refused the request.

"Why was it up to him?"

No answer needed. He looked at me and apologized.

"I don't know how you do everything you do. You are never late with an assignment. You come early and leave late. You take everything in stride, including Nigel's assignment of the acting cultural resources position to you." Then he said in a serious voice, "You need to not work so hard. It makes others look bad."

I got up and went outside. I will never forget the depth of emptiness I felt as I remembered the words my dad always said to me.

As I watched our State Conservationist stumble from his vehicle in the parking lot, with a shit-eating grin on his flushed face, I knew it could only mean one thing. I stood there as he approached, slurring his words as he spoke to me. I turned and walked away.

In the fall of 2009, the head of the regional soil program retired, and the State Conservationist promoted Justin to be the soil leader for the state. I was proud of him. How could I fathom the ultimate ramifications of this promotion? Could Justin?

After Chessy died, it was too difficult to get another cat. Cat-less, we were free to travel without worry, until the red-back voles invaded my strawberry and vegetable garden with a vengeance. Every beautiful, plump red strawberry had tiny chew marks. Slender shoots of broccoli, radish, and spinach were grazed to the ground. We needed a cat.

On a sail trip with friends on their boat on July 4, 2010, we stopped in Seldovia. I noticed a woman sitting near the bow, flanked by two large mounds of fur. They looked like baby muskox. I stopped and asked her what kind of cats she had. She told me they were Maine Coons, both male.

A friend who fostered at a local cat rescue told me there was a Maine Coon kitten, so I checked the place out. Among the many kittens, there was this little ball of multicolored gray, black, and white fur, with a long, wooly tail. The four furry feet looked like those of a lynx, and her eyes were emerald green. There was a very tiny orange-and-black kitten with a stubby tail, jumping on her sibling, sending them both rolling.

Justin and I took them both, even though the owner was hesitant when we selected the tiny orange kitten with the stubby tail.

At home, they sprang off the back of the couch, nearly hitting Justin in the head. We sat in the living room as these fur balls used us as launching pads.

"What were we thinking?" Justin exclaimed, drinking a beer.

He named the dark kitten "Nitro," because she was fast. The orange kitten, he called "Cricket" because she jumped like her namesake. They loved being outside, and there was no way we could keep them indoors. They went out during the day when we were home and came in every night, even if it meant me looking for them at dusk into the wee morning hours.

One day, as the snow was melting, Nitro came home with a baby snowshoe hare in her mouth, almost as big as she was. She was so proud, but it left us backtracking her prints in the snow to find where the baby had come from. She loved showing us her catch of the day, while Cricket was a hunter who ate what she caught.

These two provided comfort and companionship, and proved to be loving. Nitro, Maine Coon, but Cricket? Her stubby tail, which we thought had frozen when she was a kitten, and her stocky stature, with feather-like fur, confirmed her bloodline was Russian Kurilian Bobtail. Two totally different personalities—same mom but different dads.

These cats filled the void I had been feeling since Chessy died. Life at home and work was improving, because, in 2010, five regional ecologists were to be hired across the United States. The Office of Personnel Management (OPM) evaluated the ecologist positions, as a GS-13. Finally, I would get a promotion. Maybe my dad was right?

Besides my current role, the National Range Conservationist and National Soil Program leader asked me to assist in the program's transition. When the National Range Conservationist called to tell me, he thought I would be thrilled. He asked me, "What's up?"

"I wish the leadership would have announced these out of Lincoln and not left it up to the State Cons. Big mistake. My position still has not been announced. I keep asking when, and all I am told is, 'It will be later.'"

I had relayed my concern to him a year ago that our State Conservationist was not supportive of my position.

In August 2010, an administrative person took me aside. She told me to talk to my boss, before he transferred to Idaho, about the status of the regional ecologist position in Alaska. She'd heard from an excellent source that, as soon as he left, the State Conservationist was planning to remove me as the regional ecologist.

The agronomist was the leverage to do that. They offered her the SRC position, a promotion. In exchange for that promotion, she would remove me from my position.

I waited while my boss was busy on the phone. Then I decided to have a chat with the agronomist. In that conversation, I confided in her that Nigel had told me I would not get the GS-13 promotion. I waited for her response.

Her expression told me what I already knew.

She stammered, "I know, Michelle. I am so sorry. The State Conservationist said he would not have a GS-13 ecologist." Tears formed in her eyes.

I sat down in my supervisor's office and asked him why he'd never let me know the State Conservationist would never hire a GS-13 ecologist. He said he knew nothing about this situation. I looked at him and asked, "If you knew nothing, then why does your agronomist know?" Dumbfounded, he shook his head.

He met with Justin and the State Conservationist and was informed there would not be a GS-13 ecologist, but he promised nothing else would change. I would keep my position. There was not much I could do, as the other ecologist positions had been filled.

In December 2010, two weeks before Christmas, they removed me from my position as regional ecologist. My new supervisor gave me the reason.

"That is ridiculous. We are two single individuals."

She had a statement ready. "Yes, but you live together."

I was removed because the Agency considered Justin and me married. That was interesting, because I had tried to get on Justin's federal health insurance plan when I was in graduate school. I was making a point at the time, when Justin refused to commit, and it was costing me more than $5000 for health insurance. The administrative office for the Agency told me I did not qualify because Justin and I were not married. We were living in sin, but we were not married.

My new supervisor could not look at me as I got up and said, "I hope the GS-13 is worth it."

I reached out to program leaders in DC, but it was the Christmas holidays, and no one was around except for one woman, who was part of the soil program review team. I explained what happened. She was speechless, but she got right on it, just as I thought she'd do.

After a month, the director of soils got hold of me. His response, ". . . there is no conflict. The SRC can supervise. We have at least one female ecologist who was hired, and her husband is the soil leader." I let him know the SRC had always supervised me.

I called the EEO Division, where I learned there was nothing I could do after a 45-day window, except mediation. With the Christmas holidays, and waiting on the decision by the soil program leader, the 45-day window had expired.

My only recourse was mediation.

And the marriage proposal? A couple months after he proposed, Justin found out his dream job was not such a dream. The previous occupant spent his time traveling and sampling soils all over the world. The job was in the lab analyzing the soil samples, so he decided not to take the job.

After endless attempts at "proposing" a wedding date, two of my girlfriends tried their hardest to persuade him: "Just show up," they said, "and we will do the rest."

Marriage can be wonderful, but it is a team sport. If Justin wanted to get married to me, he would. Should I surprise him with a Justice of the Peace? I did not dare.

CHAPTER 28

Trials and Tribulations

M*ediation was an inconvenience.* The air of superiority in the room and the aloofness of the man on the other end of the phone line was appalling. It was also well scripted.

I imagined the man on the phone, the State Conservationist's boss, at headquarters, lying on a couch, in a suit, taking a nap. Or maybe enjoying a late lunch.

The mediator was sharp and well-seasoned. He was from the National Park Service (NPS), as the Agency had no one available.

"Why was I removed from my position?"

"You know why."

"No, I do not. Explain."

"There was a conflict."

"According to who, and where is that written?"

"Headquarters."

"Could you explain, please?" I asked the man on the other end of the line. Dead silence.

Finally, after the mediator asked a few times to respond, he finally answered. *Did he really step out of the mediation?* I thought to myself.

Of course, he agreed with what the State Conservationist said, word for word. It went on like this until we took a break for lunch.

The mediator was stunned. He could not believe what he had witnessed.

"They're doing this to someone like you? This makes no sense. NPS never would have done this to an employee of your caliber."

After lunch, as we sat in the room, I glanced at the mediator and smiled. He shook his head.

At the end of the mediation, I signed the mediation agreement form. The agreed-to items were a joke, and we all knew it. And so did the Equal Employment Opportunity Commission (EEOC), as they rejected the mediation agreement and required a second mediation. The Agency delayed the second mediation for nearly six months.

At the end of the second mediation, I refused to sign the agreement. It was obvious that this process was exactly what I was warned it would be: a joke. I was also warned it would cost me, and it did.

The director of the soils program did respond to the State Conservationist's refusal to hire a GS-13 regional ecologist. He eliminated the regional status of the soil program in Alaska and included it with three states in the west. The State Conservationist lost the soils-program positions, and, most importantly, he lost the money the soils program received each year.

It made no sense to me. Why not just hire a GS-13 regional ecologist for Alaska out of headquarters?

In 2010, Justin began storing large Styrofoam blocks in the garage. He said a friend who worked at Lowes had asked him to store them for him.

In May, he was using a post-hole digger and strategically laying out holes on the ten acres next door that he'd bought. When the parcel came open, I was excited. Justin always wanted this parcel, and it would be a perfect birthday gift for him. I was surprised when the current owners said he'd already purchased it.

I asked him what he was doing.

"Why do you think what I do is always of your concern?"

His anger was real. Did he hold me responsible for the loss of the soil region in Alaska?

In fact, since 2002, while working as the field office manager in Anchorage, I was asked to be a member of the Alaska wetland supplement team. The work I performed to develop national guidance for the determination of jurisdictional wetlands within the state of Alaska provided me with national recognition as an expert in the field of wetland science.

In 2004, I was assigned to a national interagency hydrophytic-vegetation team. I was ecstatic and humbled. As a member of the team, I had the opportunity to exchange expert knowledge with professional scientists. The knowledge I gained was invaluable for my duties in Alaska.

I remained on both teams until the State Conservationist removed me in 2013.

Isolating a person is a well-known strategy, stripping a person of knowledge, dignity, and respect. It was cruel, and it was intentional.

When the rumor spread that the resources staff was being eliminated, I applied for the national wetland coordinator position after the state engineer informed me that it was open; he strongly encouraged me to apply.

Justin returned from the field after two weeks in late August. Two of his staff members joined him to hunt moose behind the house. Afterward, they hung out, having a few beers. The next morning, Justin was not feeling well and stayed home—something he rarely did.

On Friday, he saw a doctor and called me at work to pick up a prescription for him. As I was leaving, I made the mistake of answering the phone. It was the director of the ecology program in DC. She was asking me if I wanted the wetland coordinator position.

She insisted I give her an answer right then. I said I couldn't do that but that she could call me next week, at her convenience.

Saturday morning, Justin was admitted to the hospital with a twisted intestine. Curled in a small chair, I did not leave his hospital room except to run home to change and put the cats on feeders. On Sunday night, they operated on him. He was lucky, as the intestine showed no signs of gangrene. I spent the night in the chair, and the next morning, I went to work directly from the hospital.

The first thing I did was meet with our human resources coordinator about the strange phone call I'd received on Friday.

She looked at me and told me to take the position in DC.

"He removed your name from the required beneficiary form in early August when he submitted his retirement paperwork."

"You had no right telling me that," I said as I left her office.

I called the woman on the phone in DC and accepted the position.

After Justin got out of the hospital, I confronted him about the beneficiary form. His eyes spoke the truth, although his words did not. He said my information must be mistaken—he said he hadn't made any changes.

A couple days later, he gave me a copy of his "new" beneficiary form with his signature and me as his designated beneficiary.

It was not signed by the administration officer, so it was not certified. Another subterfuge, but this time I didn't fall for it. But I didn't understand it. I could not fathom what I had done.

During the next four months, my life was hell. I could not eat. I could not sleep. Every second of the day was spent trying to get the paperwork for my transfer to headquarters. My hell went something like this:

Out of the blue, I was offered a position in DC as a GS-13 wetland coordinator. The position was currently held by a GS-15 who teleworked daily from another state and was retiring. He recommended me for the position. He later apologized to me.

I accepted the position, and my future supervisor informed me that I had to be in DC by the first week of January. She informed me that they would approve only minimal moving expenses—no mover expenses and no shipping or driving of a vehicle. However, I could snail-mail personal belongings.

During this time, I spent endless hours trying to find a place to live near headquarters on a GS-13 wage, with no vehicle. With a deadline date looming, there still was no transfer agreement from headquarters. I could do nothing more until that paperwork was completed.

After a few dozen phone calls, I finally found a person who sent me not the official transfer paperwork but a moving request form, to estimate the cost of my move.

Coincidently, the State Conservationist appeared early one morning and told me to be sure to list Justin as my spouse on the paperwork.

So, I did.

A week later, I signed a one-year lease at a cost of $23,000 for an apartment within biking distance or a short metro ride to the office. I let my new supervisor know I'd met my obligation. At the same time, I called the department secretary and asked her where and how I was to mail my boxes for my move to DC. I still did not have my transfer paperwork, but I decided to push the process ahead. I was tired of getting the runaround.

After a few minutes of silence, she asked, "What move?"

As I explained, there was more silence. Then she said the position had been terminated.

An hour later, the Alaska administrator officer received a fax that said that the position had been terminated.

The State Conservationist, a smile on his face, leered, "Guess you are out of a job?"

I smiled. I had kept my end of the agreement; they had not.

This time I knew the procedure, and I filed an informal grievance against the woman who hired me in DC, and then I waited. There was no response. The next step was to elevate the informal grievance to a formal grievance, which goes to the Chief of the Agency. Again, no response.

An employee cannot file a grievance and file an EEO complaint at the same time, so on day 44, I withdrew the formal grievance and filed a complaint with the EEO. Then I called an attorney in DC.

Meanwhile, Justin retired, along with six other employees, three of them on the resources staff.

A few months later, the agronomist and I received a memorandum informing us of our reassignment to the Wasilla field office in two weeks. If we did not show, we would be considered AWOL, with the possible consequences of removal.

On the first day, my new boss, the field manager for the Wasilla field office, informed me that my one-day-a-week telework agreement had been terminated. He also informed me that, because I had been falsifying my time sheet under the flex-schedule—the same schedule I had worked my entire career with the Agency, with no problems—the flex-schedule was also being terminated.

He informed me that I had to work five days a week, eight hours a day, which would require me driving 80 miles a day for work.

My previous boss, the SRC, apparently had been informed of my alleged falsification of time sheets by the human resources person. However, she called bullshit and refused to do anything, including telling me. She knew it was a witch hunt.

In response, for her disloyalty, she lost her staff. After talking with her, she told me to call the telework coordinator in DC.

During the conversation, the national telework coordinator said any employee without a conduct or performance issue can work a telework agreement. Apparently, she made a stink about what was happening to me. It started to make sense as I dug deeper into the shit. They had to find a conduct issue where there was none.

The following Monday morning, I received a warning of suspension from the State Conservationist for contacting headquarters.

Then the field offices received a copy of a memorandum stating that no individual can contact anyone outside their line of command in Alaska. The consequences of such an action were suspension or removal. The memorandum was signed by the State Conservationist.

Also, my knees were excruciatingly painful; driving to work every day and sitting at a computer was wreaking havoc on those joints. I saw my surgeon. This time, he said it was time for knee replacement—not one, but both.

Before I left his office, he had my worker's compensation form completed and faxed a reasonable accommodation form to the Reasonable Accommodation coordinator at headquarters. After knowing my surgeon for more than 17 years, I confided in him that I was not allowed to contact anyone in my agency outside of my supervisor.

I drove back from Anchorage, feeling anxious and worried about having both my knees done at the same time. I walked into the office, where I was immediately assaulted with angry words from the secretary.

"You finally did it!"

I calmed her down as she told me the State Conservationist was going to suspend me because I'd contacted headquarters.

"Really? I never contacted anyone at headquarters."

It was the truth; my surgeon had, but I had not.

Instead of worrying about the surgery, I was pissed. So, I did exactly what they accused me of doing—I called the Reasonable Accommodation coordinator.

When I hung up the phone, my supervisor called me into his office. In his need to prove his authority over me, he had spoken with the State Conservationist, who was going to suspend me. But there was a chance that he would let me take 12 weeks of sick leave during my recovery.

We will fucking see about that, I thought, as I watched this asshole try to intimidate me.

My surgery was scheduled for mid-September, and the Reasonable Accommodation coordinator had the paperwork signed, sealed, and delivered before she went on maternity leave.

I received Reasonable Accommodation, teleworking from home. Incidentally, at the same time, I was offered a four-month detail assignment in DC with the Conservation Easement program. I would only need a month of working from home—if the surgery went well.

One small detail I neglected to tell anyone was that my surgeon required me not to be alone while in DC. He assumed Justin was going to be with me.

After surgery, I woke up in the rehabilitation wing for orthopedic surgery patients, a private room with a guest bed, where Justin could sleep. The first night after surgery, the nurses woke me every 20 minutes, as my blood oxygen was dropping critically low. Justin had gotten no sleep, so he went back home.

A couple hours later, I was walking. The physical therapist helped me walk down a flight of stairs, and we entered the reception room of the rehab clinic. I was feeling dizzy, and I must have

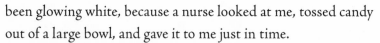

been glowing white, because a nurse looked at me, tossed candy out of a large bowl, and gave it to me just in time.

"Thank god you rescued the chocolate."

Finally, home, I walked our two-mile trail, slowly, and with my poles. And I was back to work, teleworking from home. My pitiful excuse for a boss demanded I keep my time in 15-minute intervals and to report what I accomplished every Friday. The good thing about pain medication? I really didn't care what the men in my life cared about. My only goal was to get strong, physically and mentally.

A month later, Justin and I arrived in DC the day before Veterans Day, after a grueling 18 hours of traveling. Blood clots, even a month after surgery, can be another complication and a major concern for my surgeon.

Once I settled into my office, I needed to thank the two women who helped me—the reasonable accommodation and the telework-program coordinators.

As I chatted with the Reasonable Accommodation woman, I mentioned that my supervisor required me to keep my time in 15-minute increments and do weekly reports.

Her eyes got big. "I told your State Conservationist, as well as that jerk supervisor, that they cannot discriminate. That State Con of yours actually told me I had no authority over him."

Next, I met with the telework coordinator, and she expressed similar issues with the idiots in Alaska. She informed me she was retiring. She could no longer do her job because she continually was forced to implement protocols outside the rules of her position.

I thought of her words as I walked down one of the many, dismal, vacant hallways, back to my cubicle. At least, I really enjoyed the staff I worked with.

My life revolved around work and physical therapy. Slowly, I could see some hints of muscle starting to appear on my skinny legs. Sometimes I would meet a couple friends for a drink or hang with my co-workers for a beer at a local bar they visited. My weekends were spent reading in the Botanical Gardens Atrium, admiring art, visiting the free zoo, while watching the pandas play in the snow. And I always visited a new museum every weekend.

A few weeks before my detail ended, I made an appointment with one last person. I asked him to keep our conversation private. He was a coordinator for employee and human resources and was involved with developing the manual on administrative procedures.

As I sat down, I pulled out a large binder containing several documents, including my time sheets over the last few years. I asked him to show me what I'd done wrong in recording my time.

I patiently waited. Then he shook his head, took his glasses off, and rubbed his eyes. I gave him a list of my accomplishments and what had happened to me since December 2010.

He confirmed what I already knew, but I needed to hear it. There was no discrepancies or inaccuracies with any time sheet from 2010 until 2015.

I showed him every performance appraisal. All were at the highest level of performance, with no conduct issues in my entire career. I also showed him references and recommendations especially in regards to the position as regional ecologist. One was from one of the soil scientists I worked with who had quit after what happened to me.

I had every right to work a telework and a flex schedule. Everything I showed him supported the harassment and sexual discrimination I had endured for the last ten years.

There was never a conduct issue recorded. He also knew about my current EEO complaint as well.

And there was no merit to remove me from my ecologist position, even if I had been married to the leader of the soils program for Alaska. Of interest, my current supervisor in DC was the program leader, and, yet, her husband was on her team. He was supervised by another person, but he was on her team.

And his next comment surprised me.

"After that civil rights fiasco he was involved in, he should have retired."

I looked at him and said, "You know about that? And yet, this man has ruined the lives and careers of good, hard-working, productive employees like me? I am on the Civil Rights Team. He directed us to sign a form that we had approved the closing of the remote field offices, after the fact. All of us on that team refused to sign the form. It was a damn civil rights violation against two villages!" I was pissed. "Retired? Him and his followers deserve to be fired."

"He is that powerful."

"No one in this agency should be that powerful," I spewed.

"I'm sorry. You did nothing wrong in any of this," he said.

"I know I didn't."

I thanked him for his time, and I left the office. I was so mad; tears were falling down my cheeks. I walked to my Senator's office, where I met with a staff member. I explained the situation, and then I made a request.

"There are more than 3,000 civil rights and EEO complaints in this Agency, a cost to the taxpayer. The process benefits no one, and it helps incompetent, bad people stay in charge."

I continued, "They simply move them up the food chain. I am asking for a Bill that prohibits internal manipulation of EEO complaints within an Agency. I expect nothing on my behalf, but we can prevent hard-working, passionate, smart public servants from being bullied and forced to leave. Isn't that worth it?"

Senators do not get involved in personnel issues. It wasn't worth it all.

The Agency paid the legal fees for my EEO complaint. I got $3,000, which was reported as income, so it was taxed. I signed another ridiculous agreement, listing most of my demands.

It was a battle I would not win, and, after ten years of persecution, I settled. Although the program leader of the ecological sciences division and her attorney said there was never an offer of a position, only an offer of interest, I had evidence that disputed that. I had a letter from headquarters, congratulating me on my new position, with the pay grade and start date. It did not matter.

I went back to Wasilla, and the first thing my jackass supervisor did was require me to record my time in 15-minute intervals during my one day a week of telework. I called the new telework coordinator and relayed what my supervisor was requiring me to do. She said he couldn't do that.

"Are you venting?" she asked me.

"No. I want you to do something about it."

"Are you sure? Because, it probably won't turn out so good for you."

"And I know that all too well. And your job is to correct the situation and make sure they understand the consequences to them for what they are doing to me."

"Do you want me to talk with your supervisor?"

"Yes. I do."

"Okay. This is a first."

I heard the screaming coming from his office. Then I got a phone call.

"He is one angry man. I am warning you to avoid him until he cools down. Do not go near him or into his office."

I think back on that discussion and the danger she'd put me in by not informing anyone else. She did not tell me to leave. She did not call Federal Protection. She did nothing.

A few weeks later, I received an email on a Sunday, from my boss. He was being transferred from Alaska to another state. However, in this email he informed me that the State Conservationist had assigned him as acting State Conservationist for the weekend, and in that capacity, he was reassigning me to the position he was vacating, the field manager for Wasilla.

He also stated in his email that he was ending my telework agreement and that I would have to drive to work every day. The throbbing began between my eyes.

On Monday, I called my attorney. He confirmed that an "acting" position can be assigned to an employee—but only if said employee agrees to the acting position. He also apologized for not listening to me. One of my demands was the right to telework, but he refused to list telework because it was already understood that it is a right for employees who meet the requirements.

Another one of my demands was I had the right to contact anyone in headquarters.

On Tuesday morning, the State Conservationist called me into his office. His southern charm could not mask the red face and the slurring of words. He told me he needed me to take the acting position in Wasilla.

"What would I get out it?"

"Nothing. I had hoped you would accept it."

"I do not."

"Well, too bad. I am assigning it to you."

I looked at him and didn't say a word. Then I smiled. "I am declining the position. And according to my lawyer, the only way you can force me to take it is—well, you can't."

His face got redder as he stood up. He then motioned for me to leave.

I waited, and only then did I get up and walk out the door, with a full-on nauseating migraine. I had applied for dozens of positions since 2011 in the federal government, but I was never selected. I retired January 1, 2017.

CHAPTER 29

The Last Adventure
of Us

Justin planned a retirement party on New Year's Eve. His Jekyll-and-Hyde behavior still shocked me. Around others, he did big, amazing things, but, with me, he was distant and moody. He planned this wonderful party, and I appreciated it, but he refused to give me what I wanted most: spending time with him.

Clearing the forest around the cabin, he created two enormous brush piles towering 30 feet high and 15 feet wide that he wanted to torch. My only request was to celebrate with neighbors and friends. It was a clear, chilly night with snow on the ground and a slight breeze, with embers twirling bright red toward the heavens, as the northern lights danced across the night sky. It was a new year, and I yearned for a new beginning. How many times had I said that?

As I hugged and laughed with friends, I watched Justin stoke the fire. He seemed happy, and yet, I felt such deep sadness.

For months, I had suggested a retirement-celebration trip. It would be my first vacation in a long time, and it would be one without the fears of retaliation at the end of the vacation. After his trip to China and Tibet in July, I reminded him to renew his passport, along with another pitch for a trip in January after I retired.

Every November, for the last 15 years, he went deer hunting on Kodiak Island. Nothing kept this group of guys from that trip. They planned almost a year in advance, and during that time, Justin spent hours every day shooting his bow.

Because of the *use or lose* annual leave policy, I always booked a trip in October, after the field season. I booked two weeks on Molokai, an Island of the Hawaiian chain we had never visited. He screamed at me for booking a trip without consulting him.

"What the hell," I said as I looked at him.

After that, I would ask him once, and if he was not interested in traveling, I started going on trips with friends in October.

The following year, after Molokai, I went with a girlfriend to Thailand, Cambodia, Laos, and Hong Kong. The October after that, to Morocco with another friend. We visited ruins in the Atlas Mountains, rode camels, and camped in the Sahara. As temperatures plummeted below 30 degrees, we all curled together in the Bedouin tents, nestled in layers of thick woolen blankets.

At night, we sat around a fire, drumming with our nomadic friends to keep warm. We saw amazing country and met some wonderful people and ended our trip riding the train from Marrakesh to Casablanca.

When I got home, Justin looked at me with a forlorn expression. He told me he would have liked to have gone to Morocco. Yes, he would have enjoyed it.

The next October, I asked Justin if he would like to do a trip. He did not want to, so I mentioned to a girlfriend I was researching small-boat travel in the Galapagos, but they required double occupancy. Shocked that Justin did not want to go with me, she said "Yes," and the trip was spectacular. And to see Darwin's Station? If only I had my copy of the book *The Origin of Species* with me.

We snorkeled through the arch with hundreds of hammerhead sharks below and booby birds diving into the water, nearly missing us. We had black sea iguanas and sea lions swimming around us, playing and feeding.

A month later, when I asked Justin if he would like to go on a winter vacation, he quickly said "Yes." And then he said he would like to go to the Galapagos. Stunned, I booked a trip—before he changed his mind—for late April, breakup time in Alaska. He loved it!

Finally, in 2016, Justin explained to me his rules for traveling. Apparently, I never gave him specifics. Instead of me asking him where we should go on vacation or where he would like to go, I needed to provide a place and a time. And then, he could decide if he wanted to go or not.

Knowing the travel rules, I proposed my retirement trip to Tanzania, Kenya, and Rwanda with a selection of dates for travel with a tour group I used for Peru.

He refused to commit. As spring turned into summer and summer into fall, he neither inquired nor responded when I asked.

It was the second week of November 2016, and he was leaving for Kodiak. When I got to work, I checked the tour-company website, something I did every morning. There was one slot left, so I called Justin as he was driving to Anchorage. He said "Yes."

The trip left the first week in February 2017.

Word spread in the office about my Africa trip, especially to Rwanda, and still, when I unwrapped my retirement gift, I fought back tears. It was a picture of this black ball of hair, with two bright eyes staring back, with the name Kundurwanda; my new, adopted baby gorilla. And she was in the Pablo Group.

Our administrative assistant knew I had adopted gorillas over the years, through the non-profit Dian Fossey Gorilla Fund International. She also remembered the name of a large silverback I had mentioned, Cantsabee, the leader of the Pablo group. This was one of the most special gifts I had ever received. Cantsabee was one of the few remaining gorillas that knew Dian. I had followed his activities for decades.

This trip required three visas, and Justin had not renewed his passport. I had to expedite his renewal and then each visa document. It was very expensive, even though the trip was very reasonable for three countries and a month of travelling, including the costs of the parks.

It was worth the effort. Our group was small and fun. As we traveled through Kenya, I noticed the impact and severity of droughts, leaving dying and dead cattle along burnt, brown rangeland. My new friend, Bonnie, an outgoing artist from California, whose husband had taken her on this trip as a gift, noticed tears in my eyes.

"What's wrong?" she whispered.

"I'll tell you later," I said. In fact, our guide asked me to explain what I'd seen later, at happy hour.

During a visit to a Masai village, we visited a one-room, plaster-sided school with no glass in the windows. Justin and I noticed immediately the words scribbled across the blackboard. The kids, aged 5–16, were learning about—and living with—climate change.

As one young, thin boy pointed, he said, "The snows no longer come."

He was pointing to Mt. Kilimanjaro, in the distance, whose summit stood bare, with only a few patches of white. Their tribe was suffering from the lack of water, with so little snow melt to feed the aquifer. These kids, with their one-room schoolhouse, built with the money by the nonprofit arm of the group we were travelling with, understood more about our world threat than most kids in the United States.

The Masai culture, where a man shows his wealth and power by the number of kids, the number of cattle, and the number of wives he owns, was the driver to overgrazing and starvation for both bovine and human.

During my travels to Africa, exploring more than 8 countries, and 7 trips over the last 25 years, not counting this one, I had never seen such a positive movement in women's rights as I was observing now. Not only in Kenya, but also in Tanzania and Rwanda.

In the Masai village, a few of the women expressed their feelings quietly to us women. They were tired of burying babies, and the jealousy among some of the younger wives was murderous. They wanted change.

There would be more than dying cattle, I murmured as we left the village, but I expected these women would succeed.

As we stood on the crater of Ngorongoro, I walked away from the group and took a plastic bag out of my pack. I slowly shook out the dusty contents, thinking no one would notice me. I turned as James, our guide, walked over and was sorry for my loss. Justin had told him. *Whew, I was unsure if what I was doing was a horrible offense.* It was my mom's wishes that, if I ever went to Tanzania, to spread her ashes there.

The hundreds, if not thousands, of zebras, gazelle, wildebeest, and buffalo migrate to the open grasslands of the Serengeti to give birth. It was breathtaking to watch, and the show did not end with the migrations.

We spotted this flicking tail, midway up the trunk of an umbrella tree. Slowly, our driver approached but kept a safe distance, so as not to disturb that flicking tail. We spotted the leopard sprawled along the lower branch. After 20 minutes, the leopard yawned, stood up, and half-crawled, half-jumped to the ground. Then he sauntered over to us and sat, looking up, half bored, half inquisitive, just like a domestic cat.

And then, he lifted his nose, got a scent, and wandered into the grass. About that time, there was a radio call about a leopard and a baboon. It threw me against the open top as the driver quickly sped off.

Two other land cruisers were stationary, as we slowly moved forward a couple hundred feet past them. The scene when we arrived was a troop of baboons, near a baobab tree; two large male baboons were sitting on a log, staring toward a lone umbrella tree. Up in the branches, we saw the tail swooshing, as the leopard, with four paws dangling from the trunk, slept. Quietly, the two large baboons jumped off the log and ran to the tree. And then, the scene flashed into chaos as the leopard sprang off the branch and ran, with the baboons screaming and chasing the leopard.

We were all shocked and did not know what we were witnessing. When we saw the two baboons approach the tree, we were all holding our breaths, assuming the leopard would attack the baboons. We could not have been more wrong.

The guides were screaming into their radios in a language we could not understand. As the baboons chased the leopard, we followed suit in the land cruiser.

Soon, the leopard disappeared, and the two baboons stopped the chase. Once the dust settled, our guide, those bright white teeth and smile stretched across his face, looked at us.

"This has never been witnessed. But we knew it happens," he said, catching his breath.

"The leopard must have killed a member of the troop during the night. With a full stomach, he took a nap. The baboons, no doubt the leader and his second, waited until the leopard was asleep. If they had caught the leopard in the tree, those baboons would have torn him to pieces," he said, shaking his head. "What you saw? None of us has ever seen."

Not a whisper among us, as we left the Serengeti.

And then we flew to Kigali, the capital of Rwanda—a modern city, with a powerful presence of military guard. This small country was doing everything it could to prevent another genocide of its people. If you asked a Rwandan what tribe or clan they were from, they answered, "Rwandan."

We toured a Catholic church, a place where, during the attack, people from the surrounding villages hid. They thought they would be safe, even as the priest locked the doors on the outside. Their bones remain, piled in a pit, as do the bullet holes in the mud walls. Our local guide did not go into the church. Justin went outside, and I saw him staring at nothing. He told

Justin his family had been murdered. He'd escaped to nearby Uganda as a boy.

We met with survivors, who told their stories.

It reminded me of that hot, muggy day in Phnom Penh at a gravesite, still littered with shattered bones, crunching below my feet as I walked to a glass tower filled with human skulls.

Our guide, when he was a young boy, had watched his family being shot in the head. He survived because his glasses had fallen off into the understory. A person who wore glasses was considered intelligent and killed.

From Kigali, we were again silent as we drove to the base camp of the Virunga Mountains gorilla guides. What we had seen and heard left us with heavy hearts.

Our group of six stood together, among several others, as guards with clipboards observed us. This took about an hour, as Bonnie and I giggled, joking that the gorillas must be picky about who they let into their community.

Our guide called us over, and a fit man jumped into the land cruiser as we departed quickly, before any of the other groups. Our guide, James, looked back and said, "Michelle, we are going to the Pablo group."

I looked at Bonnie. They had told James about my adopted gorilla. The Pablo group normally were not visited by tourists, but my companions had urged James to get us into that group.

Our guide, after observing us, agreed we were fit enough to make the climb, as it was a very arduous trip, by vehicle or on foot. James had called the Head Guide the night before to request the Pablo group.

The road to the trailhead was rocky. We walked upwards, through bamboo growth and then into the jungle. Just before we'd left Alaska for this trip, I got a message from the Dian Fossey Gorilla Fund, saying that Cantsabee had disappeared. The hypothesis was that he was old and had wandered off to die, leaving his group with a reliable leader. I mentioned this to the guide as we were hiking up the slope.

"You know Cantsabee?"

"I have followed him for decades. Do you know what happened to him?"

"He came back," he whispered.

As we approached a thicket, our guide stopped. He told us we were close. He then got excited and told me to come ahead. Justin and Bonnie were with me.

He pointed.

"Cantsabee," I murmured. I knew him. He was smaller, not as muscular, but his silver hair was thick, down his back, like a skunk.

"Cantsabee, the leader of Pablo," I whispered to Bonnie.

We walked a little further and then sat down. And among the thick greenery, we were not alone.

Grunts. Gorilla language—the guides understood more than 200 words. A large female, picking at vegetation and chewing on a stalk, paid us little attention, with a six-month-old playing with a newborn. The baby, intrigued, started toward me, and then mom grunted. Slowly, the baby went back to her. Then the older one came toward us, and again mom grunted. It, too, obeyed and then jumped on the baby as they both rolled in the vegetation.

Our guide asked several times if the baby could come close, but mom shook her head. He told us that the troop is on guard and that they had been this way since Cantsabee came back.

"They are nervous," he said and got up.

We slowly stood and walked along a path, and then we heard a commotion behind us. Bonnie's husband was holding up traffic, according to the juvenile gorilla who'd slapped him on the butt. Surprised, he complied and moved off the trail.

A slap? These animals are powerful and could be very persuasive if they want. The intelligence and the gentleness of these creatures deserve our respect, at the very least.

There was a rustle in the vegetation, and the guide looked at us and pointed. At that moment, I saw a small baby with her mother dart through the thick vegetation. The guide whispered to us, "Be still."

I felt pressure on my leg, as a medium-sized gorilla walked by me, and this little ball of fur hit my leg and looked up. It was Kunderwanda. She stopped, those beautiful golden eyes so inquisitive, looking at Justin and me. And then she was gone, following her mom through the dense vegetation. I hugged Justin.

"You told her to do that, didn't you?" I asked our guide.

He laughed. I cried.

Normally, these animals tolerate our presence for only about an hour; one minute more than that, and it could be dangerous. However, the same juvenile that had slapped Bonnie's husband had other plans. He had climbed a branch that hung over our path as we were departing. He was hanging, first with one arm clinging to the branch, and then he would drop and do it again. We couldn't move.

"The clown," our guide smirked.

We waited until we heard a loud grunt, as Cantsabee appeared, with a look of understanding, but also, sadness?

What he must have witnessed in his life! Does he remember his time with Dian? I wondered, as we slowly made our way back down the mountain's path. Eye contact is not allowed, but I looked back over my shoulder at him, smiled, nodded my head, and headed downslope through the bamboo forest.

Once home, for the first time in years, I did not rush or stress about getting back to work.

I relaxed on the couch with a cup of coffee and rubbed Nitro's belly as she slept on my lap, while Cricket curled by my head. I reflected on how I felt and what I had learned during the last month. All the pain, all the love, all I had endured in my 61 years of life—had it steered me to the very experience I had always dreamed of?

A few days later, James sent me an email, letting me know Cantsabee had died shortly after our visit. The guides had found his body.

"They knew. His troop knew," I told Justin.

Justin spent most of his time at the cabin, shooting his bow and building the garage, now connected to the solarium. I had hoped my life would be simpler once I retired, but Justin got more estranged. As his dinner was getting cold, I found him sitting in the solarium, looking exhausted.

"Dinner is ready. I thought you might have fallen off a ladder or something," I said.

He got up, said nothing, and walked away.

"Justin, what is going on? Talk to me. What's the matter?" He was scaring me. This is how he acted when he found out the moose he shot the year before was not legal. I thought there was something horribly wrong, like he had cancer or something. He would visit the place he killed the animal every day, sometimes twice a day. He thought someone was moving the gut pile and the antlers around, sending him a message. He finally told me what happened. I hugged him and told him to report it to wildlife control. It was an accident; he did nothing wrong.

When he continued walking away, I grabbed the arm of the baggy Carhartt jacket to get him to stop. He did, and I did not recognize the man who stared back at me.

"Don't you touch me," he screamed, his face red. I saw the whites of his enormous eyes, exuding hate. He looked like a rabid dog, spit spewing as he screamed.

I froze. I watched him get in his truck and drive away. I was shaking so hard I could not walk. I had not seen him since he came home for lunch. What did I do? It was getting worse.

He came back, quiet, as if nothing had happened. He spent more and more time with our neighbor, in the solarium, drinking. The neighbor, a Christian man, had recently graduated with a therapy degree. He was a janitor at a hospital where and when he met his wife, a nurse. From there, he'd worked as a counselor at a correction center while going to school for his degree. He had moved to the mountain a few years earlier, with a troubled and ill wife, 15 years older than him. Initially, I thought he would be a beneficial influence, but I was terribly wrong.

In June, the wife of an ex-coworker friend and I were talking about boating. They owned a beautiful powerboat that they would take out on the sound, but they had never sailed. We schemed and then proposed to the boys that we bareboat a sailboat in Tortola in January. Justin was a little hesitant, as I watched his eyes. And yet, he agreed. *Things are getting better,* I thought.

In May, Justin had also agreed to a trip to Panama and Colombia after hunting season in November. It was a trip he had talked about for years, and with the tour company, it would be relaxing.

By August, we had the paperwork submitted for the sailing trip with Justin as captain, since he had the most sailing experience. We rented a beautiful 37-foot sailboat. I rented a bed-and-breakfast for all of us on Tortola a few days before sailing.

Justin and the neighbor were sitting in the sunroom when I let Justin know I had completed the booking for the sail trip in January. The neighbor looked at me with a confused look on his face, and then he looked at Justin.

"I thought you were going to Panama in November after hunting."

Justin had this sheepish look on his face as he looked at the neighbor.

"Don't worry. I only have him two weeks in January and two weeks in November. I promise. You can have him the rest of the time."

As I said this, I saw an exchange between Justin and the neighbor. Was it a look of understanding? And the tension in the room changed.

They both knew there would be no trip to South America *or* the Caribbean.

Epilogue

My Dear Friend,

It was a frustrating day, starting with no internet. I can see you rolling your eyes and shaking your head. And you know why? My answer to everything anymore:

Too many people and inadequate infrastructure to support all these people!

Something so minor, in the big picture of things. It was the timing and, truthfully, a culmination of frustration. Eighteen months, to be exact, since Justin's temper tantrum on my birthday.

Where do all these people come from? OK, yes—I am one of them. But in my defense, I am a family of one! I only need one home, a small one at that. Not a mega-home. I looked everywhere. OK, not everywhere. I will not live in the wheatfields of eastern Washington or the swamps of Missouri. We know that about me.

Was I delusional? Okay, don't answer that. I really thought I could find what I needed. A home in a community. Near the water, but close to an airport. And good medical care. Is that too much to ask? And it would be nice to be in a college or university town. And, honestly, in a blue state, not red. I would settle for purple. I lived in Alaska for 40 years.

Port Townsend. Bellingham. White Salmon. Wenatchee. Walla Walla. Spokane. Boise. Ashland. Yes, all the nice places where I expected to land. And crazy expensive. By the time I talked to the realtor to see a house, it would be gone. Some guy from Texas with an offer $30,000 above asking! Or the manufactured home in PT for $450,000, cash only, because it was ancient. And yes, some misgivings. The old condo outside of Bellingham? I could not trust myself to make a decision. That was the nagging battle inside my brain. I could not decide.

Why? We know why. I lived with Justin longer than anyone else. Deciding involved two. I was now one.

And since I am being honest here, it is all the people. It frightened me in a claustrophobic way. And being in Washington? So close, so easy to go home. And the absurd increase in real estate? An excuse? No, I don't think so. It is legit, as I have a reason for hesitancy in buying in an inflated housing market. I did it in 1983. And then the market crashed.

I digress. It is easy to get sidetracked these days.

My frustration, at least for today?

My writing coach and I had a Google meeting to discuss my manuscript. I was looking forward to seeing her, hearing what she had to say, and yes, I was nervous, but excited. She is so intuitive, it's freaky how she gets me. Of course, she'd read my manuscript.

And then, as if by magic, with twenty minutes to go, I heard the beeps. The electronic Google gods of the web. The sound made my heart miss a beat as Rebecca's warm smile appeared on my laptop.

She loves the story, but—as she paused and looked at me. In her serious voice, with a stern face, she scolded, *"Enough with the narcissistic man."*

She wanted to read about *me* in the end. *Not him. How did I end up where I am?*

She was right, as I closed my eyes.

"I am done with you. You are toxic."

And so predictable, as he stormed out of the house and refused to talk. I asked him if we could do some counseling or mediation.

"Mediation? You don't know what mediation is. I told you what you are getting."

He refused to get a real estate agent. How else could he make a backdoor deal to sell our home to the neighbors—and then use his charm on me to do his laundry and take him to his outpatient surgery, without even a thank-you. He just walked away.

He signed a legal agreement with his terms of sale. And yet, he demanded I pay him the difference when his backdoor deal fell through.

It's insane, right? I know you are shaking your head. I can feel it.

If it were not for you, for being there, I might have given in to his demands, a habit for me. I did not give him what he wanted, and even if I did, you are right. He still would have used my cats as leverage against me.

And, what I have not told you, although I think you know, is the reason I left my home, my community, my life, and my cats. Justin would still be around. I would not deny him seeing the cats, but what would that do to me? Could I be free of him? We know the answer to that. He would still use them to get to me, as he is doing now. I miss them terribly. You know that.

As crazy as it sounds, it was me who needed to run. To break that cycle of behavior.

Some have mentioned it to me frequently that my relationship with Justin is like some offshoot version of Stockholm Syndrome. Have you heard of that? I have a feeling most women, and even some men, have.

I did leave, and I always came back. I knew Justin was not the domestic sort of guy.

All my life, I did what was expected of me. I was responsible. I worked. I saved my money. I was the protector. I was the fixer. And to survive, I lost myself in the world of imagination. I gave all my love and loyalty, without question, without demands. And yet my most trustful companions were four-legged, not two-.

And then Rick appeared. And my life changed. Do I regret that decision to marry him?

No, I don't. I regret the cruelty of people I loved and how they treated me. How I treated myself. But *regret being married to Rick?* I hate that word, don't you?

No. I was loved, and for that, I am grateful. Many people cannot say that. And me? I was loved by not just one man but two men, as I felt true love from DG.

Why did I stay? Why did I come back? Are you ready for this? I wanted someone like Justin. I was able to keep my promise to Rick—*what was taken away from him, taken away from me.* Justin enabled me to finish my story. To live, to explore, and yes, to try and love again, to *love me* again.

I saw the world. It was no longer in my imagination. I have done amazing things. I swore I would never say those words my mother always said, *"I wish I would have."*

And Justin helped me with that endeavor. Believe it or not, he helped me to go beyond that hurdle, to push my limits. I had it in me, but it was so taboo in my family. He always did what he wanted. I was envious of that.

And *I made a home*. I hoped it would be a home for us, but I knew better. I felt it. It was so hard with Justin, for him to give himself to me, to love me. It is my stubbornness or maybe my need to fix those who I think are broken, especially those I love. I have always felt this way.

As you know, my friend, I am compulsive. Justin wanted me to take care of *his* house, but he could not care less if it was *our* home. Deep down, Justin was a lost puppy, all alone and cute. But I could not fix him. For him, there was nothing to fix.

I was born with flaws; I am human. At least in my dysfunctional family, I knew my parents loved me. There might have been anger, and even hostility, but there was affection. Affection was hard for Justin. For years, I used his family as a reason for that, an excuse. I blamed myself, but it was his lies and lack of commitment that ended us. And for that, I feel sorry for him, for what we could have had. Such a cliché.

I stayed because I wanted to. The adventure, the travel; it was exciting. Rick and I would have done that if he'd lived. And there you have it. I promised my husband I would do what they took away from us, from me. To live our adventure.

I am a determined and loyal woman, whose passion and empathy overrules logic. The veterinarian I worked for understood that. He knew being a vet would take a toll on my emotional health. My mother understood that; I was too sensitive. Hell, she would rarely allow me to watch shows like *Lassie*.

I know you want to ask me, "What drove you to move from the northernmost shores of the western edge to the southernmost eastern shore of the Continental U.S.? What the hell were you thinking?"

I will tell you the obvious reasons I thought of Florida. Justin and I discussed seeing Maine again, and the Northeast. Maybe I discussed it, and he just tolerated me. Whatever. I researched where we could leave a trailer and a vehicle. That led me to the warmer sections of the east coast, such as Florida, North and South Carolina, even Georgia. To counter, I did the same thing in the PNW. Bellingham became the perfect place because of the ferry.

Of course, that put me on every list server, from 55 communities to trailer and RV parks. For two years, it inundated me with crap, which, I admit, went into the garbage or wood stove.

And then he, on my 63rd birthday, rocked my world.

I hired a real estate agent in Palmer, Alaska, in October 2019. When Covid hit in 2020, I still had not found a place. It was a game of roulette. No supply, and then demand.

Honestly, I listened to my girlfriends in Washington. The anxiety and stress took a toll, as I lost several pounds, while Justin told me, *"You will be out of the house by May."*

After Covid hit, I made the decision, and, on May 6, I left Alaska. I could not drive, as planned, due to border closures.

Did you know that, when asked that question about driving, many people do not know that to drive to Alaska, you go through Canada? Wow. I am lucky I have not lived in a bubble.

Anyway, I had to leave everything that could not fit inside my Subaru Forester, which was shipped to Seattle by barge.

It was the extreme opposite of the real estate market in the PNW. The demand was through the roof! After months, I was frustrated and anxious, so I finally flew to Florida when Covid was on the downside, on Labor Day. It was so extremely different from where I had lived for the last 40 years.

Washington was familiar. Maybe too familiar. There was no challenge to learn new things. Florida was the opposite. I kayaked in the mangroves and saw manatee. I felt like I was on vacation. Maybe that was the problem. *Vacations end. This will surely end.* Then I spent a week looking at housing, primarily townhomes, condos, and villas. All new. Clean, manicured, tamed. How strange.

I thought maybe I could reinvent myself. *It's so different; it will not be home. There is an airport, medical care, a university, an aquarium where I could volunteer, a rowing club where I could learn to row, community activities. Not a 55-and-older community.* I was not quite ready for that, but I looked at one in Tucson. But, and yes, no family.

One of my reasons for moving to Washington, as you know, was to be closer to family and friends. And as you also know, that blew up in my face!

In Florida, I would not feel the pain of not being invited to a family function. Chalk another one up for the shrinks.

It intrigued me as I left the green and blue of Florida. I arrived in Seattle in a thick cloak of gray, as smoke permeated my senses. The PNW was on fire. I finally made it back to Wenatchee and grew depressed and frustrated with my choices. It was not just the outrageous price of housing; it was something else. I just didn't feel connected. I did not feel *at all*. In fact, being so close to home, that illogical conclusion to go back to Alaska was all I could think of. To see my cats.

It must be what drives a zebra or a wildebeest, that instinct to survive, the place they know—to give birth, to feel protected, despite the hardship of the journey. I felt compelled to go home to the safety of people who *knew* me and animals who loved me. Justin was not part of my compulsion—not really, or so I told myself.

Oh, how that scared me, my friend. I wanted it so badly. The instinct to survive.

Then the sales rep called me from Florida for one village I'd looked at. As he spoke, I looked at the brochure for the village. This one was not on my radar. It was an impulse, nothing more. I remembered that, as I'd driven by, it looked kind of cool. I pulled a U-turn and checked it out. The look was colonial in a gated community.

Really, I thought? It reminded me of *The Stepford Wives.* It was quiet. A pool. Fitness club and pickle ball? A lot of my tennis friends have switched to that game. I have never played.

The sales rep explained that they would build the townhomes in the fall, a brand-new place. I even had the option to select what I wanted in the interior. There was only one exterior unit left, on a larger lot. It was across from the fitness center. My brain was in hyper mode, calculating all the pros and cons. I fought that instinctual desire to go home. *What home? Where?* I had no home. All of this was going in my brain.

And then I said those words. *I want it.* I. Want. It. *What the hell? Did I say that? I did.*

I hung up and was ecstatic. I did not expect that.

And yet, here I am in Florida. Of all places. Was it because of the Pandemic? Or something else? What was I thinking, you ask?

This is what Rebecca wants from me.

I absorbed what she had to say, and, when we finally hung up, I was anxious and energized to incorporate Rebecca's wisdom into my last few chapters. You know that compulsion.

As you also know, food comes first, and I was starving, so I fixed a sandwich and I turned on live TV, something I had not had since

I left Alaska last May 2020. It was the French Open, and it was the men's semi-finals between Rafael Nadal and Novak Djokovic.

Okay, I thought, *I can watch this for just a little.* The volley between these athletes went on and on and on. The match was addicting, and when my cell phone rang, it astonished me. An hour had elapsed. It was my worker's compensation adjuster. She was sorry, but she had bad news.

The last hope for a surgeon within my area turned me down. She said it was not uncommon, but even she was amazed that I could not find an orthopedic surgeon who would take my case. She recommended calling the Fort Myers area, and, because of the time difference, we signed off to reconnect the following Monday. I had already been trying for more than a week, calling every clinic and surgeon I could find. What did I say about medical being important? WTF? Is this a sign? Oh, my god!

I was in Florida? Where older people end up.

So, guess what I did? I called my now-retired orthopedic surgeon's office in Anchorage. How insane is that? Although Dr. Ryan had retired, they at least had all the files. I did not know the surgeon who took over, but, heck, if I had to fly back to Anchorage every other year? How bad could that be?

And now, I need to go outside. I abandoned my cell phone for my bike. As I rode the bike trail along the Manatee River and looked out at the wide, slow-moving water, I took a deep breath. I waved to my friend James, a social magnet, who hangs out on his favorite bench, with his bike, his belongings tied securely to every free space, including a cat carrier strapped to his handlebars, for his three-month orange tabby, Mr. Kitten.

James told me the story one day as the kitten cooed in my arms, purring. He lived in the woods and heard this mournful cry. It had rained extremely hard, and he ran to the overflowing canal. He saw the tiny, orange ball of fur clinging to a rock. Its littermates and mother were not so fortunate. He loves animals. I saw this as I rode my bike by him daily. So, when he told me his story, it hit home.

He had suffered a head injury in a work accident. He'd lost his home, his bikes, his vehicle. I watched him gently playing with the tiny kitten. He fed the malnourished feline with a bottle, and the kitten survived. He took him to the Humane Society to get his vaccinations. *Really?* Shit, I know people with money who are not that responsible. He was distraught when he had to pay $20 for the shots and worried about the cost to have the little guy neutered. I called the Humane Society when I got home. They'd lost many of their volunteers during the Covid pandemic and now had to charge $20 for the shots, but the vet charged nothing for spay and neuter. I relayed the information to James.

Usually I stop and chat, but today, I needed some air, and he had company. So, I waved and said "Hi" as I rode by. I slowed down near the marina docks to catch the nightly show of the Egret and the Green Heron. I don't know if they choreograph this, but it is hilarious to watch as they balance, together, on a boat line, their beaks steadily aimed just above the water, hoping to spear one of the small, sardine-like fish swarming just below the surface.

Sometimes, I can see manatee swimming by the rock edge or dolphins surfacing and then diving. Mostly, I see ibis wandering through the grass, eating insects, along the river trail. As the sun was setting, I headed back to my current Air BNB, one of many I have rented since early May. As I started my turn from the main street toward the driveway, I quickly swerved.

There, on the edge of the street right in front of the driveway, was a small fledgling. It did not move, and I nearly hit it. I quickly jumped off my bike and ambled over to the small, stunned creature. Still, it did not move. I saw the soft down poking through its gray feathers. A young Mockingbird, it seemed to me, the State Bird of Florida.

I watched this young bird, no doubt scared, in a new place, not in his nice, safe nest with his siblings.

"I feel your pain. Don't be afraid. You'll be okay. I promise," I breathed, as I gently enclosed my hands around his tiny body. "Oh, you'll have some challenges, especially these cats, ready to pounce on you," I whispered. "Be strong."

And then, as I safely set him down, at least out of the driveway and away from the street, I heard the harsh *krrdee*, and then a *clack*. I looked toward the overstory, and as I had hoped, there in the branches, was mom, the Mockingbird.

A new adventure, my little one, for you and for me. Although alone, I will do my best not to be lonely, I said to myself.

Before Justin left, I asked him why we never married.

Do you know what he said to me?

"You never followed the marriage protocol."

As I look across the Atlantic Ocean, digging my feet into the soft, white sand with the texture of flour, I celebrate our 42nd wedding anniversary. There is not a day I do not shed a tear for my husband and for what we both lost. Love, respect, honesty, and companionship. That is the only marriage protocol I know.

I don't know what the future holds for me, but I will survive, and I will grow. I just returned from Alaska, and it was bittersweet. My friends kept me busy, but they were afraid for me, as I ached to see my cats.

Justin refused.

My wish is that they are happy and loved; my love will endure.

Although Florida is a new adventure, I'm not sure it will be home for me. Maybe that's the key. Maybe home for me is not a structure or a place. Maybe it comes from within. The people I meet. The things I do. I am welcomed here, and, once I get settled, the itch to travel and to explore will begin all over again. I hope I am wiser, and smarter, but who knows, right? If I have you, my dear friend, I will be okay. We will grow and learn and suffer and be happy. Because that is what we do.

Acknowledgments

Life is a journey, either alone or with many. I endured unfathomable loss at 25, and yet, I found the strength to move forward. But, writing about my life? This was a challenge like no other, that dug deep into my soul.

I began writing my story in October 2020, a year after the man I trusted walked out on my 63rd birthday. It has taken nearly 2 years, living in 11 locations and 3 states, before I found a place to settle, with nothing more than what fit in my Subaru.

I mourn the loss of my life in Alaska. A home we built, the soil we worked by hand and grew our food. The miles of trails we skied in the dead of winter, following the tracks of lynx and wolf. And the serenity, waking every morning to the architectural magnificence of nature. I mourn the loss of unconditional love from my furry felines, Nitro and Cricket, and the security and joy from my Alaska friends and community. And yet, I had to walk away, leaving all I loved.

It has been one of the toughest challenges I have faced, writing this story. And I could not have accomplished this feat without the help of many. So, to those not named, I thank every one of you for your validation and love.

I owe a special thanks to my writing coach, editor, therapist, philosopher, cook, clown, and friend Rebecca Bloom. I could not have finished *The Understory* without her patience, her expertise, and her encouragement.

A big thank-you to Connie Jackson, who shared such wisdom during our Writing Workshops with Rebecca, and who continues to inspire me with her beautiful words.

And to Greg Smith, my childhood friend and superman extraordinaire of many talents, who volunteered to edit every chapter, from start to finish.

For Pamela Weiss, who gives hope through her vision, that someday, *we* will be accepted for our strength, our talents, our creativity, and respected for our empathy, our passion, and our intelligence. I am so grateful.

And, to Story Summit, and organizations like it, for providing a platform for the most talented, brave women who are the summit, who have a voice to share.

And to my dear friends, Julie, Karen, and Malia, who patiently provided their critiques and observations to my endless inquiries on cover design.

I am so grateful for those who give me strength to confront the whirlpool of emotions each day—to live for all those I have lost in the physical world and whose memories are my motivation for life's potential. And thank you, to the natural world, for giving me your mysteries of beauty, for without you, I could not exist.

About the Author

Michelle *was raised* in a rural town in Eastern Washington. Her passion for nature and travel steered her to an adventurous career in wildlife biology in Alaska. While recovering from a helicopter accident, she discovered her love of writing and published *Jaguar Moon*, a novel of suspense deep in the rainforest of French Guiana. After she retired, she wrote her memoir, *The Understory: A Female Environmentalist in the Land of the Midnight Sun*. Her life story was optioned by a female-forward production company before it hit the presses.

Made in United States
Orlando, FL
17 November 2022

24670889R00186